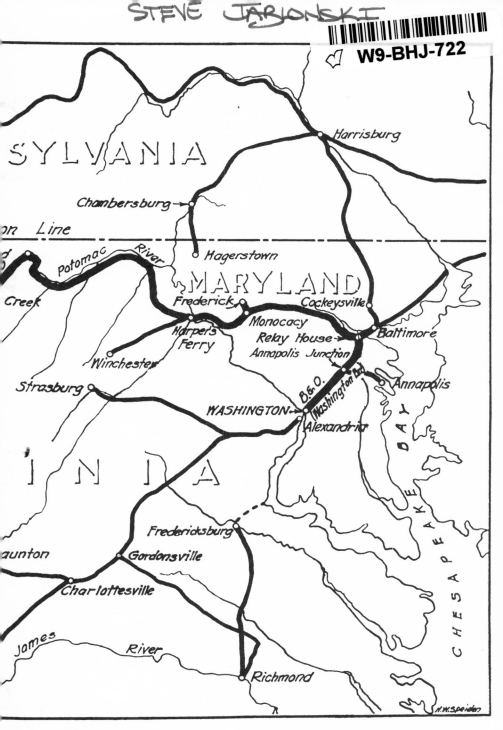

Harrisburg

SYLVANIA

Chambersburg→

on Line

Potomac River

Hagerstown

Creek

MARYLAND

Frederick Cockeysville

Harpers Ferry

Monocacy Relay House→

Baltimore

Winchester

Annapolis Junction

Strasburg

B.&O. Washington Bd.

Annapolis

WASHINGTON→

Alexandria

CHESAPEAKE BAY

I N D A

Fredericksburg

aunton Gordonsville

Charlottesville

James River

Richmond

n.w. Speiden

OHIO (1861)

THE BALTIMORE AND OHIO
IN THE CIVIL WAR

President Lincoln, General McClellan, and John W. Garrett at Antietam, October 3, 1862. An arrangement by Bendann of figures in an original Matthew B. Brady photograph in the Garrett Collection (Courtesy of the Honorable John W. Garrett)

THE
BALTIMORE AND OHIO
IN THE
CIVIL WAR

BY
FESTUS P. SUMMERS
Associate Professor of History
West Virginia University

 Stan Clark Military Books
Gettysburg, Pennsylvania

Reprinted with permission in 1993 by:

STAN CLARK MILITARY BOOKS
915 Fairview Avenue
Gettysburg, Pennsylvania 17325
(717) 337-1728

ISBN: 1-879664-13-5 (Hardbound)
ISBN: 1-879664-14-3 (Softbound)

Front Cover Illustration: "GUARDING THE
THOMAS VIADUCT" by Hubert Stitt, courtesy
The B&O Railroad Museum, Baltimore, Maryland

Rear Cover Illustration: "SOUTHBOUND"
by Alan Fearnley,
courtesy American Print Gallery,
Gettysburg, Pennsylvania

Introduction

The Civil War – by whatever name we remember it, from whichever side we favor, no matter which interpretation we choose for its cause – remains a central theme in our national consciousness. It is a reference point clumsily, but effectively, dividing the history of the United States into two epochs. Even without explicit reference, the War and its aftermath weaves through politics, popular culture, social relations, and the dozens of other topics that together form the fabric of American life.

Railroads, too, played a central role in creating the modern United States from a fractious collection of English, French, and Spanish colonies uneasily coexisting on the edges of an immense wilderness. Railroading is arguably the defining technology of the nineteenth Century. It took form from emerging "American" values and in turn railroads changed the way we grew as a nation. Simply by existing as a network at the time of the Civil War, railroads had a profound effect on the course of the war, as they had already on the development of society at large.

Taken together, railroads in the Civil War constitute a useful and important framework for understanding the conflict and its resolution. The war itself made extraordinary demands upon the railroad network. The availability of railroading completely changed the conduct of warfare. This combination is a powerful tool for academic historians and Civil War enthusiasts alike. Surprisingly, it took nearly a century to create even the most basic body of reliable literature on railroads in that war. Festus Summers' *The Baltimore and Ohio in the Civil War* was the first major study bringing together railroading and its role in the Civil War.

The American Civil War has become a bona fide industry in some parts of the United States. In the historical profession, it remains both a crowded field and a subject of continuing fascination for seasoned scholar and neophyte alike. For a large segment of non-professional historians and the American public with some stated interest in history, the Civil War is the one single subject that they identify of primary interest. The epic public television documentary program of the same name is but one example of the war's popularity. It is also the manifestation of a peculiar phenomenon.

All wars and military actions have their followers and historians, amateur and professional. Yet I am not aware of large groups of passionately interested civilians dressing the parts and assembling to re-enact battles from the Crimean War. Nor the Franco-Prussian War. Veterans and interest groups commemorate significant events from the First and Second World Wars, but not with the fervor of Civil War aficionados. Surely, there must be die-hard fans of the Hundred-Years War, or the War of the Roses, or any of a dozen equally historic human conflicts, but they do not keep so high a profile as Civil War re-enactors. To the best of my knowledge, in general citizens of other countries do not display the zeal for and make a leisure-time hobby of their particular wars as we do for our War For Southern Independence or Southern Rebellion.

We treat the Civil War differently from other American wars, perhaps because it indeed was so different from those which came before and after. While we might dress for Revolutionary War skirmishes in select locales, ordinary folks do not decorate their pick-up trucks with the battle flag of the Continental Congress of 1776. They do, however, proudly display the battle flag of the Confederacy, arguably a less-successful and shorter-lived entity. The Civil War has become part of the cultural landscape in ways that other wars perhaps have not.

In all of the other significant conflicts, the enemy was someone else. Although we were a nation largely descended from the English in 1776, we inhabited a different continent and had become different enough from them and enough alike as "Americans" to sustain a fight for independence. In the same fashion, at the time of the First World War a substantial proportion of the United States population was of German descent. Nevertheless, we success-fully characterized Germany as an enemy with a different language and different politics which had to be checked.

Southern secession was different altogether. How could one part of the United States dare to declare war on another part, with the express purpose of defending the very principles of freedom and rights upon which the Union was founded in the first place? There were perfectly sound and understandable, although lamentable, reasons for the Civil War, and one can argue that the cataclysm or something very much like it was required to both dispose of chattel slavery and establish the primacy of the federal government. We continue to be fascinated by that wrenching experience long after the root causes and direct results have faded from our consciousness.

This was the first war made easily accessible to most Americans during and after the fact. The armies fought on American soil in both the North and South, ranging from the Eastern Seaboard to Texas. An unprecedented number of non-combatant Americans saw, heard, or in some way participated directly in fighting, siege, or evacuation. Most of the rest of the country was touched by the war effort in ways similar to, but far more immediate than, the Revolutionary War or the later European contests.

It certainly was well documented as it happened, thanks to a lively press and the perfection of photography two decades previous. Reporters and artists made money, careers, and thousands of pages of prose and images as they followed campaigns back and forth across what became familiar territory. Some worked for newspapers, some for magazines, and some freelanced. Many shared the risks and inconveniences of war, and some died. The record that they created stands as a rich, but undisciplined and often untidy resource for historians.

Likewise, the governments themselves took pains to create official records of the war, as did various lesser sovereign entities. These "official" records provide a reliable, if usually dull, basis for other types of history. The U.S. Government was especially concerned and ably equipped to document its actions and preserve the records of both sides. For railroad historians, these files offer rich but difficult sources. Much of the documentation was created and is preserved by unit, agency, campaign, office or other functional division. Railroads in war, as well as in peace, cross and transcend such artificial categories. The researcher must be intuitive and dogged to get all they have to offer.

Letters, diaries, and personal memoirs comprise a rich but dangerous resource. They can be like spice to a balanced meal, adding flavor, color, and an especial point of view or poignancy. They often stand on their own as primary documents, or as valuable records of a particular fight or activity. They must be used with caution, however, for they are subject to the human temptations of error, selective recall, and attitude as well as the truth of immediacy and participation.

A work of scholarly history, such as *The Baltimore and Ohio in the Civil War*, must use as many of those sources as possible. Such a work may also be packaged a number of ways. This book originated as Festus Summers' doctoral dissertation at West Virginia University, accepted in 1933. It served its creator well and established Dr. Summers as a full-fledged scholar and card-carrying academic historian. The fact that it was also a very good narrative account of a popular subject distinguished it from the larger crop of rather dry, specialized history dissertations and led to its subsequent publication for a popular audience.

Festus Summers began his career as an educator instructing elementary school children in some of the most rural parts of West Virginia. He served as principal of a number of secondary schools and as Superintendent of the Jane Lew school district. After a brief stint in the Army during World War I, he remained in the Officer's Reserve Corps. In 1922, Professor Summers received his Bachelor's degree from West Virginia University; in 1927, he completed the Master of Arts degree from the University of Chicago. For a while, he taught history at Morris Harvey College at Barboursville, West Virgina. Entering West Virginia University in 1931, Summers required only two years to complete his PhD.

This was one of, if not the first, instances of a scholar choosing to unite Civil War and railroad histories in a single major work. Summers had few secondary works to use as models and but a thin body of research from which he could select approaches or draw conclusions. Even more ironic is the fact that there are probably more – and better – primary sources of research material available to writers today than a half-century ago.

It would have been quite reasonable for a young scholar at WVU to choose either the B&O or the Civil War as a dissertation topic in the early 1930s. Summers himself had grown up in Nicholas County, in central West Virginia just west of the Allegheny Mountains. The lifeline for that part of the state in the early twentieth century was the Coal and Coke Railway, which was absorbed into the B&O in 1917.

The B&O line from Burnsville to Richwood, off the Coal and Coke Railway, traversed the hilly terrain of Nicholas County. At Allingdale, the Strouds Creek and Muddlety Railroad branched off for a 23-mile wander through coal mine country, including the town of Summersville. As a boy growing up, and later as an elementary school teacher in Clay and Fayette Counties, he would have depended on the B&O and other railroads as today we rely on automobiles.

In a broader context, the B&O Railroad had just celebrated its centennial in 1927, which closely corresponded with the centennial of the railroad industry in the United States. The railroad industry peaked as a social, economic, and cultural force in these years. The B&O loomed especially large in the commerical and cultural life of northern West Virginia. It enjoyed a historical cachet that its counterpart railroads in the southern West Virginia coal fields lacked. Indeed, the very presence of the B&O in the Eastern Panhandle counties caused them to be annexed to the new state of West Virginia in 1863. It would seem natural for Summers to consider a railroad topic for scholarly research.

The Civil War, on the other hand, was subject to renewed popular and scholarly interest on the coattails of a renewal of interest in American history (evidenced by the Colonial Revival style) and post-World War I scholarship. The last of the veterans were making their last hurrahs, and with their passing the personally felt and vividly remembered first-person war gave way to the historian's more distant analysis. Summers grew up in an area literally shaped by the war, and the ghosts of John Imboden and George McClellan were not far removed.

Summers chose to treat both topics simultaneously. Aside from a few articles in historical society journals and cursory accounts in larger railroad histories, practically no one had examined in depth any of the major parts the railroad played in the war. Yet it took a certain degree of courage or hubris to attempt so daunting a task. Thousands of Civil War books and increasing numbers of dissertations treated increasingly smaller slices of the conflict. To work, this one would need to synthesize military history, railroad history, political history, and any number of sub-disciplines not fully articulated at the time.

The book appeared on the eve of the Second World War, which itself helped mark changes in the ways we write and interpreted American history. After the war, a new generation of scholars and students took up anew the large questions of the causes and conduct of the War. Yet at the same time some historians were producing works of grand sweep and narrative prose, others were successfully coaxing a finer level of detail and new understanding of the actual conduct of the war from the tangle of sources.

With *The Baltimore and Ohio in the Civil War* as a precedent, a dozen books appeared in the two decades following the Second World War. They competently treated the northern and southern railroad systems in wartime, railroads of individual states, the overall strategy and tactics of railroads in the Civil War, and even the lives of particular wartime railroad men. The popular and railroad enthusiast book publishers came forth with photo albums, reprints of railroad memoirs, and compilations of varying quality and worth.

This spate of activity simply was part of a larger trend. By now, something like 50,000 books on the Civil War have been published, most of which were so narrowly focused or of such ephemeral quality that they quietly vanished from the shelves of all but the most devoted collectors. *The Baltimore and Ohio Railroad in the Civil War* did not vanish, nor has it lost its usefulness as a tool for other historians, railroaders, and the literate public interested in the war.

The fact of its republication may be taken as evidence of the quality and continued utility of Professor Summers' original work. For decades, it has been the standard work on the B&O Railroad in the period and the pattern for many subsequent Civil War railroad history books. It holds up well today, and it will likely be a while before someone attempts a reinterpretation of his work or a restatement of the role of the B&O in the war. Good scholarship stands up against the vicissitudes of time, popular opinion, and scholarly fashion.

The Baltimore and Ohio in the Civil War also is a fine piece of railroad history, valuable for its cogent account of one of the most tumultuous periods in the B&O's long existence. While the literature of the railroad is vast, and that on the B&O more complete than most individual companies, this remains one of surprisingly few works of scholarly railroad history concerned with the B&O.

Dr. Summers enjoyed a distinguished career as a professor of American and West Virginia history, author, and advocate of the past as a window to our future. His slightly revised dissertation found a much wider audience in the form of this book, published first by G.P. Putnam's Sons in 1939. Original copies became scarce and highly coveted as both a historical resource and a collector's item by railroad and Civil War aficionados alike.

The current reissue will diminish the collector's value only slightly, and will make the work available to a new and broader audience. I believe that Professor Summers would have been pleased to see his work again in print. I know that I, and thousands of fellow railroad and Civil War buffs, will be.

John P. Hankey
The B&O Railroad Museum

PREFACE

THIS volume belongs to the history of the Civil War rather than to the history of transportation. The Baltimore and Ohio, like its competitors, the Pennsylvania Central, the New York and Erie, and the New York Central, profited from the traffic windfall of the storm years. Its Washington Branch had a monopoly of land transportation between Baltimore and Washington. But the company did not enjoy the full fruits of war prosperity because a large part of its main line lay on debatable ground. Although United States troops endeavored to keep the road open, it was repeatedly cut by the Confederates. Advance and retreat in the contest for control furnish interesting sidelights on the conduct of the war. Significant was the part this railroad played in military strategy and in the shaping of Federal and state policies. In these fields its action was conspicuous and unique.

Many have assisted me in this study. I am especially indebted to the Honorable John W. Garrett of Baltimore for helpful suggestions and permission to examine the private papers of Robert Garrett and Sons; to Mr. Robert M. Van Sant, Director of Public Relations of the Baltimore and Ohio Railroad Company, for many of the illustrations; to Dr. Thomas P. Martin, of the Manuscript Division of the Library of Congress, who facilitated my research in Washington; and to Dr. Roy Bird Cook, of Charleston, West Virginia, who permitted me to browse in his private manuscript collection and library. Messrs. Millard K. Bushong and William E. Nels corrected errors of detail on the manuscript. I owe also a special debt to Mrs. Helen Swindler Sowers for expert secretarial assistance. Professors Albert T. Volwiler and Thomas N. Hoover, of Ohio University, and Professors Charles H. Ambler, David D. Johnson, and Allen W. Porterfield, of West Virginia University, gave me helpful advice on style and format. If errors remain, I am alone responsible.

FESTUS P. SUMMERS.

West Virginia University,
June 1, 1939.

CONTENTS

ILLUSTRATIONS

45. Trestlework near Rowlesburg with a blockhouse in the background.
46. Trestlework near Rowlesburg with a blockhouse in the background.
47. The Battle of Philippi, 1861.
48. Bridge #112 over the Monongahela River, Fairmont, West Virginia.
49. 16th Ohio Volunteers crossing the Tray Run Viaduct.
50. The Cavalry's method of destroying railroads.
51. Twisting the rails.
52. A powder car of Civil War days.
53. A railroad battery.
54. Confederate cavalryman Harry Gilmor helping a Union soldier off the train.
55. Theater of Operations of Sheridan's artist, James Taylor.

MAPS

THE BALTIMORE AND OHIO
IN THE CIVIL WAR

CHAPTER I

From Tramway to Trunk Line (1827-1857)

THE Baltimore and Ohio Railroad Company was chartered by an act of the Maryland general assembly on February 28, 1827. John Quincy Adams then occupied the executive chair at Washington, although he was not the choice of a united people. Currents of the new nationalism, born of the War of 1812, still swept the American scene but chilly drafts of economic sectionalism already had begun to cool the passion for unity. This adverse influence, however, restrained but little the unifying zeal of the people of Maryland. With patriotic impulse they explained the founding of their railroad on the ground of national necessity; they earnestly professed that it would contribute "to the permanence of the union of the United States." [1]

The chief design of the founders, however, was to promote the economic prosperity of a particular state and city. Baltimore had long nursed an ambition to become a great commercial emporium; and the opening of the National Road to the Ohio River in 1818 had seemed an important step in this direction. Baltimore's commercial expansion however faced the prospect of a standstill in the early 1820's. With lengthening transportation systems, both New York and Pennsylvania were reaching into the Ohio Valley and diverting Trans-Allegheny trade from Maryland; New York City and Philadelphia indeed appeared to the people of Maryland to be growing unduly at the expense of their metropolis. Marylanders too were alarmed at prospective action by Virginia, which contemplated the construction of a system of communication to boost her own commercial centers. The chartering of the Baltimore and Ohio was Maryland's reply to the encroachment of enterprising neighbors; it was Baltimore's answer to the challenge of her seaboard competitors.[2]

Yet Maryland was poorly situated for a contest. Both Pennsylvania and Virginia stood athwart her path. Virginia however proved friendly at the inception of the railroad enterprise and actually proffered assistance. But the charter which she granted specifically forbade the Baltimore and Ohio to strike the Ohio River lower than the mouth of the Little Kanawha.[3] Later as her own system of internal improvements seemed endangered she raised other jurisdictional barriers. When the Baltimore and Ohio applied to the Virginia general assembly for an extension of time to comply with the terms of the original charter, that body answered with a statute so weighted with qualifications and conditions that the stockholders refused to accept it.[4]

It was not until 1847 that Virginia grudgingly yielded and enacted a measure that the railroad company would accept. But this was not done without a price. The act contained a provision that the road must not touch the Ohio River "at any point further south than the mouth of Fish Creek," [5] which is eighty miles north of the mouth of the Little Kanawha. This restrictive clause not only denied the company a direct approach to Cincinnati, but also gave notice that Virginia meant only to tolerate the Baltimore and Ohio.

But it went forward; and within a decade the Baltimore and Ohio Railroad attained the proportions of a system.

FROM TRAMWAY TO TRUNK LINE

In 1858 it boasted a main stem, an auxiliary line, and an important branch. The main line, 379 miles long, extended across Maryland and Virginia, from Baltimore to Wheeling. This road opened locally a convenient outlet to the forest, the farm, and the mine; and it provided nationally a new avenue for the expanding trade between seaboard and interior.

The main stem crossed the Potomac River at Harpers Ferry; ran northwesterly through three of Virginia's northeastern counties; re-entered Maryland for easy approach to Cumberland; paralleled the meandering upper Potomac for a score of miles; curved suddenly into Virginia; and finally after traversing the south bank of the Potomac for approximately ten miles, again returned to parental jurisdiction to ascend the first defiant mountain. The road then remained in Maryland to the western limits of Allegany County. From the top of the Allegheny plateau it threaded a serpentine course through northwest Virginia, passing over mountains, under hills, across streams, and through valleys.

Geographically, the Baltimore and Ohio was situated to compete for the trade and travel of the industrial North, the planting South, and the agricultural West. Its strength lay in supporting connections. If the Ohio River trade was declining, the volume of business swelled at railroad junctions. At Benwood, situated four miles south of Wheeling on the eastern bank of the Ohio, the road received passengers and freight that came by steamer from Bellaire, a river town opposite on the Ohio side. Bellaire was the eastern terminus of the Central Ohio Railroad and the southern terminus of the Cleveland and Ohio.

The Baltimore and Ohio company maintained at Grafton a connection with its only auxiliary, the Northwestern Virginia Railroad. This line lay wholly within Virginia and penetrated a hilly region rich in coal, oil, and timber. The western end of this important arm was at Parkersburg, situated on the Ohio, a scant hundred miles below Wheeling. Through the medium of the steamboat this road maintained at Parkersburg a connection with the Marietta and Cincinnati Railroad; and there, too, it intercepted a share of upstream commerce.

The most eastern junction point on the main stem in Virginia was Harpers Ferry, where it was joined by the short Winchester and Potomac Railroad. This road was a convenient vehicle for the commerce of a half dozen of Virginia's lower Shenandoah Valley counties.

The most easterly connection was a short but important branch that had sprung from the very roots of the main stem. It was the Washington Branch Railroad. This line joined Washington and Baltimore; and by means of tramways in streets of the latter it utilized inconvenient and inadequate connections with the Northern Central and the Philadelphia, Wilmington and Baltimore railroads.

The Washington Branch was the last link in the chain of railroad communication between the North and the National Capital. It was also the only way by rail. Main stem and Washington Branch ran parallel between Baltimore and Relay House, a point nine miles west of the city. The remaining distance of thirty-one miles was traversed by a single track road, joined by a lone connecting line. This was the Annapolis and Elk Ridge Railroad which connected midway between Baltimore and Washington. It was this road and the southern half of the Washington Branch of the Baltimore and Ohio that provided a direct overland route between Washington and Maryland's capital; and it was this channel, as will be seen, that proved opportunely efficacious in 1861, when the seat of the Federal government was threatened.

Although three-fourths of the Baltimore and Ohio Railroad lay on Virginia soil, it retained its identity as a Maryland public work. Both the State of Maryland and the City of Baltimore had invested heavily in its securities. On more than one occasion state and city in their corporate capacities had come to its relief. Both had driven hard bargains in the public interest. With only two-fifths of the capital stock of the company in their possession, they counted a majority of six on its board of directors; [6] and under the guise of a capitation tax, the state garnered one-fifth of the gross passenger receipts of the Washington Branch.[7] Of the remaining shares, practically all were in the hands of Maryland residents.[8] There was substance indeed in the current claim that the Baltimore and Ohio was a Maryland enterprise.

When the main stem reached Wheeling on December 24, 1852, it was commonly believed that completion of the road to the Ohio would insure it full quotas of both freight and passengers. The gross receipts of the fiscal year, 1852-1853, seemed to confirm the correctness of this belief.[9] Then came warnings that the company could not long rely upon river commerce as a source of through traffic. Both Pennsylvania Central and New York Central railroads had reached Cincinnati over connecting lines; and both had begun to draw off freights that otherwise might have found a way east over the Baltimore and Ohio. Moreover, travelers deserted the elegant, slow-going Ohio River packets for more rapid transit over Northern rails.[10] To keep pace with events, the Baltimore and Ohio

19

simply had to intercept much of this traffic and divert it into its own channels.

The road was strategically located to accomplish this result. In fact it held the advantage of interior lines. Over three short routes it could strike its opponents in as many sectors.

These were soon salients of attack. With the aid of the Baltimore city council, the company first fostered the extension of the Pittsburgh and Connellsville Railroad southeasterly to the Maryland border to connect with its own main stem at Cumberland.[11] This extension seemed likely to recapture an appreciable volume of eastbound through traffic from the Pennsylvania Central at Pittsburgh; and it would give the lower Monongahela basin a competitive seaboard route. The Northwestern Virginia Railroad was hurried westward from Grafton toward Parkersburg by the urge of the same beneficent patronage.[12] The obvious purpose was to reach Cincinnati over the Marietta and Cincinnati Railroad, the eastern terminus of which was established on the west bank of the Ohio ten miles north of Parkersburg. The third forward thrust was the Central Ohio Railroad which drove deep into the competitor center.

This line, 138 miles long, was being laid from Bellaire to Columbus. At the latter point it made connection with the Columbus and Xenia Railroad, which in turn joined the Little Miami at Dayton. These three constituted the segments of an uninterrupted line between Bellaire and Cincinnati. The Central Ohio was also the axis of a wedge that penetrated to the center of an expanding traffic territory. Columbus was indeed more than a way station for Cincinnati trade; it gave promise of becoming an important distributing point for much of the Central West.

FROM TRAMWAY TO TRUNK LINE

The Baltimore and Ohio management looked cheerfully to the opening of the strategic Central Ohio. There was radiant optimism in a letter written June 12, 1854, by John H. Done, the Baltimore and Ohio master of transportation. It was addressed to the president of the road:[13]

... I do not hesitate to express my conviction that the completion of the Central Ohio Rail Road will open a new era for us. After that event shall have happened, the time from Cincinnati to Wheeling—now by steamboat fully 36 hours—will be reduced to 9 hours at fartherest. A moderate and entirely safe speed upon the Baltimore and Ohio Road will then place the traveller in Baltimore at least five hours earlier than by any other route, and in Philadelphia or New York fully as soon as by any of the routes now travelled by those cities. In this state of things it is fair to presume that this route will command at least an equal share of the great travel between the East and West. ...

The Baltimore and Ohio soon took steps to consolidate its advantages. In the same season, despite its own impecuniousness, it voted a loan of $400,000 to the Central Ohio.[14] If this act contributed to an early opening of the new road, it also smoothed a way for closer relations.

The Baltimore and Ohio did not attain its final objective in this sector without a fight. And oddly the most stubborn opposition came not from competing lines but from an offended third party. As the Central Ohio neared completion in the closing months of 1854, the Baltimore and Ohio and the Central Ohio entered into agreement to establish a ferry connection between Bellaire and Benwood.[15] Fearing isolation the City of Wheeling saw danger in the contract and promptly sought to prevent its consummation; and under authority of alleged statutory rights she sued out an injunction in the Marshall County circuit court. Although the writ was granted, it was dissolved by

THE BALTIMORE AND OHIO IN THE CIVIL WAR

Virginia's highest tribunal.[16] The ferry was then established. In keeping with terms of the accord the transfer was placed under control of the Baltimore and Ohio company, which was authorized to collect sixty cents per ton on freights, mail and express, and twenty-five cents for each passenger, carried either way across the Ohio.[17]

The establishment of this route was however not the last word on western connections. In 1857 the Baltimore and Ohio leased the Northwestern Virginia Railroad, just opened from Grafton to Parkersburg. Although the road had its inception in local initiative and had received impetus from home capital, it had been completed under Baltimore and Ohio Railroad auspices, with financial aid from the City of Baltimore.[18] With the eastern terminus of the Marietta and Cincinnati Railroad fixed at Scotts Landing, it was easily reached from Parkersburg by water. Because of this fact the Northwestern Virginia seemed now the final answer to Baltimore's demand for a more direct route to Cincinnati.

Early in 1857 the Baltimore and Ohio and the Marietta and Cincinnati companies concluded an agreement which officially closed the gap between their terminals. The transfer between Parkersburg and Scotts Landing was placed in the hands of the Marietta and Cincinnati Railroad. It was granted a ferriage for each passenger and for each ton of freight and express equivalent to the charge collected for through traffic of like kind and quantity over fifty-six miles of rail.[19] By this arrangement the tariffs on through traffic between Baltimore and Cincinnati were made approximately equal to prevailing rates between the same cities by way of Benwood and Bellaire.

Not unnaturally the cry went up at Baltimore that the agreement had been negotiated in the interest of the more

22

indirect central route via the Central Ohio Railroad. Obviously it deprived the Northwestern Virginia Railroad of advantages inherent in its geographical location; and the protest rang out in Baltimore that it took from both the city and the Baltimore and Ohio *"all the advantages of the shortest line between the seaboard and the Great West."* [20]

Of no little concern during these years was the financial condition of the company. To discharge floating indebtedness incurred in reaching the Ohio and in making improvements, it had in 1854 borrowed $5,000,000 from the City of Baltimore; [21] in turn it lent two-fifths of a million to the Central Ohio Railroad; and at the close of the ensuing three years its grants-in-aid and loans to the Northwestern Virginia exceeded a million and a half.[22] Another item of embarrassment in Baltimore and Ohio bookkeeping was a high operating ratio which kept net earnings at a low figure despite substantial increases in gross receipts.[23]

Although the financial structure tottered, the board of directors was not deterred in its spending. On December 17, 1856, it voted a thirty per cent bonus dividend on the mere assumption that net earnings absorbed in construction properly belonged to the stockholders. This was paid in certificates of indebtedness bearing interest at six per cent from June 1, 1857, to June 1, 1862. On the latter date the certificates were convertible into common stock of the company.[24] Then as a consideration in the lease of the Northwestern Virginia Railroad, the board contracted to pay the interest on a bond issue of that company that had been guaranteed by the City of Baltimore in 1853.[25]

This liberal policy compounded the company's difficulties during the panic and depression years just ahead; and it narrowly missed insolvency. Although the gross receipts suffered no diminution for a time, net proceeds were not sufficient to meet maturing obligations.[26] In fact, from October 1, 1856, to April 14, 1858, the whole of the net earnings, amounting to approximately two and a quarter millions, was absorbed by pressing demands upon the treasury; and for the same period the floating debt soared to a million dollars. In 1857 dividends were suspended but it was not until March 1, 1858, that the board voted a reduction in rates to stimulate traffic.[27]

By the close of 1857 the road's financial condition became obviously critical. The board consequently appointed a special committee to diagnose the ills of the company and to prescribe remedies. This committee submitted majority and minority reports on April 14, 1858. The majority group, composed mainly of city and state directors, urged immediate liquidation of the floating debt and recommended sharp curtailment of expenditures for construction, excepting only the arching of tunnels. They also condemned the practice of extending financial assistance to connecting lines.[28]

The minority likewise urged retrenchment. To effect it, however, they recommended drastic reductions in both wages and services. Because of "the great competition for business, and the existing reduced and low rates of transportation," they stated, "every practicable economy and reduction of expense, in each department of the service, shall be effected." But their report defended the program of expansion. They emphasized the importance of maintaining friendly relations with the Central Ohio Railroad and illustrated that importance with statistical data; called attention to the fact that that road was dissatisfied with the amount of through traffic it was receiving from

24

the Baltimore and Ohio; and tersely prophesied that unless the Central Ohio management were mollified that company would surely negotiate a traffic alliance with the Baltimore and Ohio's most dangerous rival, the Pennsylvania Central Railroad.[29]

These differences in committee only magnified the divergent principles that actuated opposing factions on the board. State and city maintained that their interests were of a public nature and in consequence superior to those of individual stockholders. Their point of view was exemplified in the attitude of the city directors who had consistently opposed any program of westward expansion which did not comprehend the Northwestern Virginia Railroad.

Quite contrary the private stockholders, under the leadership of Johns Hopkins and John W. Garrett, insisted that the interests of the two classes of owners were mutual and identical. They urged that the road should be operated with a single purpose in view, to increase net earnings. They declared therefore that the company must continue its policy of meeting competition and of reaching out for all available traffic.[30]

Events of succeeding months pointed to an impasse. The Cumberland coal trade, on which the road relied for its largest intra-line tonnage, continued to decline in spite of the recent reduction of rates on that commodity.[31] On July 15, 1858, the Central Ohio Railroad notified the Baltimore and Ohio of its intention to "invite to the eastern terminus of its road all parties representing every avenue of trade, east, to compete for the traffic which it may deliver at that point." [32] This it would do unless the Baltimore and Ohio company discontinued its practice of granting preferential rates by water on westbound through traffic. Finally, the business summary of the fiscal year, ending September 30, 1858, disclosed facts and figures that could not be ignored.

Gross receipts of the main stem had declined three-fourths of a million, while the reduction in operating expenses barely exceeded $125,000; and working expenses of the Northwestern Virginia Railroad were actually in excess of its gross receipts. There was a small increase in the revenue of the Washington Branch; but this was largely dissipated by a relative growth of operating expenses.[33]

The time indeed seemed propitious for changes of both policy and personnel. On November 17, 1858, the directors chose a new president. He was one of their own number—John W. Garrett.

CHAPTER II

Expansion and Conflict (1858-1860)

JOHN WORK GARRETT was a member of the Baltimore banking house of Robert Garrett and Sons. He had studied at LaFayette College but he owed his quick rise to the tutelage of his father and the good fortune of early initiation into his father's firm. It was in fact this connection that gave him a place on the Baltimore and Ohio board of directors in 1855; the house of Garrett held high rank among the private stockholders. Robert Garrett and Sons had also invested heavily in stocks and bonds of the Central Ohio Railroad. This background alone added strong leaven to Baltimore and Ohio policy. Nor could Garrett's personality easily go unnoticed. In physique he towered above his fellow men with Bismarckian proportions. His forehead was high, his jaw heavy, his face sometimes stern. While his business upbringing conduced to suavity of manner, his heavy tread and ponderous fist marked him as a man of direct action.

Garrett's first concern was to place the railroad on an earning basis. He promptly cut operating expenses by effecting sharp reductions in both wages and personnel. Next he adjusted rates and schedules to meet competition of rival trunk lines and to obtain from local traffic the highest compensating return.[1]

Garrett was soon able to demonstrate the wisdom of his strategy. Although the gross receipts showed a decrease over the preceding fiscal year, he reported on September 30, 1859, net earnings of two and a half millions. This was $857,054.55 more than had been earned during the previous year.[2] He now liquidated the company's most pressing obligations. Next he nonchalantly announced that the "return to regular payment of semi-annual dividends has been judiciously accomplished, and can hereafter be confidently relied upon." [3]

Garrett did not accomplish this result without opposition. He early aroused the antagonism of local shippers, Baltimore merchants, a number of state and city directors, and others, all of whom had felt the sting of his Peter-to-Paul policy of discrimination against the short haul.

None could deny that the Baltimore and Ohio was hard pressed by the aggressiveness of Northern rivals. Despite the existence of an agreement establishing uniform rates for through traffic, each of the four trunk lines—the New York Central, the New York and Erie, the Pennsylvania Central, and the Baltimore and Ohio—was encroaching upon the traffic areas of the others and by the use of rebates, drawbacks, and other ingenious means, was diverting traffic to its own lines. It was inevitable that repeated infractions of both the letter and spirit of the compact should render the agreement useless. It was indeed dissolved in March, 1859.[4] The immediate result was the intensification of competition. In the contest which ensued the Baltimore and Ohio was pitted against its natural rival, the Pennsylvania Central Railroad.

Since the opening of the Northwestern Virginia Railroad in 1857, the Pennsylvania Central had pursued a program of aggression on the Baltimore and Ohio western front. The Pennsylvania early inaugurated a policy of paying a drawback equal to the cost of boating on freight carried by water from Parkersburg to Pittsburgh, and employed similar means to draw off through traffic from the Baltimore and Ohio at Wheeling.[5]

One of Garrett's first official acts as president was retaliation. He offered similarly attractive terms to river trade between Pittsburgh and Wheeling and made rate reductions that turned a stream of through traffic into Baltimore and Ohio channels. No small tonnage was soon passing between Pittsburgh and Philadelphia by way of Baltimore. The Pennsylvania Central however answered in kind and routed freights to Baltimore over its main stem and connecting lines at rates equally close to suicidal.[6]

After the disruption of the compact, this feud expanded into a hotly contested rate war that extended far down the Ohio. The Baltimore and Ohio accepted consignments for Philadelphia and New York delivery at Louisville, Cincinnati, and other Western cities at figures far below the charges imposed on similar quantities shipped from the same points to Baltimore.[7] It carried flour from Parkersburg to New York at the incredibly low rate of seventeen cents per barrel.[8]

If these practices resulted in a larger through tonnage, they boded only ill for the company's financial health. For the month of April, 1859, the gross earnings of the Baltimore and Ohio main stem were $101,174.74 less than for the corresponding period in 1858.[9] It was not unnatural that out of desire to recoup its losses on through traffic the company should maintain local rates at customary levels and raise them substantially at noncompetitive points.

The most persistent objectors to Garrett's policy of charging more for the short than for the long haul were Baltimoreans. They dissented, it is true, because Baltimore was forced to pay higher rates; but their chief objections were to the lower rates accorded Philadelphia and New York. Garrett's rate policies were making "Baltimore only a tender to New York, and her merchants mere brokers living here," [10] gibed the Baltimore *Daily Exchange*. The Baltimore and Ohio itself was caricatured in this newspaper as "a stepmother to Baltimore and a handmaid to Philadelphia and New York." Business men believed that Baltimore was rapidly losing advantages inherent in her geographical position; they were not slow in reminding Garrett that he was in the habit of proclaiming the city's geographical superiority.[11]

Opposition to Garrett's policies took definite form and assumed threatening proportions in the January session of the Maryland general assembly, 1860. That body received numerous petitions and memorials praying relief from burdensome and unfair rates imposed by the Baltimore and Ohio company; and in logical sequence it entertained measures looking to effective restraint on the rate making powers of that corporation.[12]

First it appointed a special committee to collect data on approved methods of railroad administration. Then it called Garrett before an investigating committee and requested him to answer whether his company had discriminated against Baltimore in the manner alleged.

Garrett replied that the Baltimore and Ohio was making a "constant effort to contribute to the welfare and prosperity" of the city "by making the largest practicable differences in its favor." He stated with characteristic emphasis that under no circumstances would the tonnage carried through the city to Philadelphia and New York have found a market in Baltimore. In any event, he said, the revenues accruing from through traffic were beneficial to the local shipper, for they enabled the company to keep local rates "generally below the rates authorized by the charter, and below the average rates of other roads." [13]

He then made a summary retort that mirrored his economic philosophy. He coolly expressed the opinion that rate making was a "matter which involves the theory of trade, and more than this, the very freedom of trade" and suggested cogently that the subject matter of the investigation was beyond legislative competence. [14]

Garrett also drew fire from another angle. He was accused of unduly favoring the central route to Cincinnati. The Baltimore Corn and Flour Exchange passed a formal resolution excoriating the Baltimore and Ohio management for indifference to advantages offered by the Northwestern Virginia route to the West, which the City of Baltimore had subsidized with both cash and credit. [15] In a message to the city council, Mayor Thomas Swann, himself a former Baltimore and Ohio president, weighed the relative merits of the Northwestern Virginia Railroad and the main stem as competing routes for the Cincinnati trade. [16] He produced figures showing that the distance from Cincinnati to Baltimore by way of Parkersburg was forty-nine miles shorter than the more northern route via the Central Ohio Railroad. He demonstrated that the southern route held an advantage of five miles over that of the Pennsylvania Central between Philadelphia and Cincinnati, while conversely the latter boasted an advantage of forty-four miles over the Baltimore and Ohio central route. He also emphasized obvious advantages in connections.

With these factors in its favor the arguments supporting Baltimore's chosen route to the West seemed unanswerable. Certainly they were of sufficient moment to warrant immediate improvement of the Northwestern Virginia railway with a view to making it a first class road. There was in fact urgent reason for this. Between Pittsburgh and Steubenville a new railroad was being built. The existing lines between these points were the Pittsburgh, Cleveland and Chicago, and the Cleveland and Ohio, which joined at Wellsville, Ohio; both were convenient auxiliaries of the Pennsylvania Central Railroad; but the route formed by them paralleled the curving northern bank of the Ohio. The projected road followed the chord of the Ohio River arc and saved the Pennsylvania Central twenty-five miles.

This prospective advantage in running time was not all that disturbed interested parties at Baltimore. What appeared ominous was the unpleasant prospect of a junction at Steubenville of this new line with another, the Steubenville and Indiana Railroad. If effected this connection would give the Pennsylvania Central an advantage of sixty-nine miles over the Baltimore and Ohio main stem route between Philadelphia and Cincinnati; and by the same token it would turn the scant advantage of five miles held by the Northwestern Virginia route into a disparity of twenty.

These considerations led to the inevitable conclusion that the southern route via Parkersburg was the only possible competitive one available to the Baltimore and Ohio company. They led straight to the recommendation that the Baltimore city council should insist upon a more convenient connection between the Marietta and Cincinnati and the Northwestern Virginia railroads. Swann's specific proposal was that the council should lend its assistance in the construction of a branch road from Scotts Landing to Belpre, a river town opposite Parkersburg.[17]

EXPANSION AND CONFLICT

Garrett also saw an obstacle to his program raised in still another quarter. The City of Wheeling had not relented her determination to compel the Baltimore and Ohio to abandon its ferry connection at Benwood and effect a junction with the Central Ohio Railroad within her own corporate limits. In fact the Wheeling program had been expanded and it now contemplated the development of an important railroad center to which the Hempfield Railroad and the Cleveland and Ohio Railroad were expected to add prestige.[18] The entire network that converged upon her limits was to be integrated by a railroad bridge across the Ohio.

The main obstacle to the plans of Wheeling was the traditional attitude of Virginia toward bridging the Ohio River. In fact that state had long regarded the lower Ohio Valley as her own special trading preserve. She had "always carefully guarded the passes of the Ohio River, and . . . rejected every effort of other Atlantic States to bridge its waters. . . ."[19] In 1860 there was a special reason why Virginia should interpose objections. The Covington and Ohio Railroad was auspiciously started toward the Great Kanawha Valley and it was expected soon to strike the Ohio near the Kentucky border. With the completion of her own road Virginia's day of battle with the Baltimore and Ohio and the Pennsylvania Central for dominion over Cincinnati traffic would be at hand. As the deciding factor in the contest Virginia correctly pinned hope on the greater directness of her route. In face of accepted belief that a railroad bridge over the Ohio would eliminate the equivalent of fifty miles of running distance, it is not strange that the commonwealth had no bargain for her competitors.

Virginia had last asserted her resolution in the early

33

1850's. With the opening of the Pennsylvania Central Railroad to Pittsburgh, the embryonic Hollidays Cove Railroad applied to the Virginia general assembly for a charter. It requested authority to build a railroad from the Pennsylvania border across the Virginia panhandle and to bridge the Ohio at Steubenville. There was great anxiety in Wheeling; for her business men saw in the move designs of both Pittsburgh and the Pennsylvania Central Railroad to cripple their trade and deny their city advantages inherent in its position as the western terminus of the Baltimore and Ohio. Despite Wheeling's obvious interests, however, the fight against the proposed charter was conducted on grounds of state policy. Mainly through unflagging efforts of Charles W. Russell, a talented Wheeling lawyer in the pay of the Baltimore and Ohio Railroad Company, the general assembly was persuaded that the construction of the proposed Hollidays Cove Railroad and Steubenville bridge was "a commercial ruse, designed to bring commercial advantage to Philadelphia in competition with the Covington and Ohio Railroad. . . ." [20] The charter was denied.

The defeat of the Hollidays Cove Railroad charter aroused bitter feelings in Virginia's most northerly panhandle counties, Brooke and Hancock. Resentment smouldered for almost a decade. By 1860 however the partisans of Wheeling and advocates of the Steubenville bridge had composed their differences. They agreed upon compromise measures and caused two bills to be introduced in the lower house of the Virginia general assembly.

These measures authorized the construction of two bridges.[21] One chartered the Hollidays Cove Railroad and gave that corporation power to span the Ohio in the vicinity of Steubenville; the other incorporated the Wheeling Bridge Company and empowered it to erect a bridge over the same stream at Wheeling. These bills contained numerous qualifications and restrictions which made the construction of the Hollidays Cove Railroad and the erection of the Steubenville bridge contingent upon progress *pari passu* of the Wheeling bridge and other public works embraced in the Wheeling plan of municipal growth. To many, Wheeling seemed to be driving a shrewd but unscrupulous bargain which if consummated would deprive the Covington and Ohio Railroad of its natural advantages. Although opposition was sharp in both houses, the bills passed by substantial majorities.[22]

Debate and final vote on these measures reflected legislative logrolling, but their passage was not due alone to political manipulation. Virginians were already aroused by hostile antislavery sentiment and unfriendly legislation at the North; and they were advocating policies of self-sufficiency and self-defense. Although the hour was late, the general assembly now saw the wisdom of conciliating regional differences and the necessity of binding all sections of the state by commercial and social ties. The appropriation of funds for the survey of a railroad from White Sulphur Springs to Grafton and the rise of sentiment favorable to connecting the Alexandria, Loudoun and Hampshire and the Baltimore and Ohio railroads were symptomatic of the growing demand for unity and security.[23] To all appearance it was these considerations which caused seaboard Virginians to execute a belated about-face and clear the way for the authorization of the Wheeling and the Steubenville bridges.

The Wheeling Bridge charter contained provisions incompatible with Garrett's policies and he sent a lobbyist to Richmond to combat it.[24] His effort was however of

35

no avail, for the general assembly refused to delete the objectionable features. The statute specifically provided that upon completion of the railroad bridge at Wheeling no exchange of freights and passengers across the Ohio River from one railroad to another was to be permitted within twenty-five miles of the city except within the corporate limits of that municipality.[25] This provision nullified a decision of Virginia's highest court and sounded a knell for the Benwood-Bellaire connection, in operation since 1854. On the other hand the Baltimore and Ohio company, in common with certain other railroads, was allowed to subscribe to the capital stock of the bridge company without restriction as to amount. Garrett's company was thus given an opportunity to own and to operate the bridge. But the use of the structure by the Baltimore and Ohio was conditional upon its agreement to abandon discriminations against the short haul in the state and to transport at fair rates the freight cars of any Virginia railroad authorized to connect with its lines.[26]

Virginia was destined never to put these statutes to the test. None of her projected railroads succeeded in effecting a junction with the Baltimore and Ohio in the months that intervened between their passage and the opening of the Civil War. Nor was the Wheeling bridge completed in the interim. The statutes were however not without effect. The railroad management categorically listed them as "inimical legislation," alongside other regulatory measures which Virginia had enacted. They indeed revived the impression that that state was unfriendly and had not abandoned its policy of keeping close watch over every activity of the company; and it was this alleged unfriendliness that was to give added force in wartime to the movement to deprive Virginia entirely of her jurisdiction over it.

It was in this unhappy season that Garrett turned to internal reform. From the beginning of his official connection with the road, he had thundered against the arrangement which gave Maryland and Baltimore majority control of its affairs. He contended that their supremacy on the board of directors was unfair to private interests; and he saw danger in political control. Upon elevation to the presidency therefore he schemed to emasculate this public influence. Opposition of a number of state and city directors to his policies, alleged espionage by some, and the actual meddling of others in the administrative affairs of the company urged him on.[27] Fundamentally, the situation which seemed to demand a reconstitution of the board was the fact that the private stockholders with a voting strength of approximately fifty-nine thousand shares were represented by twelve directors, while the state and city with only forty thousand chose eighteen.[28]

To remove this inequality Garrett caused a bill to be introduced in the Maryland senate in the January session of 1860. It was framed to change radically the basis of representation; it provided for one director for each block of twenty-five hundred shares of common stock. The measure contemplated a board of directors of forty-one members. Of these, twenty-three were to represent the private stockholders; the remaining eighteen, the State of Maryland and the City of Baltimore.[29]

There was a shower of petitions and memorials for and against the passage of this measure. The Baltimore press became immediately the vehicle of a spirited discussion; and a few pamphlets were issued to fan the flame. Garrett's supporters emphasized obvious benefits in private

37

management and the potential dangers of political influence. They held up the uncertain business qualifications and the limited political tenure of public appointees on the board as notorious weaknesses.[30] Garrett's followers had much to say too about the positive virtues of individualistic control. The incentive to earn would be the primary motive of the railroad management; and with increased earnings all interested parties—state, city, and individual stockholders—would receive commensurate returns in dividends. Even local citizens would share in this prosperity; for they would receive direct benefits from relative decreases in taxation.[31] At best, they urged, the state and the city should maintain only a nominal representation on the board and that merely to serve as a sentry for the public interest.

Arguments were equally pointed on the other side. It was held obviously unreasonable to expect Maryland and Baltimore to relinquish control of a public work in which each had almost vital concern. Spokesmen for the state and the city emphasized the fact that the board as constituted had saved the company from bankruptcy and was at present leading it out of the financial wilderness. Because the company was firmly established on a substantial dividend basis, they recommended that its policies should be shaped toward the relief and welfare of communities it served rather than the accumulation of greater profits.[32] They also gave biting rebuttal to the charge of political interference in its affairs. They answered that the removal of state and municipal supervision would place the road in the hands of a small group of Baltimore capitalists who would build up "an oligarchy as dangerous, odious and irresistible as any that ever ruled or ruined a people." [33]

Next Garrett's opponents sounded a note that was an

38

echo from the "irrepressible conflict." In the event the
bill passed, they stated, Northern interests would surely
acquire working control of the road and use it not only
to their own advantage but to the detriment of both Baltimore and Maryland. More particularly they expressed
fear of the Camden and Amboy Railroad, a corporation
already reputed to be in possession of the Baltimore and
Ohio's most direct eastern connection—the Philadelphia,
Wilmington and Baltimore Railroad. They professed to
believe that the Camden and Amboy interests had also
acquired control of a number of steamship lines south of
Baltimore and had an acquisitive eye on both the Richmond, Fredericksburg and Potomac and the Ohio and
Mississippi railroads. These forebodings stirred apprehension that with the enactment of Garrett's policies into law
the trade of the South and the West would pass into the
hands of Northern rivals of Baltimore.[34]

Whatever the immediate causes, the bill failed. But the
effort was not without significance. It emphasized the importance of the Baltimore and Ohio as a factor in the commercial and political life of Maryland and of Baltimore;
and it impressed upon Garrett the necessity of closer attention to state and municipal politics, if he were to enjoy
tenure in the presidency and shape the destinies of the
company to his liking.

Undaunted by this reverse Garrett pressed forward along
other lines. One of his main objectives was the acquisition
of controlling interest in the Central Ohio Railroad, of
which, as noted above, his own banking house had already
obtained a large fraction. Aside from personal and business motives, there was indeed likelihood that the Central
Ohio might become an arm of the Baltimore and Ohio's
ever watchful rival, the Pennsylvania Central. In fact the

Cleveland and Ohio Railroad had extended its line from Bridgeport to Bellaire and the danger was imminent. Moreover, before midyear the Central Ohio was in great financial need and was receptive to any alliance that promised relief.[35]

Garrett used these facts to advantage in promoting his scheme to establish a great competing line to the Central West. He redoubled his efforts in the purchase of Central Ohio Railroad securities, acquiring them as they came on the market.[36] It was not until 1863 however that the Baltimore and Ohio obtained a majority control of this natural westward extension of its own main stem.

Garrett's plans also comprehended expansion toward the south. One of his pet schemes was to bridge the Potomac at Washington and there effect a connection between his own Washington Branch and the Orange and Alexandria Railroad. From this he might well expect a substantial increase of passengers and tonnage on the Washington Branch. His plan was not without political motives; it gave promise of placating a bloc of Maryland public opinion which was insisting upon closer economic relations with the Southern states. The time indeed seemed propitious for consummation of this plan; and as a first step Garrett applied to the United States Congress for authority to extend his lines in the District of Columbia to the point of junction.[37]

Here he encountered not wholly unexpected resistance. On April 5, 1860, Senator Anthony Kennedy of Maryland introduced in the upper house a bill authorizing the Baltimore and Ohio Railroad Company to build the extension.[38] The measure was almost immediately attacked by Senator Simon Cameron of Pennsylvania. He gave notice that he could not give assent to its provisions unless important qualifying clauses were added; and he announced that he himself would embody them in an amendment.[39]

Cameron's position was a natural one. In its fight with the Pennsylvania Central Railroad for through traffic the Baltimore and Ohio had persistently pursued the policy of favoring the Philadelphia, Wilmington and Baltimore Railroad as against the Northern Central, a road with which the name of Cameron had long been identified, and of which he was still one of the chief stockholders.[40] Nor was this all. The Northern Central was in reality a convenient southern outlet of the powerful Pennsylvania Central Railroad, the officers and employees of which were Cameron's constituents.[41]

But the opposition of the Senator from Pennsylvania was not actuated solely by implicit motives. As a watchful public servant it was plainly his call of duty to obtain a redress of grievances which the traveling public without doubt desired. The Baltimore and Ohio was charged with the practice of refusing to check through baggage tagged to points on the Northern Central Railroad and beyond. This refusal caused both delay and inconvenience to passengers who transferred to that road at Baltimore.[42]

Although the Kennedy Bill failed to advance on the calendar in that session, it came up for consideration early in the next. It was given final hearing on December 21, 1860. On that day Senator Cameron introduced the amendment of which he had given notice seven months before.[43] It provoked heated debate, and the major grievances which it was intended to redress were hotly discussed. The amendment suffered some change of language but it was not emasculated in context. In its modified form it read: [44]

THE BALTIMORE AND OHIO IN THE CIVIL WAR

That all the provisions of this act shall be inoperative unless the said Baltimore and Ohio Railroad Company shall check baggage over their main line or branches to and from Washington city, with and over all railroads terminating at Alexandria, Washington city, or Baltimore, and with the connections of the same, on terms as favorable as the said Baltimore and Ohio Railroad Company may make with any other terminating or connecting lines.

Although the amendment was undoubtedly Cameron's, it might well have been from the pen of Thomas A. Scott, vice-president of the Pennsylvania Central; for on December 24, 1860, Scott wrote Cameron a letter in which he enclosed a copy of a similar amendment that he had composed for certain Pennsylvania members of the House.[45] Cameron was however in strategic position where with concurrent effort he could serve his own interests and promote the public welfare. He pressed the amendment with vigor and it was incorporated in the bill which passed the Senate.

Garrett was highly displeased with this result. He made an effort to persuade the House of Representatives to pass the original as a substitute but failed. He would have no other and frankly notified the lower branch of his dissatisfaction.[46] His plan to connect Baltimore and "principal southern cities" died with the Thirty-Sixth Congress. The crowding of events in the succeeding months relegated the strategy that gave it birth to the limbo of forgotten schemes; but the coming of the war made the union of the Washington Branch and the Orange and Alexandria Railroad a military necessity. The roads were joined via the Long Bridge before the first year of the conflict had passed.

Nor was this the only Garrett scheme grounded in dual

42

EXPANSION AND CONFLICT

motives. To curry favor locally he formulated plans for the completion of the Pittsburgh and Connellsville Railroad from Connellsville to Cumberland, in which the Baltimore city council had already invested heavily; in keeping with local current demand for Southern economic independence, he purposed to establish a line of steamers between Baltimore and a leading European port.[47]

By 1861 the Baltimore and Ohio seemed cured of financial ills. A swelling traffic volume augmented gross receipts; and as the management cut down working expenses, net earnings piled high in the treasury. The company was not only meeting its creditors but was also gratifying the expectations of public and private stockholders. Besides putting aside sums for the various sinking funds and paying semiannual dividends with clock-like regularity, it made heavy expenditures for machinery, rolling stock, second track, bridges and other improvements.[48]

In light of previous conditions and current competition, these accomplishments seemed but little short of miraculous. It was indeed unknown at the time that Garrett was juggling the accounts. Expenditures which the company made for repair and new construction he charged to a "Surplus Account," an unknown quantity that reacted with tonic effect upon the market price of Baltimore and Ohio stocks.[49] In 1861 his policies stood vindicated before a Maryland public that had been both wary and critical. Garrett was proclaimed as one of the foremost of railway executives.[50]

At the beginning of the Civil War the Baltimore and Ohio represented an investment in excess of thirty millions.[51] Construction and maintenance, the use of heavy rails, and the employment of up-to-date types of rolling stock and machinery involved expenditures that made it

43

one of America's most costly railroads. The management
had at its command 513 miles of line exclusive of sidings and second tracks, 236 freight and passenger locomotives, 128 passenger and express coaches, 3,451 coal, freight
and ballast cars, and sundry appurtenances in the shops.[52]
This tangible property lay entirely in slave territory but
close to the Mason and Dixon line. With roots fixed in
slave soil and tendrils already reaching into free states the
Baltimore and Ohio in truth occupied at the beginning of
hostilities an unenviable position. Its case resembled "that
of the amphibious animal that could not live on land, and
died in water...." [53] It could be "neither flesh nor fowl—
neither for the Government, nor completely with the
traitors...."

CHAPTER III

Dilemmas in 1861

I F the geographical location of the Baltimore and Ohio suggested a policy of benevolent neutrality in the impending conflict, John W. Garrett's position on burning political questions reflected a partisanship that identified his road with the Southern cause. Until late 1860 his actions seemed to corroborate his sympathies. Few, indeed, had shown greater concern than he over the John Brown affair at Harpers Ferry in 1859. Garrett enthusiastically offered his company's facilities to Washington and Richmond authorities; in truth it was his railroad that made a prompt suppression of the insurrection possible. He was so much alarmed over contingencies that he urged upon the Federal and the two state governments the necessity of maintaining strong military guards in both Virginia and Maryland.[1]

Conveniently enough, Garrett's attitude and behavior during these stirring months were calculated to win favor with a board of directors dominated by proslavery influences; because of civic and corporate interests at stake his co-operation with the constituted authorities was not unnatural. Yet it can hardly be doubted that his action was sincere and his sentiments the product of his Southern background.

Whatever his motives, Garrett made commitments of a rash and positive sort. Not long after the John Brown raid he delivered a short speech before a Baltimore audi-

45

ence. In it he outlined the course his railroad would pursue if sectional war came. It reflected the white heat of the proslavery argument: [2]

> It is a *Southern line*. And if ever necessity should require—which heaven forbid!—it will prove the great bulwark of the border, and a sure agency for home defense.
> It has the ability, sir, with its equipment of 4,000 locomotives and cars, to transport daily 10,000 troops and with its disciplined force of 3,500 men has always in its service the nucleus of an army.
> During a period when agitation, alarm and uncertainty prevail, is it not right, is it not becoming, that Baltimore should declare her position in "the irrepressible conflict" threatened and urged by Northern fanaticism?

This effervescence was however soon supplanted by studied decision; for the heart soon gave way to the head. Garrett's change of front first became public knowledge when the Washington railroad convention assembled on January 23, 1861. Here it was apparent that he had about-faced to a more judicious temper. He joined representatives of leading railroads of the Northern and the Border states in their plea to Congress for adoption of the Crittenden program. They extolled this as "such a settlement of the slavery controversy as would banish the slave question from the Halls of Congress and the arena of Federal politics." [3] Nor did he change position with the failure of the Crittenden compromise. During the ominous weeks that followed, he eschewed political activity and kept his own counsel on vital public questions.[4] He wrestled instead with problems that arose because of the difficult position of his road.

One of the first of these resulted from a change of mind by President-elect Abraham Lincoln. Contrary to first reports that the incoming President would proceed to

Washington via Wheeling and the Baltimore and Ohio main stem, announcement was made on January 27, 1861, that a more northern itinerary had been definitely arranged.[5] This change, it was believed, was dictated by threats of violence by bitter-enders in both Virginia and Maryland.

Garrett deplored this wholly unexpected turn; he rushed forward to defend both his railway and the region it served. "Our road is regarded, both in Maryland and Virginia, as a monument of the common enterprise of their people, and as the means of a common prosperity," [6] he declared. "This feeling is of itself sufficient to protect the travel and freight of the road from all annoyance," he explained. "You may be assured that whatever is done in Maryland or Virginia will be done with a steady regard to all the rights of persons and property of all sections of the land," he asserted with some exaggeration.

Garrett's parting shot was the flat statement that his railroad had been victimized by agents of rival lines who were spreading alarm in the West "for the sole purpose of interfering with the trade and travel on the shortest route to the seaboard, that they might secure it for themselves." Nor did he end his expostulation without expressing regret that the man of the hour should unwittingly contribute to the perpetuation of this venality.

The "irrepressible conflict" had in fact already begun to take toll of the Baltimore and Ohio's through tonnage. As early as mid-January, 1861, Western shippers had countermanded bills of lading and re-routed consignments over competing Northern trunk lines. They professed to believe that Maryland was on the verge of secession and that the hazards of exportation at Baltimore were too great for risk.[7] Even greater seemed the probability of the

47

detention or loss of goods in transit through Virginia. To combat this apprehension, Garrett relied solely on stock assertions about the inimical designs of rival roads. His explanation fell flat and receipts from through traffic continued to decline. Suffice it to say, by February 1, 1861, the slump had become so pronounced that he was called upon to compound a new remedy.

Garrett did so and applied it in his own inimitable way. Calling up his earlier assurances, he again declared that his road was safe and free "from all apprehended warlike dangers." [8] Then he pledged absolute guarantee that the Baltimore and Ohio company would indemnify shippers for all losses incurred on its road from "political or military causes." This announcement brought quick restoration of confidence. Despite the fact that uneasiness persisted in some sections of Baltimore and Ohio territory, the company soon recaptured its through traffic; it enjoyed a profitable Western trade until the very beginning of hostilities.

Whatever hope Baltimore and Ohio officials entertained for continued tranquillity among Western shippers was however shattered by April events. On the fifteenth President Lincoln issued his first call for volunteers. Following this proclamation opinion quickly spread that the secession of Virginia was only a matter of formality. [9] Garrett acted quickly. He repeated his assertion that his line was entirely safe and renewed the guarantee of compensation for losses. His telegram to an inquiring patron is typical of many replies he sent out from Baltimore during this critical period: [10]

There is no occasion for such fears. Business is proceeding on our road, and in this city, with usual regularity and reliability. . . . This company continues to guarantee all shipments against damages in transportation upon our road, arising from political or military causes. You are aware of the abundant financial ability and safety of this company.

But before these assuring words could dry on paper, Garrett faced a knottier problem. A report of the most insidious nature was making the rounds at the North that the Baltimore and Ohio management had refused to carry Federal troops for the defense of Washington. Since it first became current in the West, Garrett impulsively nailed it as the handiwork of the Pennsylvania Central Railroad.

Again he turned to the telegraph. First he issued specific instructions to his Western agents; then he outlined carefully his policy to officials of connecting lines. His directions to the company's agent at Bellaire are worthy of the leisure of a professional soldier. "Until further orders you [are] to take all troops or munitions that offer at regular rates," [11] he stated. "Our company fully recognizes the present legal authorities State and National under which we live, and as common carriers propose to promptly and safely transport all passengers or freight that those authorities may desire. . . ."

Before the rumor could be laid however more substantial evidence appeared to give it color. Soon after President Lincoln's call for volunteers, Garrett and Governor William Dennison of Ohio concluded arrangements for the transportation of approximately eight hundred Ohio volunteers from Parkersburg and Wheeling to Washington. Preparations for the movement were all but complete when in the evening of April 17 Garrett notified Dennison that his road must withdraw from the undertaking because of lack of facilities. He then explained that he had just received notice of the arrival in Baltimore next day of 2,500 Federal soldiers en route to Washington; all available cars

49

would be needed on the Washington Branch.[12] Dennison could not conceal his mixed emotions over this sudden change of plans, and his message to the War Department

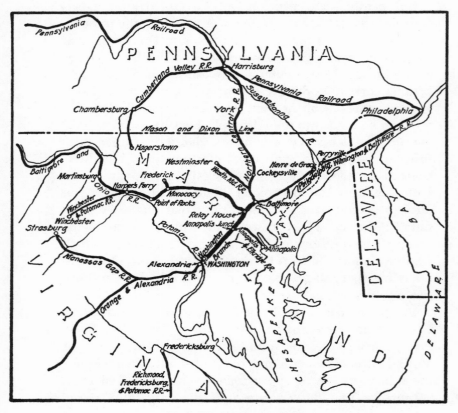

THE WASHINGTON BRANCH

undoubtedly gave weight to the charge that the Baltimore and Ohio management was of doubtful loyalty.[13]

The situation which caused Garrett to change his mind had developed without warning during the afternoon of

April 17. Between four and five o'clock William P. Smith, master of transportation, received notice that not fewer than 2,000 troops would arrive at Baltimore over the Philadelphia, Wilmington and Baltimore Railroad next day.[14] He was also informed that about the same number would detrain from the Northern Central. Dispatches conveying this information had scarcely been read when J. Edgar Thomson, president of the Pennsylvania Central Railroad Company, alighted from a train at Baltimore. He came as a personal agent of the United States Secretary of War, Simon Cameron, to co-ordinate transportation agencies centering in the city. Baltimore and Ohio officials promptly gave him assurance of their co-operation.[15]

The negative side of the picture also supplied facts which supported Garrett's position. Without doubt the political situation along his road from the Ohio to the Chesapeake was critical by the evening of April 17. News of Virginia's secession flashed over the telegraph and headlined newspapers; word came that Virginia militiamen were marching on Harpers Ferry; both passengers and trainmen arriving from the western end of the line reported a hostile, threatening citizenry in some of Virginia's counties.[16]

It was thus easy for the Baltimore and Ohio president to find justification for refusing the Ohio troops; probably he welcomed the opportunity to do so; but it is doubtful if he was actuated by improper or unpatriotic motives. In fact, the safety of the troops and the integrity of the railroad seemed to command a strong measure of caution. If Garrett was chargeable with duplicity or insincerity, a more tenable indictment could have been brought against him for his misrepresentations to inquiring shippers who were assured during this same period of uncertainty that

51

tranquillity prevailed along the entire extent of his road.
If Garrett needed vindication for failure to keep his
engagement with Dennison, it was forthcoming in events.
On April 18, he received a message from the local Baltimore and Ohio attorney at Clarksburg stating that the
war scare was spreading in western Virginia and that residents were preparing to prevent the passage of Federal
troops from the West; [17] on the same day he received at
his office in Baltimore a messenger that had been sent by
the mayor of Charles Town, Virginia, who wished to obtain assurance that the Baltimore and Ohio would not
transport government troops through Virginia or move
arms and munitions from the United States arsenal at
Harpers Ferry. The messenger hinted that if some guarantee were not given there was grave danger that the company's long bridge spanning the Potomac at Harpers
Ferry would be destroyed.[18]

The last occurrence of the day was however the event
which gave Garrett's decision the force of wisdom. Late in
the evening Virginia troops reached Harpers Ferry and
occupied the town. They posted guards at the railroad
bridge and established a watch at the telegraph.[19] Through
traffic on the main stem thereafter passed only with the
consent of Virginia.

In Baltimore events moved quite as rapidly. Throughout the evening of April 17 and the forenoon of the following day, Baltimore and Ohio general officers worked
beaver-like to complete arrangements for forwarding the
United States troops to Washington.[20] None came until
the afternoon of April 18, when a small detachment of
regulars and some Pennsylvania volunteers arrived at the
Northern Central Station. These were transferred to the
Baltimore and Ohio's Camden Station without difficulty,

although there were hoots and hisses from the swelling crowds along the line of march. A few bystanders threw stones at the volunteers. But all were entrained without serious injury.[21]

Next day the temper of Baltimoreans was put to a stiffer test. It was the eventful nineteenth of April. Too well is it known how the Sixth Massachusetts regiment was moved from the President Street Station through city streets; how it was attacked by a mob infuriated by the spectacle of Northern soldiery on Maryland soil; how the troops finally reached Camden Station, although not without spilling blood; and how in a shower of missiles they boarded Washington Branch trains for the last leg of their journey.[22]

Meanwhile other units came in on the Philadelphia, Wilmington and Baltimore Railroad and stood at the President Street Station awaiting orders. None seemed to be forthcoming and civil authorities seized the initiative. At a conference of city officials in which sat Governor Thomas H. Hicks of Maryland it was decided to close Baltimore's streets to military forces. The decision was sent immediately to Garrett who had accepted responsibility for making the transfers. The message contained notice that "the troops now here be sent back to the borders of Maryland." [23]

Garrett promptly telegraphed this information to Samuel M. Felton, president of the Philadelphia, Wilmington and Baltimore Railroad, and indicated his intention of carrying out the policies of the civil power. The waiting detachments were then sent back toward Philadelphia; and troops that arrived at the Northern Central Station during the afternoon were promptly ordered to return to Pennsylvania.[24] That night both the Northern

THE BALTIMORE AND OHIO IN THE CIVIL WAR

Central and the Philadelphia, Wilmington and Baltimore railroads were cut near the city by direction of municipal authorities.[25] Thus ended an episode which severed rail communication between Washington and the North.

These events brought no end of trouble to Baltimore and Ohio officials. From the arrival of the first detachments on April 18 to the departure of the Sixth Massachusetts next day, Garrett and his assistants put forth every effort to allay disorder and prevent bloodshed. They shared police responsibilities with city officers and only good fortune seems to have saved them from harm. Like the police they interposed themselves between the rioters and the soldiers; [26] this was done despite the fact that there was growing belief in the mob that the Baltimore and Ohio was in large measure responsible for the presence of the invaders.

In sober truth, this belief evolved with such uncommon rapidity that by the second day it had reached the stage of open antagonism. In the afternoon of April 19, a ruffled, menacing crowd gathered at Camden Station and tried to force entrance to the company's general offices. Unsuccessful in this attempt, the ringleaders denounced the railroad in unmeasured terms and warned its officials that the building would be burned if they moved other Northern troops.[27] This spirit was manifest far down the tracks toward Washington. From various points came disconcerting news that unfriendly groups of watchful men were stationed along the line ready to tear up the tracks.[28]

These were not the only attempts at intimidation on this memorable day. The president and other executive officers of the company received many anonymous letters. The uncertainty of the times is reflected in this specimen, written in a bold distinctive hand and addressed to John W. Garrett personally: [29]

One Hundred of us, Firm Respectable, Resolute men—have determined & Sworn to each other, to destroy *"every"* Bridge & tear up your Track on both lines of your Road—(the Main & the Branch) between this City & their head points—If you carry another Soldier over either line of your Road after Saturday April 20th. We trust Dear Sir that you will hearken unto the request of your Southern Fellow Citizens & save us this labour which we will very much regret to undertake. This organization of ours extends from here to Grafton & Washington & your trains will be watched. Spare us Dear Sir this to us unpleasant duty. Many of our Committee know you personally, some intimately, but the nature of our Oaths prevent us from seeing you in person. I am requested Sir to thus notify you. We have a large force ready to answer our calls.

Garrett received another communication that was framed in even uglier mood. It purported to be the collective sentiment of fifteen hundred residents of western Maryland. It demanded the summary dismissal of all Republicans holding positions on the main stem between Monocacy Bridge and Harpers Ferry.[30]

The company drew other fire. Garrett's telegram to Samuel M. Felton in the afternoon of April 19 had made it plain that because of the attitude of city and state authorities the Baltimore and Ohio could take no further part in making troop transfers at Baltimore. His message was garbled in news channels and again the Baltimore and Ohio management was held up in the Northern press as disloyal.

On April 20 the nationalistic Wheeling *Intelligencer* issued an extra which gave this report momentum. It contained a bald statement that although the company had refused to carry government troops it was willing to transport the soldiers of Maryland and Virginia.[31] This unhappy item immediately focused suspicion on Baltimore and Ohio officials; [32] and for many months Garrett and his associates were dogged with imputations of a most unsavory sort.

The Baltimore and Ohio was at the crossroads. It was under suspicion at the North and the South alike. Secretary Simon Cameron notified Garrett that the transportation of "rebel troops" over his railroad would be held a treasonable act.[33] Then came this pungent notice from John Letcher, governor of Virginia: "In the event that you allow Federal troops to be passed over your road, I will take possession of so much of said road as lies within the limits of this State. It is due to the South that your road, located within slave territory, shall not be used to the prejudice of the slaveholding States, and especially the State of Virginia." [34]

Further embarrassment was in store because the War Department still held to its purpose of passing troops through Baltimore. In truth late in the afternoon of April 19, Secretary Cameron directed Samuel M. Felton to send "them on prepared to fight their way through, if necessary." [35] But no troops were sent until Sunday, April 21. Then approximately three thousand men under the command of Brigadier General George C. Wynkoop unexpectedly alighted from Northern Central trains at Cockeysville within fourteen miles of Baltimore.

The effect was electric in the city. Churchgoers left their pews, congregations were dismissed, citizens flew to arms. Garrett soon heard the news and wired it to Mayor George William Brown who was at that very hour in Washington trying to convince President Lincoln of the impolicy of sending troops through Baltimore.[36]

Garrett's telegram must have closed the discussion, for the President agreed to return the troops to York, Pennsylvania. Secretary Cameron transmitted the order to their commanding officer but not without writing in an important qualifying statement. In its amended form it directed the commander "to take care to leave force sufficient along the road to keep it safe from depredation of every kind and within his entire controll [sic]." [37]

The main body soon recrossed the Mason and Dixon line; but the Northern Central, commonly called "Cameron's road" because of his personal interests in it, was kept open almost to Baltimore's suburbs.

The United States however did not persist in its first plan and temporarily abandoned the Northern Central route. Instead, the War Department fell back on a supplementary line of communication. On April 23, it established a military route from Perryville on the Susquehanna to Washington by way of Annapolis.[38] Troops and supplies routed over the Philadelphia, Wilmington and Baltimore Railroad were transferred to steamers at Perryville, then carried down Chesapeake Bay to Maryland's capital. From this point to Washington movement was by rail. The land segment of the route embraced the whole of the Annapolis and Elk Ridge Railroad and twenty-two miles of the Washington Branch of the Baltimore and Ohio.

The Federals took formal possession of this route on the day it was established. Detachments were stationed at various points south of Annapolis and guards soon patrolled the tracks to Washington. The United States forces seized all railroad equipment in sight and put it to military use.[39] Four days later Secretary Cameron appointed as superintendent to operate this military railway none other than Thomas A. Scott, vice-president of the Pennsylvania Cen-

tral Railroad. The order which announced Scott's appointment carried explicit directions to local railroad authorities to "conform to his instructions in all matters pertain-
ing to their management." [40]

Thomas A. Scott had energy and imagination. One of
his first official acts was to dispatch recommendations to
the Secretary of War. He urged that the revenue cutter
"Harriett Lane" or any other well-equipped vessel be
placed on the coast to blockade Baltimore and to protect
transports and passenger steamers between Perryville and
Annapolis; that Fort McHenry compel all passing craft to
heave to for inspection; and that all suspicious ships carrying contraband of war be confiscated and placed in government service. His final words foreshadowed coming
events: "You may rely upon it that action—decisive measures are necessary to satisfy all that you depend upon
North of Mason & Dixon. Isolate Baltimore and subjugate
Maryland—do it promptly." [41]

Garrett was now in another dilemma. If he permitted
southbound trains to leave Baltimore, they would surely
be commandeered for service on the military railway. On
the other hand if he obtained assurance that these trains
would not be molested, there was strong probability that
secessionist sympathizers in Maryland would not permit
them to move. In fact Southern partisans in and near the
city were prepared to go any length to deprive the so-
called Lincoln government use of the road. Watchful, re-
sentful, and alert, they made it plain that company officials
must not suffer additional railroad property to fall into
Federal hands.[42]

Garrett tried a way out but without success. He asked
the War Department for safe conduct for his regular trains
only to find officialdom obstinate. He was curtly informed

that the entire capacity of the military railway was needed for troop movements.[43] Secretary Cameron himself wrote the reply to Garrett's application. It showed that he chafed over recent events at Baltimore; he seemed bent on punitive action. His answer was in part as follows: [44]

> ...I beg leave to say that this Department will consent to your proposal whenever the railroad lines running into Baltimore from the North and East are placed in such a condition as to admit free and uninterrupted travel over them, and when the U. S. Government can be assured that satisfactory arrangements have been made to enable it to transport through Baltimore, unmolested and without interruption, such troops, arms, ammunition, supplies, &c., as it may deem necessary or desire.

Garrett fared better with the Virginia authorities. On April 19 he sent Charles J. M. Gwinn, general counsel, to Harpers Ferry to confer with Major General Kenton Harper, commander of the Virginia militia. Although Governor John Letcher had notified Garrett that his road must not be used to the prejudice of Virginia, he was equally determined to maintain and promote cordial relations with Maryland. There was a minimum of fencing in the negotiations; arrangements acceptable to both the railroad and the commonwealth were quickly concluded. Harper gave tacit promise that his troops would not interfere with the normal business of the main stem.[45] A few days later Governor Letcher issued a special order approving all his subordinate had done.[46]

There was indeed no interruption of traffic. But the Virginians were on the alert for Federal troops from the Ohio. Nor did they limit their actions to strictly defensive measures. They used the road as a line of communication and supply. Military as well as civilian merchandise was

59

purchased in Baltimore and shipped by rail to Harpers Ferry. On a single occasion at least Harper forwarded to Southern men in Baltimore a consignment of muskets.[47]

While the eastern part of the main stem was momentarily serving the cause of secession, political developments in northwestern Virginia pointed to the probability that the western end would pass into Federal hands. Union feeling was strong in most of Virginia's forty-five Trans-Allegheny counties. In fact, northwestern Virginians had promptly shown displeasure at the action of the Richmond secession convention.[48] This part of the Old Dominion was geographically situated to invite invasion from its pro-Union neighbors; it was a veritable wedge driven sharply between Ohio and Pennsylvania; for military reasons alone it was unlikely that these states would permit such strategic territory to be annexed by a foreign confederacy.[49]

At the end of April, 1861, along the Baltimore and Ohio main line there was indeed a marked diversity of opinion and allegiance. The unique position of the road was the subject of a trenchant editorial which summed up picturesquely the basic cause of the railroad's troubles. It was written by Archibald W. Campbell, militant editor of the Wheeling *Intelligencer:* [50]

This road in its geographical position, is to be deeply sympathized with. . . . The main stem runs through 379 miles of country, and through every kind of country, at that. And the public sentiment which it traverses, is not less varied than the soil it passes over. The terminus at one end is among the mobocracy; at the other end, here in Wheeling, among good, order-loving Union men. At Harper's Ferry it is completely under military despotism, and every train has to run the gauntlet of cannon and armed espionage. At Cumberland it passes through loyalty and Union, and from that point on West, it might be said to be all right.

This anomalous situation also disturbed Washington authorities. Even the uninitiated recognized the political and military importance of that part of the main stem held by the hostile Virginians. On April 23, 1861, J. Edgar Thomson, president of the Pennsylvania Central Railroad, wrote Secretary Cameron that "The War Department should at once destroy, if it has not already done so, the bridges on the main stem of the Baltimore and Ohio Railroad as high up as Harper's Ferry." [51]

In view of traditional trunk line rivalries and existing competition, one may doubt whether his recommendation was prompted entirely by unbiased judgment and strong patriotic motives.[52] If the military situation in the vicinity of Washington called for just this kind of advice, there were equally compelling reasons why the United States should not accept it. There was still hope that Maryland might be conciliated by indulgence; Lieutenant General Winfield Scott hinted that he might need the road for an early advance against Harpers Ferry.[53]

While the War Department adopted a policy of watchful waiting, it made preparations against the day when the main line should be closed. General Scott sent a staff officer to Chambersburg, Pennsylvania, to ascertain from Major General Robert Patterson "the means of breaking two bridges . . . , somewhere below Frederick." [54] He undoubtedly meant the two very costly viaducts at Monocacy Junction. Scott, however, only asked Patterson to make a reconnaissance and to "pause a few days for further instructions."

Patterson complied. He detailed soldiers in disguise who proceeded without difficulty to the vicinity of Monocacy Junction and Frederick. They found the railroad well guarded at the bridges and Patterson made plans to strike further west. Before he could do this however his calculations were rendered obsolete by other events. In line with Thomas A. Scott's recommendation the United States had at last resolved to strike Maryland a direct blow.

On May 5, 1861, Brigadier General Benjamin F. Butler moved a Federal force along the Washington Branch Railroad from Annapolis Junction to Relay House. At this junction point, only nine miles from Baltimore, this officer established a position which commanded east-, west-, and southbound traffic. The redoubtable Butler promptly took possession of the main stem with its telegraph lines. He ordered a strict censorship over telegraphic communication. Next he subjected trains to search for contraband; but he permitted the railroad authorities to carry on according to schedule.[55]

This phenomenal tolerance did not last. On May 7, only two days after the occupation, the Federal commander issued orders forbidding the transportation of provisions westward. He also instructed his subordinates to exercise special care in examining express.[56]

Garrett made a vigorous but tactful protest. He informed Butler that more foodstuffs were being moved east than west and called attention particularly to possible retaliation by the Virginians at Harpers Ferry. He also emphasized the impolicy of penalizing the mining population of the Cumberland coal field which leaned heavily on the Baltimore market for subsistence and supplies.[57] Butler was strangely moved by this pleading, and on May 8, modified the order. Thereafter groceries and dry goods, except uniform cloth, were permitted to pass without restriction.[58]

The Federal government was now ready to turn the entire Washington Branch to national use. On May 7, the

War Department granted the company permission to operate trains between Baltimore and Washington on regular schedule. Next day a water route was opened from Perryville to Locust Point in Baltimore.[59] There was now provided a line of supply more direct than the military route via Annapolis. It gave timely relief to the Annapolis and Elk Ridge Railroad, then overloaded with government traffic. On May 9, the first detachment of Federal troops was shunted over this route. In sight of Baltimore wharves 2,700 men disembarked at Whetstone Point under cover of the guns of the "Harriet Lane" and boarded special trains on the Washington Branch of the Baltimore and Ohio.[60] It was left to the realistic Butler to re-establish the broken railway connections at Baltimore.

On May 13, 1861, the Federal commander moved quietly into the city, occupied Federal Hill, and planted his artillery.[61] Without delay the Northern Central and the Philadelphia, Wilmington and Baltimore railroads were repaired and reopened. Their connections with the Baltimore and Ohio were as promptly restored.[62]

The United States now possessed an all-rail route between Washington and points north. Secretary Cameron's determination to establish a line of supply through Baltimore had at last borne fruit.

Despite Federal control of the eastern part of the main stem, Virginia continued her tolerant policy of passing regular traffic at Harpers Ferry. Inspection there was mere formality. In most instances the word of conductors was accepted in lieu of search.[63] The regular passenger, freight, and mail services were maintained throughout the greater part of the month of May; flour from the mills of the Shenandoah Valley was allowed to proceed to the Baltimore market during the same period;[64] and long trains of steam coal for the United States Navy were permitted to pass unmolested to the seaboard.[65] It was not until May 23, 1861, that Virginia saw fit to change her policy. That day she laid a heavy hand on the Baltimore and Ohio.

CHAPTER IV

Opening the Corridor

THERE was indeed drama at the next turn. Virginia's voters ratified the Ordinance of Secession, May 23, 1861. On the same day the leader of the secessionist forces at Harpers Ferry anticipated the result with an act so novel that it was striking.

Since April 27 the command of troops on the northeast border had reposed in Colonel Thomas ("Stonewall") Jackson, a taciturn officer, who but recently had left a professorial chair at Virginia Military Institute. From his post at Harpers Ferry he had watched the frontier with a meager force of militia. Yet he held the lower Shenandoah and the upper Potomac firmly gripped; in his hand were fifty miles of the Baltimore and Ohio main line. It is true that his relations with the railroad company were sharply circumscribed by liberal state policy; but Jackson had not relinquished that discretion which rightly belonged to a commander in the field; and it was his use of it that early marked him as a man of rare talents.

From Point of Rocks, twelve miles east of Harpers Ferry, to Cherry Run, thirty-two miles west, the Baltimore and Ohio was double-tracked. Over these parallel lines the Virginians had permitted interstate commerce to flow with only occasional momentary interruption. Late in April they removed a Federal officer, Brigadier General William S. Harney, from an eastbound passenger train and took him to Richmond; but he was almost immediately released.[1] Yet as the Virginia troops suffered Baltimore and Ohio trains to thunder past, their commanding officer pondered a scheme that promised compensation for this politically expedient indulgence.

Jackson's plan contemplated progressive action. The coal tonnage on the main stem was immoderately heavy. Loaded train after train groaned on the eastbound track during the day as they threaded their way toward the Chesapeake; the night was filled with the strain of panting locomotives returning empty cars to Cumberland.

About May 15, 1861, Jackson gave notice that this lively night traffic disturbed his camp and must cease. His order was peremptory; he commanded the railroad company to refrain from passing any but regularly scheduled passenger and express trains through at night.

Garrett promptly but reluctantly complied. There was left to him only the obvious alternative. He could employ the double tracks to full capacity in daytime.

Jackson's next move was on even thinner pretext. In truth Garrett had scarcely put his new freight schedule in working order when the sagacious Virginian sent him a second notice. The Confederate commander complained that the daytime traffic interfered with necessary military routine and curtly directed that the train schedule be amended. Again he left the railroad management no discretion; he commanded that all freight trains should pass Harpers Ferry each day between the hours of eleven and one.

For days during these appointed hours this double-tracked portion of the Baltimore and Ohio was one of the busiest railroads in America. Then suddenly Jackson posted his actors for the climax. On May 22, 1861, he directed Captain John D. Imboden to cross the Potomac

66

next day and occupy Point of Rocks, the eastern end of the double track. Imboden was to permit all westbound trains to pass, while none were to proceed east. At precisely 12 o'clock, noon, he was to close the line. Imboden followed instructions to the letter.

The crafty Jackson dispatched a like order to Colonel Kenton Harper who, now in Confederate States service, commanded the Fifth Virginia Infantry at Martinsburg. From 11 to 12 o'clock on May 23, 1861, a long stream of coal and freight cars entered the eastbound track at Cherry Run, but none passed west. Then at noon sharp Harper closed the road and the scoop was complete. In this single hour the Virginians had bottled fifty-six locomotives and more than three hundred cars. Within the limits of their operations also were the railroad shops at Martinsburg with costly equipment. All were now held for the Confederacy.[2]

Nor had the Virginia military authorities abandoned hope of controlling the Baltimore and Ohio west of the Alleghenies. They clearly perceived its military importance to the invader but had made only gestures to protect it. As early as April 22, 1861, the commander of a local militia regiment at Clarksburg had requested Governor John Letcher to send additional arms to Bridgeport nearby and to "do what circumstances shall require to prevent the passage of troops through Virginia...."[3]

Next day Major General Thomas S. Haymond of Fairmont sent a special messenger to Richmond to obtain authority to arm and equip "at least 1,000 men, to be posted near Wheeling and along the railroad line."[4] The gravity of the situation was further impressed upon the governor by alarmist civilians who gave warning that invasion was imminent.[5]

THE BALTIMORE AND OHIO IN THE CIVIL WAR

Robert E. Lee had just assumed command of Virginia's forces. One of the first of his official acts was a step designed to make safe the Baltimore and Ohio and its only Trans-Allegheny auxiliary line, the Northwestern Virginia. He directed Major Alonzo Loring of Wheeling to muster in volunteers in the panhandle and contiguous northwestern counties and to "direct the military operations for the protection of the terminus of the Baltimore and Ohio railroad on the Ohio river." [6] Lee next sent instructions to Major Francis M. Boykin, Jr., of Weston, ordering him to raise a force of volunteers and to repair with it to Grafton. Here he was to perform the special duty of watching over the junction of the two railroads.[7]

As a final step, on May 4, 1861, Lee selected Colonel George A. Porterfield, then with Jackson at Harpers Ferry, to command all state forces in northwest Virginia. He was authorized to call out volunteers and to use them specially for railroad defense.[8] Porterfield was expected to concentrate three regiments at Grafton, one at Parkersburg, and still another at Moundsville.[9]

Lee's orders were simple and direct. But their execution proved to be difficult. In fact his subordinates faced a trying situation. Because of the prevalence of Union sentiment in the northwestern counties few volunteers came forward. Those who did found a dearth of arms and equipment. In some counties available equipment was appropriated by newly formed Federal military organizations.[10] The picture was further darkened by irresponsible rumors that United States troops would soon descend from Ohio and Pennsylvania.[11]

Major Boykin was unable to collect volunteers for duty at Grafton, and on May 10 notified General Lee that he saw "no other alternative than to send forces from the

68

east...." [12] But Lee was wary because he believed that Cis-Allegheny troops would irritate rather than conciliate the northwestern Virginians. Instead he authorized Boykin to call out the militia in the "well affected counties," march them to Grafton, and until Colonel Porterfield arrived, make such dispositions as he might deem expedient or necessary.[13]

On May 14, 1861, Colonel Porterfield alighted from a Baltimore and Ohio passenger train at Grafton. He faced disappointment. No troops greeted him,[14] for none had yet arrived. As a matter of fact even at this advanced date there were but two militia companies with rifles in the entire northwest. One was stationed at Weston, the other at Fairmont. Other companies being organized at other county seat towns faced the prospect of going to war without arms.[15] Nevertheless Porterfield ordered his puny force to mobilize quickly at Grafton; then he informed Lee of his imperative need for reinforcements and equipment.

The commanding general, now convinced, sent Colonel M. G. Harman from Staunton with a small force of cavalry and a supply of small arms. Lee also ordered other skeleton units to repair to Grafton, each of which was expected to gather recruits on the way.[16] With these accretions as a nucleus, the more visionary of the secessionists believed that Porterfield could now augment his force to 5,000 and with it occupy the Baltimore and Ohio to the Ohio River.[17]

Union men of northwestern Virginia watched these developments with grave concern. As early as the first week of May, they sent earnest supplications to Major General George B. McClellan, who commanded the United States Military Department of the Ohio. They requested him to provide armed protection for the loyal Union element and the region's only railroad. McClellan's department was extended on May 9, 1861, to embrace that part of Virginia, but he gave little heed to these requests. Like-minded with Lee, he prophesied that the use of foreign troops would stir state pride and produce adverse effects.[18]

But McClellan's inaction seemed only to inspire persistence; as the plans of Richmond military authorities unfolded, appeals became more numerous and emphatic. Perhaps the most urgent of these came from the pen of George M. Hagans, a Wheeling resident. He wrote as the First Wheeling Convention began deliberations on the propriety of reorganizing the Virginia state government:[19]

...I urge the *immediate taking possession* of the B. & O. R. R. The opinion is that the Confederates are *now* arranging for such a step themselves. *You need not fear* of wounding the State pride of West Va. The people will welcome the presence of U. S. forces. There is *no* doubt on this point for I have talked with the leading men of every county & this is their *unanimous* judgment. The U. S. arms here at Wheeling ought to be instantly distributed along the Rail Road; and decisive steps inaugurated at once. The people are with the Federal Government, and instances are narrated to me of their spirit and determination in this regard, as furnish incontestible evidence that they are *now ripe* for a movement....

Apparently afraid of border trouble, Governor William Dennison of Ohio joined the chorus for military protection. On May 20, 1861, with fresh news of Virginia's accelerated preparations at hand, he wired the United States War Department direct. To checkmate Lee, he urged General Scott to occupy strategic points along the Baltimore and Ohio Railroad. He emphasized especially early occupation of Cumberland, Maryland.[20]

Scott's reply was discouraging indeed. "The matters to which your Excellency's telegram of this date refer, except as to Cumberland, are within the competency of General McClellan to whom please refer," wrote the octogenarian chief of staff.[21] Dennison could only relay this information to McClellan's headquarters and look to that source for action.[22]

McClellan was already convinced of the expediency of occupying Cumberland and other Baltimore and Ohio Railroad points; on May 20 he wired his views to both Secretary of the Treasury Salmon P. Chase and Secretary of War Simon Cameron. Scott's reply to Dennison caused him to send another telegram asking for full authority and instructions.[23] This act evoked a stinging rebuke from the veteran Scott. On May 21 he telegraphed McClellan: [24]

Considering that Cumberland, in Maryland, is not within your command and is under the immediate consideration of Major General Patterson and the authorities here, (all of us much nearer at hand) we are surprised at your repeated admonitions to the Secretary of the Treasury, the Secretary of War and myself to occupy that point, and I am still more surprised at your complaint to the Secretary of War (against me) that you are without instructions or authority, and with your hands tied up. . . .

In the light of approaching events, it is significant that Scott also informed McClellan that the troops then being trained at Camp Dennison, Ohio, would not be expected to take the field "before the return of frost." His message likewise made it plain that McClellan should place special emphasis on the recruiting and training of at least 80,000 men, who were to be employed in an expedition down the Mississippi.

Although his authority to act was of a tacit nature, McClellan did not hesitate longer. He quickly strengthened his outposts on the Ohio River, then weakly held by

71

a single battery at Marietta and a lone infantry regiment at Wheeling. He promptly ordered a brigade of Ohio volunteers to Bellaire and moved another to Marietta. While McClellan pondered what he should do next, these troops kept watch on the border.[25]

Meanwhile Colonel Porterfield had collected a few hundred men and had established an outpost at Fetterman, two miles west of Grafton.[26] He soon had full knowledge of McClellan's concentrations at Bellaire and Marietta and concluded that the Federal commander was preparing for immediate invasion of Virginia. Naturally he took stock of his resources and hurriedly planned defensive measures. The first of these was translated into action on May 25. On that day he issued an order directing Colonel William J. Willey to proceed "on the next train" and to destroy bridges on the Baltimore and Ohio main stem "as far west on the road as possible." [27]

Willey carried out these instructions with military promptness. Accompanied by a single squad, he arrived at Mannington that evening. He at once demolished two railroad bridges that spanned Buffalo Creek. Two days later, May 27, 1861, Porterfield sent out another party from Grafton. It went west on the Northwestern Virginia Railroad and burned important bridges between Clarksburg and Parkersburg.[28]

McClellan watched these developments from his headquarters at Camp Dennison, near Cincinnati. On May 26, after receipt of news of Porterfield's first depredations, he too decided to act. He directed Colonel Benjamin F. Kelley, who commanded the loyal First Virginia Infantry at Wheeling, to move next day toward Fairmont; to repair the railroad as he advanced; and to post guards at all important bridges. Kelley was informed that the chief object of the movement was "to prevent any further destruction of the Railroad." [29] McClellan next sent a dispatch to Colonel James Irvine, commanding the Sixteenth Ohio Infantry at Bellaire, instructing him to co-operate in the movement.[30]

The commanding general also telegraphed orders to Colonel James B. Steedman, who commanded the Fourteenth and Eighteenth Ohio Volunteer regiments stationed at Marietta and Athens. He directed Steedman to ferry the Ohio on the following morning and occupy Parkersburg. He further specified that, when this was accomplished, Steedman should push his brigade eastward over the Northwestern Virginia Railroad to effect a junction with Kelley at Grafton.[31]

Before daybreak, May 27, 1861, Kelley's troops boarded trains at Wheeling. Irvine's command crossed from Bellaire to Benwood in good time and followed. To facilitate communication with his base, Kelley took possession of the Baltimore and Ohio telegraph office at Wheeling and obtained an experienced telegraph operator to accompany the expedition. As the column advanced he placed successive telegraph stations under military supervision. The Federal commander removed operators suspected of disloyalty and filled their posts with Union men. Although his troops felt their way cautiously, they encountered no opposition and before sunset reached Mannington. Here they encamped and began preparations for the restoration of the railroad bridges.[32]

The secessionist camp at Grafton was now agog. With the Federal force but forty miles away, Porterfield sent a plaintive appeal for assistance to Brigadier General Joseph E. Johnston, who had but recently succeeded Jackson in command at Harpers Ferry. Johnston's reply gave no

THE BALTIMORE AND OHIO IN THE CIVIL WAR

promise of relief and Porterfield decided to retire south to Philippi. At this point he expected to make a stand and after augmenting his force return to Grafton. In the meantime, he planned to strike the Baltimore and Ohio a heavier blow. "The railroad is unquestionably used by the company against us," he informed Virginia's adjutant general, "and I may be obliged, for the safety of the command at Harper's Ferry, to make further destruction of it." [33]

Kelley was not long delayed at Mannington. Within forty-eight hours he had raised temporary bridges and opened the way to Fairmont. Although this point was stated in orders as his destination, he was expected to exercise discretion. His force in fact was now adequate for any probable emergency. An additional regiment of infantry had already swelled his numbers; and he received word from McClellan that Brigadier General Thomas A. Morris had been placed in command of all Federal forces in northwestern Virginia and was advancing to support him with an Indiana brigade. Consequently, with little prospect of stiff opposition in his front, Kelley pushed rapidly forward and on May 30, 1861, seized Grafton.[34]

The commander of the right wing encountered difficulty in matching Kelley's feat. Less was known about the political complexion of the Northwestern Virginia Railroad counties and there was an "unknown feeling manifested by the inhabitants at Parkersburg." [35]

Equally important was the fact that the Northwestern Virginia lay upon a most difficult military topography. Throughout its entire length the road was overshadowed by innumerable wooded hills; a meshwork of meandering creeks and rills gave confusing contour to the landscape. So winding in fact were the streams and so uneven was

74

the terrain that the builders of this railway made many deep cuts and high fills; the number of tunnels exceeded a score. It is not strange that the Federals moved slowly through this uncertain country. It was perhaps due to the entire absence of resistance that they finally succeeded in reaching Grafton.

On May 27, however, Colonel Steedman set the Four-

McCLELLAN'S NORTHWESTERN VIRGINIA CAMPAIGN (1861)

teenth Ohio Infantry in motion and occupied Parkersburg.[36] With artillery attached the remainder of his brigade followed in close supporting distance. Its rear unit crossed the Ohio on May 29.

Meanwhile McClellan sent his aide-de-camp, Colonel Frederick W. Lander, to assist the movement and to report its progress. He also sent last minute instructions to Steedman. If these foreshadowed overcautious policies of a later day, they were nevertheless based on a probable situation. Steedman was directed to secure his base at

Parkersburg before moving forward; to emphasize security on the march; and to fight no battles unless success was assured.[37]

Steedman followed these instructions to the letter. As a result the movement from Parkersburg to Clarksburg, approximately eighty miles, occupied four full days, despite the fact that it was made by rail. It is true that much time was lost in rebuilding railroad bridges; over much of the distance the main body was without the services of an advance guard. Yet Steedman's studied caution caused unnecessary halts. A case in point was a prolonged delay at Petroleum, but twenty-three miles east of Parkersburg. Here after a bridge across Goose Creek had been rebuilt the brigade commander remained in position fully twenty-four hours awaiting an imaginary enemy.[38]

The column was stopped again at Tollgate, where the Confederates had burned the railroad bridge which spanned the North Fork of Hughes River. The advance guard arrived at the break in the afternoon of May 29, but its commander merely set railway mechanics to work on a new structure, then passed on. At West Union his force of two hundred boarded a train that had been sent out from Clarksburg. It reached Clarksburg early in the afternoon of May 30, 1861.[39]

The main body did not reach Tollgate until the last day of May. To the disgust of the brigade commander, he found all work on the bridge at a standstill. The civilian mechanics had been curtly dismissed on the preceding day by a local railroad authority said to entertain decided secessionist views. There was not sufficient lumber to complete the structure. Steedman detailed one hundred of his own men for work on the bridge and ordered the needed materials from Parkersburg.[40] Within twenty-four hours the structure was completed and the road was opened to Clarksburg. The column promptly moved forward and entered the town on June 1.[41]

During these uncertain days Lander had remained at Parkersburg. He was not idle. He made frequent reports to McClellan, and also did much to give impetus to the lagging column. Not only did he arrange transportation for supporting troops and order them forward but he also set up a service of supply. Naturally, he encountered difficulties with personnel. But in only a single instance, it appears, did he meet unshakable obstinacy.

When the Sixth Indiana Infantry put in appearance at Parkersburg, Lander requested its commanding officer, Colonel Thomas T. Crittenden, to entrain his regiment and move out immediately. Crittenden refused on the ground that the danger of railroad collisions was too great.[42] Already belated, Lander left Crittenden to his own devices and with fourteen men departed for Grafton. The run was made without incident in the forenoon of June 2.

Lander found great activity at Federal headquarters. General Morris had arrived only the day before and had taken command. Scarcely had the new commander entered upon routine duties when his predecessor, Colonel Kelley, unfolded a plan to surprise and capture the Confederate force at Philippi.[43]

His basic strategy was envelopment and surprise. It contemplated the movement of 2,000 infantry over the Baltimore and Ohio Railroad to Thornton, six miles east of Grafton, then a circuitous thirty-mile hike south through heavily forested hill country to the right flank and rear of the enemy position. Kelley believed that the greater part of the march could be accomplished by day without observation. Since he expected to attack at daybreak, the last miles were to be traversed under the cover of darkness.

Morris approved this plan in every particular but found occasion to amend it.[44] With an entire brigade at Clarksburg and other units coming up, he decided to synchronize a frontal attack with Kelley's enveloping movement. Thus he unwittingly introduced the fickle element of timing.

Lander came too late to witness the start of the movement. Kelley had indeed entrained his force in the Grafton railroad yards before 9 o'clock in the forenoon of June 2. Word had quietly been passed that the Federals were on their way to Harpers Ferry. The column consisted of six companies of the First Virginia, nine of the Ninth Indiana, and six of the Sixteenth Ohio. All were infantry.

Kelley detrained his force in the vicinity of Thornton within two hours after its departure from Grafton.[45] By noon the rear company of his expedition had disappeared in the overshadowing forest that blanketed the hills far to the south.

The second column formed later in the day. For the first leg of the journey it too turned railroad facilities to tactical use. But unlike Kelley's force, it then marched entirely by night over an improved turnpike straight to the enemy front. Morris's orders to Colonel Ebenezer Dumont of the Seventh Regiment of Indiana volunteers, who commanded this part of the expedition, disclose his points of strategy with commendable brevity: [46]

You will proceed by railroad this evening, at 8:30 o'clock to Webster, with eight companies of your regiment. At Webster you will be joined by Colonel Steedman, with five companies

78

of his regiment and two field pieces, also by Colonel Crittenden with six companies of his regiment. From Webster you will, with this command, march on Philippi, using your own discretion in the conduct of the march, keeping in view that you should arrive in front of the town at 4 o'clock precisely tomorrow morning. . . .

Dumont complied and by 10 o'clock his column was headed south on the Pruntytown-Philippi pike. It marched in a driving rain through a pitch-black night. Although the cannon also impeded progress, the Federals arrived at Philippi at least a quarter of an hour too soon; for contrary to plans, Dumont's advance party stumbled upon the Confederate pickets unexpectedly.[47]

While the surprise was complete, it occurred before Kelley had closed the avenue of retreat. Kelley's force arrived in time to take part in the skirmish, but it came too late to bottle up Porterfield's command. It is true that the Confederates were completely routed; but they were skillfully handled by their officers and escaped with only property loss. Porterfield led his troops over the turnpike south to Beverly and there took up a position behind Rich Mountain and Laurel Hill.[48]

Although available Federal forces in northwestern Virginia exceeded the Confederates numerically more than five to one, McClellan did not follow up his victory. Perspectively, his inaction may be attributed to an overcautious policy, but he undoubtedly exercised first-rate military judgment. Many of his troops were three months' militiamen; some of his regiments were poorly equipped; all needed further instruction in elementary tactics and technique.

None the less important was the fact that he now lacked means of transportation. The concentration at

Grafton had been accomplished only because of the strategical location of converging railroad lines. Once removed from the railway, units were compelled to rely on their own wagon trains for supplies. A few regiments had but twelve wagons, while the best equipped could boast no more than eighteen.[49] Added to these facts was the pertinent one that the next step would take the Federals deep into hostile territory. McClellan was undoubtedly justified in his decision to establish a strong position at Philippi and give first attention to strengthening his line of supply.

Despite the fact that the main Confederate force was forty miles south, the railroad was not safe. Numerous roads still lay open to raiding parties, and there was immediate danger of civilian sabotage. McClellan saw the gravity of the situation and speedily placed both the Baltimore and Ohio and the Northwestern Virginia under guard.

To this duty he assigned forty-eight companies. To protect the costly Cheat River viaduct he posted an entire regiment at Rowlesburg. He stationed smaller detachments consisting nominally of one and two companies at less exposed bridges and at the tunnels.

Guards were distributed on the main stem west of Grafton as follows: one squad at a large stone bridge two miles west of Fetterman; two companies at the long bridge over the Monongahela River at Bentons Ferry, near Fairmont; two companies at Barnesville; two between Mannington and Farmington; and two companies between Mannington and Benwood. Similarly, detachments were posted along the Northwestern Virginia Railroad at Webster, Bridgeport, West Union, Central, Tollgate, Ellenboro, and Petroleum. Regimental headquarters were established at Grafton, Clarksburg, and Parkersburg.[50]

OPENING THE CORRIDOR

As a further guarantee of security the military authorities removed a number of railway employees. Some had been avowed secessionists, while others bore marks of Southern sympathies. They were dismissed or suspended and their places were given to Union men. Removals and replacements became so numerous in fact that the efficiency of the railroad was soon in jeopardy. Consequently, John W. Garrett sent a responsible official from Baltimore to assist in "putting the right men in the right places."[51] This work progressed throughout June, 1861, and was not completed to the satisfaction of the military authorities until the first week of July.[52]

Meanwhile the Confederates schemed to cut the road. To them its destruction seemed an immediate necessity. There was now grave danger that McClellan's forces would effect a junction with General Robert Patterson's army, then training at Chambersburg, Pennsylvania; with the Baltimore and Ohio open from the Ohio River to the eastern foothills of the Alleghenies, it appeared highly probable that Federal troops from the West would be thrown into the Shenandoah Valley to support an invasion from Maryland. To prevent this, Confederate strategists resolved to destroy the road at a point where reconstruction and repair would be slow and difficult. Consequently, they planned to demolish the expensive Cheat River bridge at Rowlesburg.[53] "The rupture of the railroad at Cheat River would be worth to us an army," wrote Robert E. Lee.[54]

To Brigadier General Robert S. Garnett, who had superseded Porterfield as commander in the northwest, fell the responsibility of giving substance to Confederate policy. On June 16, 1861, he established strong defensive positions on Laurel Hill and Rich Mountain. He next turned his attention to offensive operations. His correspondence with Lee shows clearly that his main objective was the main line of the Baltimore and Ohio Railroad.

Garnett pondered two plans seriously.[55] One contemplated an advance northward from Yeager's Farm, at the foot of Allegheny Mountain on the Staunton and Parkersburg Turnpike, to Evansville on the Northwestern pike. Once at Evansville he could threaten both Grafton and Rowlesburg; his force could also strike the railroad at Independence, then move eastward and destroy the Cheat River bridge. The obvious defect of this plan was the ease with which Federals at Philippi could fall upon the Confederate rear.

The other plan called for a direct march on Rowlesburg over a rough country road leading north from Saint George. Although this road was impassable to wagons and artillery it offered convenient approach to raiding parties of both cavalry and infantry.

These schemes never advanced beyond the paper stage. Indeed they contemplated the employment of stronger forces than Garnett possessed. And before he could obtain adequate reinforcements, McClellan bore down upon him.

All along the Federal commander had vicariously watched Confederate activity on Laurel Hill and Rich Mountain. An exaggerated account of enemy strength and intentions was reported to him before the middle of June. This evoked a telegram to General Morris on June 15. "Hold your positions at Cheat River Grafton and Phillipi [sic] against whatever force attacks you," McClellan wired. "I will come in person with re-enforcements sufficient to defeat all comers," he concluded.[56]

McClellan next received news that a force of Confederates in possession of Romney was threatening New Creek. He promptly directed Morris to strengthen the position at Rowlesburg with a view to holding it at all hazards. He also fully expected a Confederate advance against Clarksburg and Philippi, and with measured words gave Morris authority to evacuate those points and to withdraw to Grafton in emergency. He, however, emphasized the fact that General Scott was being urged to intercept the enemy at Romney and gave assurance that he himself would move promptly against Garnett with a "force sufficient to fight a battle." [57]

Within the week the Third and Fourth Ohio regiments crossed the Ohio River at Bellaire and entrained at Benwood. McClellan himself arrived at Parkersburg on June 21, 1861, with mixed forces of infantry, cavalry and artillery. There with timely afterthought he summoned Brigadier General William S. Rosecrans, still at Camp Dennison, to join him with four additional regiments. McClellan then boarded a train with members of his staff and proceeded to Grafton.[58] His troop trains however took siding at Clarksburg; it was here that the commanding general expected to establish his base.

McClellan did not find the military situation to his liking at Grafton. His recent orders contemplating the reinforcement of the guard at Rowlesburg had not been obeyed and there were indications that Morris could not effectively co-ordinate railroad defense with other field duties. The situation plainly called for further experimentation. He accordingly relieved Morris of responsibility of defending the railroad and assigned that duty to Brigadier General Charles W. Hill. The latter was made directly accountable to the department commander. In assigning Hill, McClellan impressed him with the importance of his office: "The Commanding General...has intrusted to you the most important duty next to his own in this territory, viz.: That of securing the base of his operations and *line of retreat*. At any cost—that of your last man—you will preserve the Cheat River line, Grafton, and the line thence to Wheeling. On this depends the entire success of the plan of operations." [59]

He emphasized particularly the necessity of extending and strengthening the fortifications along the Cheat River. His plans comprehended a main support at Rowlesburg with strong outposts at West Union [60] and Saint George. To articulate these dispositions with scattered railroad guards, he authorized Hill to increase the number of effectives in the area to 1,000 men.[61]

McClellan next completed his plans for the offensive. By June 23, he had settled upon definite lines. His forces were to move in two columns. He himself would lead the larger one which was then forming at Clarksburg. Its objective was the Confederate key position on Rich Mountain. Simultaneously, Morris would move south from Philippi and confront the enemy on Laurel Hill. McClellan intimated that his own column would break camp on June 25.[62]

It did not move however until June 27. On that day Rosecrans's brigade took the Buckhannon pike, stringing up a telegraph wire as it advanced. Although this work delayed progress, the Federal vanguard purposely felt its way cautiously. It did not reach Buckhannon until June 30. Here it remained until July 2, when it was joined by the main body.[63]

McClellan waited five days before taking the next step. It was not until July 7 that he threw forward two regiments to Middle Fork Bridge and telegraphed Morris to move immediately against Laurel Hill.[64] The time was now at hand when McClellan demonstrated that he could strike swiftly when the hour seemed propitious. Although the remainder of his route lay through doubtful country, he quickly pressed forward with his entire force. Both he and Morris contacted the enemy outguards on July 10. Next day he turned the Confederate left and swept the entire enemy force from Rich Mountain.[65]

General Garnett soon learned of the disaster that had befallen this part of his command. He therefore decided to evacuate Laurel Hill and retreat over the Staunton and Parkersburg Turnpike while that road lay open. As he approached Beverly in the morning of July 12, however, he erroneously concluded that the town was occupied by Federal troops.[66] Promptly he retraced his steps northeastward and began ascent of the Valley Mountains with a view to gaining the Northwestern Turnpike.

Morris was in easy striking distance and might well have followed immediately; he refused, however, to move without orders from his superior. These were delayed and the pursuit did not begin until the morning of July 13. Once on its way the Federal advance guard soon came upon the retiring enemy. At Corricks Ford a lively rear guard action took place. The Confederates however extricated themselves in good order and continued to the next ford, less than a mile distant. Here Garnett was killed while drawing off the last of his skirmishers. Here too the Confederates lost approximately forty prisoners and the greater part of their wagon train. The Federal commander seemed content with his success and abandoned the pursuit. The assigned reasons were the lack of rations and fatigue of the troops.[67] After all, the demoralized enemy was headed straight toward Hill's strong outposts near the Maryland border.

In fact McClellan had already taken steps to intercept the retreating Confederates before they could cross the Alleghenies. No sooner had Garnett's intentions become obvious than the Federal commander evolved a plan to blockade the Northwestern Turnpike. Early in the afternoon of July 12, he dispatched the following order to General Hill whose headquarters were at Grafton: [68]

General McClellan, having just learned that rebel forces abandoned their positions at Laurel Hill last night, and are now making for Eastern Virginia, via the Louisville [sic] and Saint George pike, directs that you take the field at once, with all the force you can make available, to cut off their retreat. Two Pennsylvania regiments at Cumberland have been directed to proceed forthwith to Rowlesburg by a special train and report to you. You can for the time being withdraw several companies from points on the railroad between Wheeling and Parkersburg, and concentrate them by special train. No time is to be lost. It is supposed you will be able to take the field with, say, six thousand men, including Colonel Irvine's command, and at least four guns. . . .

Here was the setting for a classical maneuver. But the order was poorly executed. Notwithstanding its early issuance, it did not reach Hill until 11 o'clock in the forenoon of July 13. He however transmitted its contents immediately to Colonel James Irvine, who commanded at Cheat River, giving him also supplementary instructions. He then telegraphed orders to regimental commanders at Clarksburg, Parkersburg, Fairmont, and Wheeling, directing them to hurry their commands forward to Oakland, Maryland.[69]

This proved to be a task with unforeseen difficulties. The troops were distributed at many points along both

86

lines of the railroad and precious time was lost in the tedious stages of concentration. In addition, the railroad company was taken by surprise and had difficulty in assembling cars for infantry, cavalry, artillery, and supplies. Moreover, loaded trains had to be moved with great caution because of the confusion. In some cases conductors emphatically refused to move their trains because of fear of collision.[70]

Hill however succeeded in moving two trains out of Grafton before sundown, July 13. He reached Oakland about ten o'clock at night with approximately six hundred men. He immediately sent south three companies led by two of his own staff officers to reinforce Irvine who was believed to be in the vicinity of Chisholms Mill.

After a six-hour night march through unfamiliar country the detachment reached its destination only to find no trace of Federal headquarters. The officers in command, Major Charles C. Walcutt and Captain F. S. Bond, thereupon permitted their detachment to rest while they continued search. They soon located Irvine at West Union. Here they were informed that the Confederates had gained the Northwestern pike at Red House, eight miles east, only an hour before. Captain Bond quickly carried this information to General Hill who had all the while kept his troops motionless at Oakland.[71]

What followed was a farcical anticlimax. There was marching and countermarching to determine if the entire Confederate force had slipped through the poorly fabricated Federal net. Finally, Irvine decided to pursue. Although he moved with unnecessary caution, by noon he had crossed Backbone Mountain. Hill followed with a mounted escort and overtook him at North Branch Bridge. Here the two officers consulted and agreed to abandon pursuit. The Federal troops then trudged back to Red House and Oakland.[72]

Yet Hill had not played his last card. During that afternoon and evening the last of his railroad regiments detrained at Oakland, increasing his command to 4,000. Then early in the next afternoon, July 14, came news that the Confederates had halted at Greenland.

Hill saw a last chance to intercept them. He accordingly organized two pursuit columns. First he sent some 3,000 men by turnpike to cut off retreat to the south. He then dispatched nine hundred men by rail to New Creek to attack from the north.[73]

After twenty-four hours of forced marching, the main column with Hill commanding in person reached Greenland. The Confederates had already decamped. The supporting Federal column under Colonel Thomas Morton arrived before sunset and Hill decided to resume pursuit. Next day his forces again headed south. But he had marched only five miles when a courier handed him a dispatch from McClellan which ordered the chase stopped. Both Hill and Morton moved back to Oakland and Red House.[74] By that time the enemy had passed up the South Branch Valley and was safe at Monterey.

Failure of the Federals to intercept the fleeing Confederates marked the end of McClellan's northwestern Virginia campaign. The fumbling of inexperienced officers operating on unfamilar ground with raw troops must not however overshadow the magnitude of his achievement. When he was called to Washington on July 22, 1861, to assume higher command, his forces were virtually in undisputed possession of Trans-Allegheny Virginia.

McClellan held a tight grip on the Baltimore and Ohio Railroad from the Ohio to the eastern foothills of the

Alleghenies; his outguards covered the mountain passes, and his outposts dotted the hilly region between the Great Kanawha and the Little Kanawha rivers. It is true that the Confederates on occasion temporarily reoccupied some of this lost ground, but they were unable to hold it. They were turned back in the border counties or were maneuvered out of position in the Great Kanawha Valley. McClellan's timely campaign settled summarily the political destiny of northwest Virginia; it wiped out an enemy salient that jutted ominously north to the latitude of Pittsburgh, thereby opening wider the east-west corridor; and it cleared the way for Federal operations in the upper Potomac.

CHAPTER V

Disquiet on the Potomac

NOT the least exposed part of Virginia's boundary was the river line which extended from Fairfax Stone to Harpers Ferry. For two hundred miles the Potomac sweeps a majestic arc, the longest chord of which measures little more than half that distance. The exposed outlines of this sector invited attack from left, center, and right. The invader might strike from the east over railroad or turnpike; at the center he could advance from the southern terminus of the Cumberland Valley Railroad at Hagerstown and cross the Potomac at Shepherdstown or at Williamsport; and with consummate ease an aggressive force operating from Cumberland, New Creek, or Oakland could debouch from the mountain passes at the north and northwest.

This imperiled area was worth a stubborn defense. It was a strategic salient. If it opened a door to the fertile Shenandoah Valley, it also furnished a natural gateway to the green fields of the Susquehanna. Its military importance in offensive operations lay in the facility which it afforded for sudden invasion of Federal territory, the liberation of shackled Maryland, and the encirclement of Washington.

Not unnaturally the upper Potomac and the lower Shenandoah appeared large on the Confederate military map. In truth it was for the purpose of strengthening defenses in this region that the Confederate authorities sent a more experienced commander to replace the little known Colonel Thomas ("Stonewall") Jackson. The latter's successor was Brigadier General Joseph E. Johnston, one of the promising officers of the South. Confederate military authorities attached singular importance to Harpers Ferry, upon which they looked as a natural fortress and key to the Shenandoah Valley.[1] Because of its strategic location Jackson had advised that its approaches "should be defended with the spirit which actuated the defenders of Thermopylae...."[2]

Johnston was not the soldier to accept a conclusion of this sort without examining the premises. Soon after arriving at Harpers Ferry on May 24, 1861, he made a careful inspection of the post. He examined it with special reference to its natural strength and probable function in a regional scheme of defense.

His findings reversed accepted opinions.[3] His conclusion refuted the dictum that Harpers Ferry could be held with a nominal garrison, and of its strategic importance, he was likewise dubious. He saw little wisdom in holding the main Confederate force at a point fifteen miles removed from the Valley Turnpike, the main axis of travel of the Shenandoah.

Instead Johnston proposed to evacuate Harper's Ferry, take the field with its garrison and supporting troops, and dispute the passage of the Potomac in front of Martinsburg.[4] He would here watch enemy movements and, if attacked by superior numbers, fall back on Winchester. In any case, he believed, he could delay and perhaps prevent the junction of co-operating enemy forces in the lower Valley. Already well-grounded rumor had convinced him that Federal intentions contemplated a general advance.

While the Confederate military authorities allowed

Johnston a free hand, they were not averse to withholding approval of his plans. They did try however to allay his apprehensions. They sent him reinforcements and, as already noted, dispatched General Robert S. Garnett to Beverly to neutralize enemy successes in the Trans-Allegheny. Johnston himself was not overlooked in orders. As a further guarantee of safety he was granted full power to destroy as much of the Baltimore and Ohio Railroad as he should deem judicious or expedient.[5]

Events soon bore witness to the correctness of Johnston's views. As pointed out above, in the first week of June, McClellan's troops occupied the Baltimore and Ohio in northwestern Virginia east to the Maryland boundary; on June 7, 1861, Colonel Lew Wallace marched into Cumberland with his Eleventh Indiana Zouaves;[6] and only three days later General Patterson occupied Hagerstown with a Federal force estimated at 18,000.[7]

With the latter in easy striking distance of Martinsburg, Johnston did not hesitate to give matters a practical turn. Immediately he made preparations to move out of Harpers Ferry. First he commandeered a number of Baltimore and Ohio cars; then dismantled the heavy machinery of the arsenal and sent it to Winchester over the Winchester and Potomac Railroad; shipped heavy ordnance, quartermaster supplies and troop baggage to the same point; and destroyed all bridges over the Potomac between Point of Rocks and Williamsport,[8] including the long Baltimore and Ohio Railroad bridge at Harpers Ferry.[9]

On June 13 these preliminaries were accelerated because of information that Patterson was at Williamsport and rumor that McClellan's advance guard had passed the last summit of the Alleghenies. To meet this threat from

DISQUIET ON THE POTOMAC

the northwest, Johnston detached two regiments under Colonel Ambrose P. Hill with orders to proceed to Romney.[10] At the same time Colonel Angus W. McDonald was sent at the special request of President Jefferson Davis with a cavalry troop to destroy the Baltimore and Ohio Railroad's Cheat River bridge.[11]

In the meantime Johnston had groomed his force for orderly evacuation. He moved on June 15 by way of the Charles Town road. That afternoon his troops settled leisurely in bivouac at Smithfield. Johnston was here informed that the first detachment of Patterson's army was crossing the Potomac at Williamsport. Consequently, on June 16, he moved his command to Bunker Hill on the Valley Turnpike. But whatever expectations the Southern commander may have entertained were now dissipated by fresh news that the Federals had recrossed into Maryland. Seemingly relaxed of all tenseness the Confederates fell slowly back upon Winchester.

They had hardly halted at their new base however when Patterson's movements again became menacing. To parry a probable thrust at Martinsburg, Johnston immediately dispatched Jackson's brigade to the Potomac front to reinforce Lieutenant Colonel J. E. B. Stuart, already on watch with a thin line of cavalry.[12] Significantly enough, it was Jackson's return to the railroad that ushered it once more to the very center of the military stage.

Jackson was again to be the instrument of disaster for the Baltimore and Ohio. Indeed, the evacuation of Harpers Ferry proved to be part and parcel of a new Confederate military policy for the lower Valley and the upper Potomac. Up to the time of the strategic retreat to Winchester, high counsels in both the Virginia and the Confederate governments had correctly regarded the possession of these

93

northeastern counties as essential to the success of policies which looked to the recovery of northwestern Virginia, the secession of Maryland, and the military investment of Washington. Nor could Confederate strategists overlook the fact that control of this region also brought incidental possession of a long segment of the Baltimore and Ohio Railroad, potentially a very important Federal line of communication between the East and the West. Even though the defenders of the lower Valley faced the prospect of surrendering military and geographical advantages, they still might deny the invader the full use of important railroad communications. A few days after Jackson's return to Martinsburg the decree passed that the railroad must go.

In fact it was painfully obvious that Patterson would put the road to good use as soon as it came into his hands. Undoubtedly he would repair its broken parts and reopen it to through traffic.[13] Although Johnston's pioneers had destroyed bridges both east and west of Martinsburg, any one of the structures with the single exception of the Potomac bridge at Harpers Ferry might be replaced within a week. Consequently, the Confederates decided to destroy the road in its entirety and to appropriate such of its property as might be used on Southern railways. The Confederate War Department sent an agent from Richmond to select the best rolling stock and machinery, and to supervise its removal to the western terminus of the Manassas Gap Railroad at Strasburg.[14]

The details of destruction were left to the ingenuity of Jackson. With characteristic thoroughness the Confederate commander began the work on Sunday, June 23, 1861.[15] At the time there were fifty-six locomotives and more than three hundred cars interned on the tracks in the vicinity

94

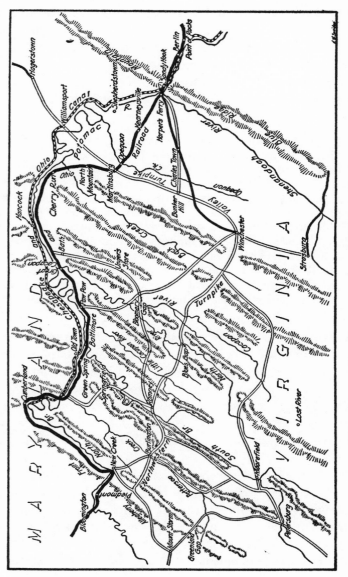

The Lower Shenandoah and the Upper Potomac

of Martinsburg.[16] Around forty-two engines Jackson's men raised pyres of wood and coal. Applying the torch, they sent up in smoke and flame not only these engines but also approximately three hundred cars. Two weeks after the event a reporter for the *National Intelligencer* visited the scene. He sent the following lurid account to his newspaper: [17]

All along the railroad were scattered coal cars in long lines, with the coal still burning, having been set on fire by the 'noble and chivalric.' They had kindled huge fires around them, burning all the woodwork and a great deal of the iron. They were all fine iron cars, holding about twenty tons each. Here and there the road led above them, and, looking down, we could see the inside—a mass of red hot coals. Some small bridges had been burnt with the cars on them, and giving way, the cars were left piled one on another in the small streams below, all battered and bent. We counted the line of locomotives that had been burnt (forty-one or forty-two in all) red and blistered with heat. The destruction is fearful to contemplate.

This exploit so nearly resembled vandalism that it produced immediate repercussions in Maryland. Union men made much of the loss of a public work in which the State of Maryland and the City of Baltimore possessed both a financial and a civic interest. Baltimore merchants, whether of nationalistic or secessionist persuasion, saw in the event the permanent passing of a lucrative Western trade.

There were however compensations. The incident afforded excellent opportunity to discredit secession and mold wavering public sentiment. Quickened by local resentment, the pro-Union press was not slow in seizing its advantage. The Baltimore *Evening Patriot,* the Frederick *Examiner,* and the Baltimore *American and Commercial*

Advertiser were especially denunciatory of Confederate policy. The latter gave vent to this comment on June 26, 1861: [18]

In view of the wholesale and needless destruction of bridges, and of some forty locomotives, belonging to the Baltimore and Ohio Railroad, and by consequence to this city, by the disciples of Mr. Jefferson Davis, we look for a large accession of proselytes here to the doctrines of that peculiar school. Looking to what Secession has already accomplished for Maryland and Virginia in its merely half-fledged condition, one can hardly estimate its blessings, supposing it had no check to its flight. . . .

It concluded in sober vein:

. . . it would be difficult to find, in the whole history of modern warfare, another instance of more unjustifiable and needless vandalism; and if anything was wanting besides this to make Maryland turn away from the threatened embrace of Secession with anger and disgust, surely it could be found in this wanton and criminal destruction of property, in the shape of the most labored and valuable works of public utility.

Many a Northern editor saw eye to eye with his Maryland compatriots. The destruction of the Baltimore and Ohio company's rolling stock was "as villainous almost as the crime of murder," [19] wrote the indignant Archibald W. Campbell, editor of the Wheeling *Intelligencer*. The New York *Commercial Advertiser* could not see how "any person of common sense in Baltimore" could sympathize with "a movement every step of which has been taken in fraud, treachery, violence, bloodshed, wanton destruction." [20] The procedure was "certainly not calculated to convey satisfactory assurances of the very fraternal regard which General Davis recently professed for the State of Maryland, whose citizens are mainly interested in the prosperity of that railroad," [21] resounded the *National Intelligencer.*

Placed squarely on the defensive, pro-Southern Baltimore newspapers promptly took on an air of reserve, but were not silenced. Both the *Exchange* and the *South* condoned Confederate policy on the ground of military necessity; the *Sun,* already steering a middle course, could not be aroused by the overworked lampoons that poured from its pro-Union neighbors.

The *Exchange* labored hard to shift responsibility for the act to other shoulders. First it published an ingenious account of the appearance of a mysterious handbill which it reported was given circulation along the Baltimore and Ohio about the middle of June. It alleged that this circular announced that the Baltimore and Ohio Railroad Company was in the market for 2,000 workmen to repair its line for immediate national use.[22] It went on to explain that responsible officials of the railroad flatly denied authorship of the circular and concluded with the statement that Southern military authorities had been provoked by an enemy of the road. It then concluded with a pointed inference that the placard was a ruse which had been inspired by Pennsylvania Central Railroad influence at Washington.

Nor could the people of Maryland themselves escape responsibility for the losses both state and city had sustained. The *Exchange* fixed the blame subjunctively: [23]

...We could not, by espousing the cause of either section, have fared as badly as we shall probably do now. If we had, at the outset, joined the North in this struggle, and had then put forth our energies in its behalf, we might, through the aid of the Government, have been in possession of the whole line of road.... If, on the other hand, we had determined, upon the secession of Virginia, to stand by the South and to share her fortunes, we could easily, with her assistance, have prevented the road from being interfered with, except at or near its Western terminus. . . . The conflict between the sections would have been decided north of Baltimore, and as our communications with the South would have been kept open, our merchants and manufacturers would have been busy instead of idle at this moment. . . .

These comments to the contrary, there is little reason to doubt that the Confederate government was actuated solely by military considerations. The Confederate president believed that the destruction of the road with its telegraph would go far to reverse the political tide in northwestern Virginia; he had stated frankly that such a consummation would unquestionably "be of immediate and great advantage" to the Southern cause.[24] Moreover, after the middle of June, 1861, military factors became paramount. With the withdrawal of the main Confederate force from the line of the upper Potomac, the Baltimore and Ohio became a prospective prize for the advancing Federals; with the road in their hands it would obviously subserve military ends. Nor could the Confederates longer respect Maryland's vested rights in the railroad. Bound hand and foot by both civil and military shackles, Maryland had unwillingly become a *quasi* enemy to the South.

On July 2, 1861, Patterson's army crossed the Potomac and the Confederate outguards under Stuart and Jackson fell back toward Winchester.[25] Their retreat gave the Federals undisputed possession of the Baltimore and Ohio from Harpers Ferry to Cumberland. For almost a month that part of the road remained in Union hands. Meantime the Confederates put to further military use the Baltimore and Ohio rolling stock that they had commandeered at Harpers Ferry and sent to Winchester. They conveyed much of it over country roads to Strasburg, where it was put in immediate service on the Manassas Gap Railroad. It was in truth this supplement of cars that enabled General Johnston to transport his army east of the Blue Ridge with comparative ease and throw it upon the field of Bull Run on July 21, 1861, in time to ensure the first striking Confederate victory.[26]

During the period of Federal occupation the company made extensive repairs and replacements and opened the line from Point of Rocks to Harpers Ferry. It also took steps to rebridge the Potomac at the latter point.[27] But with Major General Irvin McDowell's defeat east of the Blue Ridge the Confederates soon swarmed back to the lower Valley. In turn Union troops decamped to Maryland where they were destined to remain inactive for months. Their retrograde left again a hundred miles of the railroad to Confederate caprice. Baltimore and Ohio officials could only call off their workmen and wait for a turn of military operations.

The Confederates reoccupied the railroad from Harpers Ferry to North Branch bridge and resumed their work of destruction.[28] They also carted off to Strasburg the remainder of the locomotives and choice machinery that Confederate authority had spared for the Southern railroads. With thirty-two draft horses hitched to a single wagon they transported even the heaviest engines over the Valley Turnpike.[29] One of the finest was reconditioned and assigned to passenger service on a Southern railroad under the pseudonym of "Lady Davis." [30] Yet much of the railroad property was never put to use. For months it lay in rust at Winchester and gradually passed to the limbo of scrap.

Throughout the late summer and early autumn of 1861

small Confederate detachments demolished bridges and culverts, took up tracks and crossties, and burned depots, station houses and platforms.

Despite the fact that the railroad was held by a weak enemy force, Union commanders stationed at nearby Hagerstown and Frederick made no serious effort to recover it. The military authorities at Washington likewise stood aloof and seemed indifferent. Not until autumn did their attitude change. Then the nation felt sharply the first effects of traffic congestion on its trunk line railroads. Freight rates climbed quickly and the prospective closing of the Great Lakes with the approach of winter forewarned of even higher charges. The Cincinnati *Gazette* summarized the prospect editorially: [31]

The Mississippi river being closed, the produce of the entire West is driven from that channel to the Eastern railroads. In addition to this, the Baltimore and Ohio railroad is closed, and the Pennsylvania Central is largely occupied with government business. Thus railroad facilities, as compared with last winter, have been reduced very nearly one half, while business has largely increased; and if managers have put prices up fifty per cent, while the canals and lakes are navigable, without being able to move all the property that is offered, what may be expected when the water lines shall be closed? It is probable that the freight on flour to New York will advance to two dollars per barrel by the first of January, and on other articles in proportion.

Owing to this condition, the Baltimore and Ohio was elevated to national importance. Waiving only important military considerations, its reclamation became second only to the opening of the Mississippi.

Good and sufficient reasons were not lacking to those who strove to move the Federal government to action. Cincinnati's merchants' exchange as well as her newspapers

emphasized the West's need for this important thorough-
fare.[32] The Cincinnati *Gazette* emphasized the fact that
the Baltimore and Ohio company then had two thousand
freight cars and two hundred locomotives lying idle, all
of which were of inestimable value in the existing transportation crisis.[33] Others stressed salutary effects which
were sure to accrue to the government itself. Not the least
of these was the fact that the opening of the Baltimore and
Ohio would again make available to the United States
navy the high grade steam coal from the mines of western
Maryland.[34]

Nor were military considerations overlooked. A corre-
spondent of the Baltimore *Evening Patriot* wrote that possession of the road by the enemy "cripples the arm of the
General Government, adding millions to its expenses in
forwarding troops, provisions &c., and causing ruinous
delays in the concentration of its troops. . . ." [35] Another
was constrained to quote "the highest military authority in
the country" as stating that the closing of the Baltimore
and Ohio was the cause of the Federal defeat at Bull
Run.[36]

These views fell but little short of obsessions in communities touched by the Baltimore and Ohio. Both
formal and informal appeals were communicated directly
to the Secretary of War and other cabinet members urging
the army to move.[37] John W. Garrett, now an open Union
partisan, added strength to the argument. He gave notice
through the press that the Baltimore and Ohio itself
would bear the entire expense of reconstruction.[38] It
wanted only military protection.

The War Department was slow to move. Its dawdling
was quickly seized upon by the political enemies of the
Secretary of War who were already scheming to ensnare

him in a net of alleged official irregularities. They now found convenient supporting circumstantial evidence which seemed to convict him of "conniving at the disability" of the Baltimore and Ohio.[39] The charges were based on the fact that Cameron and members of his immediate family owned large interests in the Northern Central Railroad, which at the time was gathering huge profits from heavy tonnage, particularly government traffic from the West. It was alleged also that he had fixed rates and schedules for government shipments from Philadelphia to Baltimore in the interest of the Pennsylvania Central and Northern Central route as against the more direct Philadelphia, Wilmington and Baltimore Railroad.[40]

Secretary Cameron was a director of the Northern Central Railroad and owned a large block of its stock; [41] his son, J. Donald Cameron, a banker of Harrisburg, was vice-president of the company and owned "considerable of the stock;" [42] and A. B. Warford, his brother-in-law, was president.[43] Long referred to as "Cameron's road," the Northern Central since late 1860 had been controlled by the Pennsylvania Central Railroad. Thus, with the stoppage of through traffic on its rival, the Baltimore and Ohio, the Pennsylvania Central and its subsidiary held a practical monopoly of traffic between Baltimore and the West.

The Pennsylvania Central did not fail to use this monopoly to advantage. While it benefited from a general advance in rates due to wartime demands and closing of other avenues of transportation, its officials also made the most of the heavy government business which they were called upon to move from Pittsburgh to Baltimore. Government freights shipped on through consignment from Pittsburgh to Washington without change of cars were charged local rates from Harrisburg to Baltimore.[44] Since local tariffs on the Northern Central were 33-1/3 per cent higher than prevailing through rates on the same road, the discrimination was not easily explained.

If the quiescent public was not at first aware of this sharp practice, the earnings of both the Pennsylvania Central and the Northern Central companies soon reflected the prosperity which they enjoyed. Certainly the two roads held geographical advantages which insured them a virtual monopoly of the Western trade; but these were accentuated only while the Baltimore and Ohio remained closed. Critics of War Department policy pointed an inquiring finger at this fact, and some found ready explanation of it in the personal economic interests of the Secretary of War.

The War Department finally stirred in October, 1861. It created a new military area which it named the Department of Harpers Ferry and Cumberland. Brigadier General Frederick W. Lander was assigned to this command. His jurisdiction embraced the line of the Baltimore and Ohio from Harpers Ferry to Cumberland and a strip of contiguous territory thirty miles wide extending along the Virginia side of the Potomac. Although Lander had fewer than a thousand raw volunteers available for duty in his department, he was given authority to raise additional forces at Baltimore, Cumberland, and at intermediate points. He was directed to implement his force and organize it for immediate use along the railroad where civilian working parties would need protection.[45]

Lander's work had not yet begun when he fell painfully wounded in a skirmish at Edwards Ferry. His duties devolved upon Brigadier General Benjamin F. Kelley who commanded scattered detachments posted along the railroad from Cumberland to the Cheat River bridge.[46]

Kelley quickly concentrated a large part of his command at New Creek. On October 26, 1861, he marched south with 3,000 men and drove the Confederates out of Romney. He was here in position to threaten Winchester, forty miles away, and cover the railroad along an eighty-mile front. Kelley was quick to sense the importance of Romney and in his report to General McClellan insisted that a force should winter there. He also expressed belief that the Baltimore and Ohio could be opened "for trade, travel, and the use of the Government," within a few days if the Confederates were driven from Martinsburg and Harpers Ferry.[47]

The Baltimore and Ohio management strained to keep pace with military movements. First, repairing the North Branch bridge on November 14, company workmen completed the Pattersons Creek bridge, opening the line to Green Spring, sixteen miles east of Cumberland. Bridges over the South Branch of the Potomac, the Little Cacapon, and the Great Cacapon rivers were restored in order, and on December 16, 1861, the first trains ran to Hancock, fifty-five miles east of Cumberland.[48]

As early as November 26, Garrett indicated that both men and material were being held in readiness for work on the eastern end of the "burnt district" and only awaited military protection. He communicated this fact to Reverdy Johnson, then a member of the Maryland House of Delegates, inferentially requesting him to relay the information to Washington authorities; [49] he made a similar request of Francis H. Pierpont, Union war governor of Virginia, who, he believed, might also exert influence on the President's cabinet; [50] and he sent J. H. Sullivan, West-

105

ern agent of the Baltimore and Ohio at Bellaire, Ohio, to Washington to confer with General McClellan and Secretary Chase.[51]

These efforts did not produce immediate results. The only response forthcoming from officialdom, sighed a Baltimore editor, was "the bland assurance that 'something will be done soon.' "[52] Yet there was no dearth of specific plans. Both Kelley and Lander fathered schemes which contemplated concerted movements across the Potomac and the strengthening of the position at Romney.[53] Neither stirred interest at Washington perhaps because each lacked integration with general policy.

It was left to Brigadier General William S. Rosecrans, commander of the Department of Western Virginia, to evolve a plan of operations more compatible with the general military situation. Rosecrans's plan called for the concentration of troops on the Baltimore and Ohio west of Cumberland under cover of Kelley's force at Romney and a forward movement from that point against Winchester. Rosecrans correctly held that Winchester was the key to the contested salient. Not only would occupation of that town compel the Confederates to evacuate the lower Valley; it would also serve as an outpost against enemy movements down the Shenandoah. The plan comprehended still another aim. With Winchester occupied and fortified, Federals at that point could threaten the left flank of the Confederate army then at Manassas and perchance compel it to fall back to a position less menacing to Washington.[54]

Preliminary to the execution of this plan, Rosecrans quietly assembled all spare troops in his department and held them in readiness at points on and convenient to the Baltimore and Ohio Railroad. He then went to Washington to obtain from General McClellan the last word of approval. Arriving in the National Capital, he found his superior critically ill of typhoid. With no prospect of immediate interview in sight, Rosecrans turned to the Secretary of War. But before Secretary Cameron and his assistants could act, disconcerting news arrived from the upper Potomac. It was information that the Confederate commander Major General Stonewall Jackson had left his base at Winchester and was marching toward Cumberland.

Rosecrans abruptly left his conferences and scurried back to his headquarters at Wheeling. He carried instructions to rush aid to Lander who having returned to duty was at the moment holding the line of the upper Potomac.

Jackson had been in command of the Valley District since the day of its creation by the Confederate War Department on October 22, 1861.[55] From the hour of his arrival at Winchester he had busied himself with preparations for active field duty. His first care was to clear the last foot of his jurisdiction of enemy troops. With this accomplished he planned next to move swiftly across the Alleghenies and reoccupy those counties that had refused to follow Virginia into the Confederacy.

Jackson's proposed route over the mountains was the convenient one provided by the Northwestern Turnpike and the Baltimore and Ohio Railroad. Although this approach to the Trans-Allegheny was vulnerable to flank attack from the north, its weakness found compensation in the fact that it afforded quick movement, and it passed through many prosperous agricultural communities. Jackson believed that a vigorous campaign prosecuted along this line would not only result in the recovery of the Monongahela and the Little Kanawha Valley but also cause a rapid withdrawal of the Federals from the Great Kanawha Valley and from the mountain passes.[56]

Jackson's planning called for 15,000 men, a greater force than he commanded. He therefore made appeals through military channels for assistance. He asked especially for the infantry brigade that had so fortuitously given him renown at Manassas. And he urged upon the Confederate War Department the necessity of assigning to him all troops that could be spared from the line of the Alleghenies.[57]

His requisitions were filled only in part. Contrary to the wishes of Major General Joseph E. Johnston, commanding the Confederate army east of the Blue Ridge, the "Stonewall Brigade" was ordered early in November to move from Manassas to Winchester. Here it was soon joined by a brigade from Brigadier General William W. Loring's command at Huntersville; late in December, 1861, Jackson's number was further augmented by the arrival at Winchester of Loring himself with two additional brigades.[58] He now had approximately 9,000 effectives available for immediate duty.

In the meantime Jackson had not stood idle. He sent out detachments to impede railroad reconstruction and to annoy Federal communications on the Chesapeake and Ohio Canal.[59] Since this artery of trade paralleled the Potomac River on the Maryland side from Cumberland to Washington, the Federal government had imposed heavy duty on it as a line of supply after the Baltimore and Ohio was closed. At Cumberland the Baltimore and Ohio relayed to the canal heavy supplies for the Army of the Potomac and Washington's civilian population. The District of Columbia looked mainly to its craft for coal supply.

DISQUIET ON THE POTOMAC

On December 6, 1861, Jackson sent a detachment to break Dam No. 5, situated near Williamsport. Finding it heavily guarded, the Confederates turned without success to their Parrot guns. They soon fell back to Martinsburg. Not to be denied, ten days later Jackson made a second attempt. While a small force made a demonstration against the canal farther south, he led a strong body against Dam No. 5. Again he found it securely held and the river crossing well-guarded. Under cover of darkness however a detail of picked men gained the Maryland side and destroyed much of the dam's cribbing. Within a few days a freshet completed the work.[60]

Jackson showed zeal also in his efforts to frustrate work on the Baltimore and Ohio. Late in November, he sent a brigade into Morgan County to drive off the Federal railroad guards. He wished particularly to stop work on bridges west of Hancock. A Confederate raiding party struck the line at Sir Johns Run Depot and captured valuable railroad property but fell back precipitately when Federal troops put in appearance.[61]

More zealous was Jackson in his plan to remove the last vestige of railway travel between Harpers Ferry and Cherry Run. Up to December 1, 1861, the Confederates had removed practically all of the double track between Harpers Ferry and Martinsburg and seven and one half miles of one of the tracks west of the latter point.

Their work was thorough and systematic. The rails, all of which were of high English grade, they transported to Harpers Ferry and Martinsburg, there to await the call of Southern railroads; they stacked and burned the crossties on the right of way. Early in December, Jackson set men to work on the remaining track west of Martinsburg. Although his force labored only intermittently, by the open-

109

ing of the new year it had removed all tracks west to Back Creek and with them the telegraph line.[62]

By this time Jackson was convinced that his available arms were not adequate for campaigning in the Trans-Allegheny; with winter upon him he decided upon duty closer at hand. There was a special reason for this. He believed that the closing of the Chesapeake and Ohio Canal would stiffen Federal determination to open the railroad. Before this could be accomplished, it was apparent, the enemy must rebuild twenty-five miles of road between Harpers Ferry and Back Creek. Jackson accordingly concluded that his presence would be needed in his own district to prevent this consummation; for he anticipated that Kelley at Romney and Major General Nathaniel P. Banks at Frederick would attempt to unite in the vicinity of Martinsburg with a view to covering the railroad and threatening Winchester.[63] Jackson was determined to prevent their junction, and with this object chiefly in mind he took the field at the close of December, 1861.

He planned to cut communications between Banks and Kelley, threaten the latter's rear, and compel him to evacuate Romney.[64] To accomplish these ends he drove quickly toward the top of the salient at Hancock, a point on the Federal line of communication equidistant from Romney and Frederick. He attacked Union forces stationed at Bath, now Berkeley Springs, Morgan County, West Virginia, and others stationed in that vicinity guarding the railroad. The Federals crossed the Potomac to the Maryland side.

This part of the Federal line was defended by General Lander who commanded approximately 5,000 men dispersed along the railroad from Cumberland to Hancock.

DISQUIET ON THE POTOMAC

Lander had however guessed Jackson's intentions and had concentrated the greater part of his army at Hancock.

Jackson arrived on the Potomac opposite Hancock on January 5, 1862, and demanded its surrender.[65] The Union commander refused curtly, and Jackson answered with his artillery. The Confederates cannonaded the town for hours without effect.

Jackson's army remained in front of Hancock for two days. It inflicted no appreciable damage on its opponents. Yet all the while Confederate detachments worked feverishly destroying the main line of the Baltimore and Ohio which here paralleled the Potomac on the Virginia side. They removed track and destroyed railroad bridges which spanned the Great Cacapon and the Little Cacapon rivers, Sir Johns Run, and smaller streams, all of which had but recently been erected under protection of Union arms. On January 9, 1862, however, Jackson learning that enemy reinforcements were coming up from Frederick, decided to retire, and moved toward Romney.

All the while Lander had chafed in his rôle of subordinate. First he urged Banks to cross the Potomac, occupy Martinsburg, and strike the Confederate rear. But Banks thought that Jackson's demonstration against Hancock was a ruse designed to cover the movement of a heavier Confederate column down the Valley.[66] He refused to stir, and McClellan sustained him. "I would not run the great risk of crossing the River unless you see certain chances of great success and perfect certainty of being able to recross at pleasure," [67] McClellan wired Banks on January 7, 1862. "Lander is too young a General to appreciate the difficulty of a river behind an army. . . ." Lander also fell short of success in his effort to obtain permission to throw his own army across the river with a view to harassing the flanks and rear of the retiring enemy. He was sent instead to Romney to assist Kelley in evacuating that position.[68]

Lander and Kelley found ample time for orderly withdrawal of both men and property. Because of a chilling snowstorm and slippery roads, Jackson's command was delayed four days at Ungers Store; his advance guard reached Romney on January 10. The last element of the Federal garrison was by this time safe on its way to the mouth of Pattersons Creek where the main body was settling in bivouac.

On January 13, 1862, Jackson's army occupied Romney. Despite the inclement weather, the Confederate general began immediately to formulate plans for further campaigning. He would move swiftly upon New Creek, cut the railroad at that point, then strike easterly over the Baltimore and Ohio to Cumberland.

Before his troops could again take the offensive, rougher and constantly changing weather set in. Mountain campaigning was simply out of the question. Jackson reluctantly decided to conclude operations for the winter. He was now left the single choice of holding all that he had gained.

Jackson posted his battalions strategically. He ordered Brigadier General James H. Carson back to Bath with a militia brigade; placed Brigadier General Gilbert S. Meem's command at Martinsburg; scattered Brigadier General James Boggs's brigade of militia along the South Branch of the Potomac from Romney to Moorefield; assigned to Lieutenant Colonel Turner Ashby's cavalry the duty of patrolling the line of the Potomac in front of Martinsburg; and directed Brigadier General William W. Loring with three brigades of infantry and artillery, with

DISQUIET ON THE POTOMAC

a small cavalry force attached, to hold Romney. With the "Stonewall Brigade," Jackson's own, the Confederate commander marched to Winchester and there went into winter quarters.[69]

He had scarcely settled down when dissatisfaction little short of mutiny raised its head at Romney. Many of Loring's officers and men were from the deep South and unused to the rigors of a winter of far Northern proportions. Their duties on this outlying frontier were indeed of the sort that evoked strong language. They resented, too, the transfer of the "Stonewall Brigade" to the more comfortable environs of Winchester. To make matters worse, the situation was complicated by strained personal relations between Loring and Jackson.

Aided and abetted by officers and men, Loring utilized both military and political channels to gain the ear of the Confederate War Department. Due to his effort, the Secretary of War was led to believe that if Jackson had not acted with indiscretion in posting Loring's command at Romney, he had made a strategic blunder.

The upshot of the affair was that on January 30, 1862, Jackson was directed to notify Loring to evacuate Romney and to fall back to Winchester.[70] As a direct result of this shift, Carson retired from Bath and established a position at Bloomery Gap. His plans for defense now blasted, Jackson sent in his resignation and with it a request that he be returned to his professorship at Virginia Military Institute; but through the intercession of friends and officials who knew his worth as a general officer he was saved to active field service, and from oblivion.

Lander, who had but recently received reinforcements from the west, now counterattacked. On February 6, 1862, his forces reoccupied Romney and eight days later in a surprise attack sent the Confederate detachment at Bloomery Gap flying up the Valley.[71] As these movements again gave the Federals control of the railroad east to Hancock, the railroad company quickly restored the bridges and tracks destroyed by Jackson. On February 14, 1862, a train again steamed into the station opposite Hancock.[72]

Owing to the resignation of Secretary Cameron, the Baltimore and Ohio management now found a friend and mentor in the person of the new War Department head. He was Edwin M. Stanton of Ohio. Along with an aggressive spirit, Stanton carried into his high office a determination to prosecute the war vigorously. What is more, his Ohio background seemed to energize his concern over the existing traffic congestion at the West.[73] At any rate with Stanton's appointment as Secretary of War, definite plans were formulated for the reopening and military protection of the Baltimore and Ohio. This policy found a place in the scheme of things, for McClellan wished to make the lower Valley safe before beginning his contemplated Peninsular campaign. He expected also to withdraw a part of the force from the upper Potomac for service in his advance against Richmond, and he was anxious to make it available at the earliest practicable moment.[74]

The Federal advance into the lower Shenandoah was not long delayed. On February 24, 1862, Banks moved from Frederick and crossed the Potomac at Harpers Ferry. He promptly pushed on and occupied Charles Town. On February 28, McClellan directed Lander to proceed from Hancock to Martinsburg and there effect a junction with Brigadier General Alpheus S. Williams who was under orders to cross the Potomac at Williamsport.[75]

DISQUIET ON THE POTOMAC

Willing soldier that Lander was, he never executed another command. The strenuous duties of the preceding weeks had sapped his energies. Nature quickly took her reckoning; at the close of February he fell ill of pneumonia at Paw Paw. On March 2, 1862, he died. His troops under a new commander, Brigadier General James Shields, had already marched to join Williams. United on March 6, the consolidated forces of Banks, Shields, and Williams moved cautiously toward Winchester. The Federals took possession of the town on March 12, 1862.[76]

This concert resulted in the expulsion of the last Confederate detachment from the vicinity of the Baltimore and Ohio Railroad. The company immediately pressed the work of repair and reconstruction from both ends of the burned segment. Work was begun on the Harpers Ferry bridge on March 4, and despite changing weather and high water, was prosecuted with such vigor that the structure was completed on March 18. Meanwhile bridgemen moving eastward from Hancock spanned Sleepy Creek, Cherry Run, and Back Creek. Track layers followed close upon their heels and soon rebuilt the road between North Mountain and Martinsburg. On March 20, workmen began relaying iron at Harpers Ferry. Organized in shifts, the crews at either end worked night and day. On March 29, 1862, their task was completed; next day the Baltimore and Ohio was reopened from the Ohio to the Chesapeake.[77]

Through traffic was resumed immediately. The company management had already announced rates substantially lower than those imposed by competing trunk lines. As a result the Baltimore and Ohio was called upon to handle a heavy tonnage on the very day of opening. It

115

was estimated that 3,800 cars passed east and west over the Harpers Ferry bridge on March 30. Many of these, loaded with produce and miscellaneous supplies, had been held at New Creek, Cumberland, and Martinsburg ready to push forward when the last rail was in place. Regular through passenger service that had likewise been in eclipse for ten months was resumed on April 1, 1862. So auspicious was the event in Wheeling that the city celebrated with one hundred guns the arrival of the first through passenger train.[78]

John W. Garrett had striven hard to accomplish this result. He had stood at the forefront of events. The warmth of his enthusiasm was alone sufficient to lift the clouds of suspicion that had long hung over the Baltimore and Ohio management. But neither act nor spirit satisfied certain self-appointed guardians of the national destiny. They seemed to want not only atonement but a new profession of faith. Consequently, at a meeting of the Baltimore and Ohio board of directors held in February, 1862, an ardently pro-Union member offered a resolution requiring all officers and employees of the company to take the Congressional oath of allegiance. Although the resolution was promptly laid on the table by a large majority vote, the extremists were not to be denied. At a subsequent meeting one of their number presented a resolution, the substance of which required the Baltimore and Ohio company to hoist the United States flag at all of its important stations. This proposition was adopted. It was not passed, however, without the highly significant qualifying amendment that the company would follow the course outlined only "until otherwise ordered." [79]

Nevertheless by hoisting the Stars and Stripes over its

stations the Baltimore and Ohio company appeared to give
formal notice that its loyalty to the Union was thereafter
to be undiluted. The Confederates certainly viewed the
act in this light. To them it was a gauntlet thrown down.
This challenge they were determined to meet.

CHAPTER VI

The Confederates Attack

THE Baltimore and Ohio became at once fair prize for the Confederates. Already a base for Federal military operations in the Trans-Allegheny, it now began to serve a like end in the lower Valley. Its reopening also forewarned of strategic use on a grander scale. Since the Baltimore and Ohio provided the shortest route between the Potomac and the Ohio, its worth to the United States in wartime was obvious. Nor could the least alert of the Confederates fail to understand that the long coal trains which crawled east from the Cumberland yards carried warmth to a hostile people and power to a merciless navy.

The reaction of the Confederate government to an unbroken Baltimore and Ohio system was epitomized in the attitude of Virginia. On September 15, 1862, Governor John Letcher gave this warning in a legislative message: "The Baltimore and Ohio rail road has been a positive nuisance to this state, from the opening of this war to the present time; and unless its management shall hereafter be in friendly hands, and the government under which it exists be a part of our Confederacy, it must be abated. . . ." [1]

All summer the Confederates had been held at safe distance from the railroad. It is true that the Southern wave had dashed against it as General Stonewall Jackson's Valley campaign neared flood tide in May, 1862. But

THE CONFEDERATES ATTACK

Jackson's forces destroyed only two small bridges near Martinsburg and inflicted but minor damages on the Back Creek bridge.² The interruption to through traffic was momentary.

With General Robert E. Lee's invasion of Maryland in September, 1862, however, the company's good luck came to an abrupt end. On its way north the Confederate army swarmed across the line between Point of Rocks and Monocacy Bridge, destroying all bridges and rolling stock in sight; Lee's second corps under Jackson cut the road both east and west of Martinsburg as it countermarched to seize Harpers Ferry. After Antietam it struck on a front extending from Harpers Ferry to North Mountain.³ Jackson detailed Colonel James H. Lane commanding a brigade of General A. P. Hill's division to complete the work that had been so hurriedly begun. Lane's command remained at its task until late October, 1862.⁴ Smaller Confederate detachments held the road a month longer. During the period of their occupation the Southern forces destroyed most of the road from Harpers Ferry to Back Creek, a distance of thirty-five miles.

The Confederates followed a policy of thoroughness. Their aim was exemplified in method as well as in result. Already in the Bath campaign Jackson's men had demonstrated the efficacy of fire in track demolition. Other Confederate pioneers now profited by their example. Heating the rails to a white glow in improvised furnaces of crossties, the Confederate workmen bent them around nearby trees or distorted their shape against other stationary objects. In mischievous mood they encircled trees completely, leaving them weighted at the trunk with heavy collars of iron. In his next annual report President John W. Garrett informed Baltimore and Ohio stockholders of the nature

THE BALTIMORE AND OHIO IN THE CIVIL WAR

and extent of the company's losses. The following is an excerpt from his report:[5]

Great destruction of Company's property at Martinsburg. The polygonal engine house, the half round engine house, the large and costly machine shops, warehouse, ticket and telegraph offices, the Company's hotel and dining and wash house, master mechanic's house, coal bins, sand houses, blacksmith shop and tool houses, pumping engine for water station and connecting pipes were all destroyed. The destruction of tracks also commenced and continued until the main track from near the 87th to the 108½ mile, and the second track from Martinsburg to 108½ mile, and all the sidings and switches at Duffields, Kearneysville, Vanclievesville, Martinsburg, and other points destroyed, making a total of 37½ miles of track, the crossties from which were burned to heat and bend the iron.

Nor was this all. The enemy appropriated approximately ninety miles of telegraph line and destroyed the poles, smashed water stations, sandhouses and other appurtenances from Monocacy Bridge to Hancock,[6] and as a parting shot captured the railroad guard at the mouth of the Little Cacapon River and burned the bridge at that point.[7]

Relief for the distraught railroad management seemed to wait upon the shifting of the opposing military forces; for it was not until late November, 1862, that a change in the military situation east of the Blue Ridge caused the last Confederate detachment to withdraw from the lower Valley. A Federal army then followed and occupied Winchester;[8] again the Baltimore and Ohio was confronted with the singular and perplexing task of rebuilding a large part of the double-tracked portion of its main line.

The company was not entirely unprepared for such an exigency. Because of heavy traffic on its Washington

120

Branch and for other reasons,[9] the management had collected rails, crossties, bridge timbers, and accessories at points between Relay House and Washington with a view to double-tracking that part of the road. Before the grading had been completed however the company's attention was sharply drawn to the enemy's depredations. Garrett and his advisers promptly diverted the material for emergency use.[10]

It was this decision that made possible the reopening of the main stem within six weeks after the departure of the Confederates; for with materials ready at hand on the east as well as on the west end of the devastated area the rate of repair and reconstruction progressed at a double pace. The road was opened to through traffic on January 6, 1863.[11]

The next prolonged period of Confederate occupation was incident to the Gettysburg campaign. The evil hour for the Baltimore and Ohio struck on June 17, 1863. On that day the first wave of Lee's gray host rolled over the road between Harpers Ferry and Martinsburg. For five weeks the Confederates held a large part of the main line tightly in their grip. While the main body of the Confederate army crossed the railroad between Harpers Ferry and North Mountain, flank guards and roving patrols extended their operations as far east as Sykesville, into the very shadows of Baltimore, and west to Rawlings Station, at the foot of the Alleghenies. The Confederate tide swept a front of one hundred and sixty miles.[12]

Again the Southern armies burned the crossties and bent the rails; they demolished rolling stock and machinery of every kind; and as if to give a touch of finality they razed the water stations, woodhouses, fuel bins, sandhouses, toolhouses, station houses, depots, platforms, and blacksmith shops.[13] Although Lee's forces removed but seven miles of continuous track, they demolished every important bridge between Cumberland and Harpers Ferry. Spared by the advancing Confederates on their way north, the long bridge at Harpers Ferry subsequently fell victim to the hurried judgment of a Union commander. It was destroyed by a Federal force on July 5, 1863.[14]

By the end of July, 1863, the last unit of the Confederate rear guard had recrossed the Potomac and passed deep into Virginia. For a third time the Baltimore and Ohio faced the task of remaking its road. It was prepared for this emergency. Because of continuous threats of Confederate attack and actual losses from that source, the company had anticipated the day. It had not only again contracted for a replacement of materials for the Washington Branch but had also collected a reserve of lumber, crossties, and bridge timbers on the line along the upper Potomac.

The sale of timbers to the Baltimore and Ohio for emergency uses had already taken on the proportions of a business. One of the first to gather profits from this source was Henry Gassaway Davis, a merchant of Piedmont, who had left a conductor's position on the Baltimore and Ohio on the eve of the war to try his fortune in another field. He laid the foundations of an estate amounting to millions by selling crossties, bridge timbers, and accessory materials to the railroad after these Confederate thrusts.[15]

With an abundance of material at either end of the broken segment, after the battle of Gettysburg the company experienced only nominal delay in reopening. In fact the last rail was laid in place on August 11, 1863, but two weeks after the last Confederate detachment had departed. This achievement was as already indicated accomplished in part at the expense of the Washington Branch; materials that had been collected for the construction of the second track were once more diverted to main stem maintenance.[16]

Almost a year elapsed before the tide of Confederate gray again rose to submerge the Baltimore and Ohio. It was Lieutenant General Jubal A. Early's Shenandoah Valley campaign in the summer of 1864. Early's army reached the main stem between Martinsburg and Harpers Ferry on July 2 and held possession with short interruptions until the following September. Because of a brief recession in the Confederate offensive, Early's occupation of the line may be divided into two periods.

The first embraced the first half of the month of July, 1864. For two weeks Confederate troops removed selected segments of the track, cut telegraph wires, and destroyed bridges, culverts, buildings, and rolling stock. They extended their depredations as far east as Monocacy Junction.[17] On July 12, while Early's forward elements neared the defenses of Washington, a detachment of his cavalry struck the Washington Branch at Beltsville. Here it cut the telegraph, burned a camp train, and destroyed other railroad property.[18]

Between Harpers Ferry and Cumberland also, Early struck a heavy blow. Company losses included twenty-seven open culverts between Harpers Ferry and Martinsburg, a half mile of track at Quincy Siding, trestling of the Opequon and Rattling bridges, a part of the Pillar bridge near Martinsburg, and all platforms between Martinsburg and Hancock. The railroad bridges at the mouths of Pattersons Creek, the South Branch of the Potomac, and Back Creek likewise fell victim to Confederate thoroughness.[19] Not until Early had withdrawn from Maryland did the Baltimore and Ohio gain a respite. It then pushed repair and reconstruction with characteristic energy and on July 21, 1864, normal traffic was resumed.

But the railroad management had acted too soon. On July 26, only five days after the first through train moved, the Confederates again appeared between Cumberland and Harpers Ferry. They speedily put to naught all the company had done. Over a distance of seventy-five miles they systematically despoiled the telegraph; burned or pulled down engine houses, water tanks, fuel bins, toolhouses, sandhouses, stations, platforms; demolished bridges, trestles, and rolling stock; and in keeping with the policies of other years concentrated their efforts on continuous stretches of track. They worked east and west from Martinsburg; for eleven miles they removed, heated, and bent the rails. Once more they found the crossties a convenient fuel supply. In 1864, as in 1862 and in 1863, whole sections of the road were removed, almost without a trace.[20]

Early's battalions stood athwart much of the main stem north of Martinsburg until the middle of September, 1864. Then Federal countermovements in the lower Shenandoah caused the Confederate commander to draw in his outposts. On September 19, 1864, Major General Philip H. Sheridan decisively repulsed him in the last battle of Winchester. This engagement ended large-scale Confederate operations in the vicinity of the Baltimore and Ohio. The company received notice on September 20 that repairs could proceed at once; one week later the road was put in operation from terminal to terminal.

Spoliation of the Baltimore and Ohio Railroad after Antietam, after Gettysburg, and after Monocacy was in each case incidental to a larger aim. But this is not to say that Southern military authorities entertained indifferent views as to the railroad's importance. The fact is that in the interim periods the road suffered severely at the hands of smaller Confederate expeditions.

The line was indeed the main objective of many raiding parties. Small bands of irregulars were sent out to cripple the Federal line of communication, others to annoy Federal flanks and rear. They struck unexpectedly where the most damage could be done. They destroyed bridges, culverts, and tracks; pulled down telegraph wires and poles; burned company buildings, more especially shops, station houses, depots, and platforms. In a few instances they even robbed passenger trains guerilla fashion.

The railroad was however not infrequently the goal of larger detachments whose numbers were sufficient to contest a field. Although some never reached the line, others hit it in full force and inflicted heavy losses both on the railroad and on its defenders.

The most comprehensive and ambitious of these movements were concurrent raids led by two Confederate brigadiers, William E. Jones and John D. Imboden. The objectives were identical, and the commanders acted in concert. The movements were to all intents and purposes a single campaign. This colorful but menacing advance into the Trans-Allegheny in the spring of 1863 has in fact long since passed into history as the Jones-Imboden raid.

The Confederates aimed to destroy all the bridges and trestling on the Baltimore and Ohio from Oakland to Grafton; to capture the Union forces at Beverly, Philippi, and Buckhannon; to overthrow the reorganized state government at Wheeling; to recruit men for the Confederate service; and to collect supplies, particularly horses, cattle, and grain.[21]

Confederate authorities were hopeful that their forces could hold northwestern Virginia permanently or at least until they could destroy the greater part of the Baltimore and Ohio west of the Alleghenies.[22] They also believed that the shifting of Southern troops north would draw the Federal Major General Robert H. Milroy out of Winchester and reopen the lower Valley to their own quartermasters and recruiting officers.[23]

The plan of campaign originated in the fertile brain of General John D. Imboden. On March 2, 1863, he submitted a tentative draft for approval to General Lee. It called for the movement of 2,500 of his own command in two columns from Staunton. One would march over the Staunton and Parkersburg Turnpike, the other over the Northwestern Turnpike.

There was also to be a covering force. General William E. Jones was to move with his command of mixed arms, also wintering in the middle Valley, against Romney, New Creek, and Cumberland. Imboden believed that while Jones feinted at these points a detachment of his own cavalry could move through Moorefield, strike the railroad at Oakland, and then destroy the important Cheat River railroad bridge at Rowlesburg. Meanwhile the infantry, artillery, and the remaining squadrons of his cavalry would march to Beverly, capture Philippi and occupy Grafton.[24]

General Lee approved the plan, and both Imboden and Jones held their troops in readiness to move with the nod of spring. But the roads dried slowly as the Confederates waited. During this period of delay the three generals exchanged opinions on details of the campaign. Jones

126

did not relish a minor part in the expedition and asked for a major rôle.[25] Lee heeded his suggestion and granted his request.

Lee agreed that Imboden should move his entire force in a single column against Beverly, Philippi, and Grafton, while Jones would press forward to Moorefield, gain the Northwestern Turnpike, and smash the Baltimore and Ohio bridges at Oakland and Rowlesburg.[26] The revised plan contemplated simultaneous attacks on the railroad at Oakland and Grafton and an early junction of the two Confederate columns.[27]

The time of departure was set for April 15, 1863. But before either Jones or Imboden had stirred from camp, information came that Union cavalry on the Rappahannock was headed west toward a gap of the Blue Ridge. The Federal movement proved however to be only a demonstration and Lee gave the word to march within the week.

On April 21, 1863, Jones left Lacey Spring in Rockingham County. His force consisted of the Seventh, Eleventh, and Twelfth regiments, White's, Brown's, and Witcher's battalions, all cavalry, with small units of infantry and artillery attached. Three days later he put in appearance at Moorefield only to find the South Branch of the Potomac swollen with spring rains. He could not cross. There was no choice, so he sent his infantry and artillery back to the Shenandoah. With the remainder of his force, he then detoured twenty-five miles south and at great hazard to both man and animal crossed the river at Petersburg.[28]

Once on the north bank of the South Branch, Jones made haste to reach the Northwestern Turnpike upon which cavalry could move with ease. His immediate concern was to cut the Baltimore and Ohio main line before

THE BALTIMORE AND OHIO IN THE CIVIL WAR

Federal forces east of the mountains could move west. On Saturday, April 25, Jones took the road leading to the Northwestern Turnpike. He met stiff opposition at Greenland Gap [29] but after a sharp fight captured the small force of Federals which there opposed him.[30] His men then resumed ascent of the mountains. Marching into the night Jones's carefully extended body of 2,500 cavalry filed on to the high road atop the Alleghenies early in the morning of April 26. Although it was a freezing, cold night, maneuvering soon began. Near Red House, Maryland, Jones detached Colonel Asher W. Harman with the Twelfth Virginia Cavalry, Major Ridgeley Brown's Maryland battalion of cavalry, and Captain John H. McNeill's company of Partisan Rangers. Harman was directed to cut the telegraph wires and destroy Baltimore and Ohio bridges at Oakland, then to march via Kingwood to Morgantown before rejoining the main body. Jones had earlier dispatched Captain Edward H. McDonald with a squadron of the Eleventh Virginia Cavalry to Altamont, twelve miles east of Oakland, to burn small railroad bridges. McDonald had been ordered to follow and join Harman.[31] With the main body Jones himself marched west over the Northwestern Turnpike with a view to answering the challenge so long held out by the Cheat River bridge. He arrived at Rowlesburg early in the afternoon of Sunday, April 26, 1863.[32]

The Cheat River viaduct, a magnificent and costly structure, was guarded by approximately two hundred and fifty members of the Sixth (West) Virginia Volunteer regiment of Federal infantry.[33] The disposition of the defending troops had been predetermined by piles of logs and crossties at each end of the bridge and by positions of vantage on the steep hills.

THE CONFEDERATES ATTACK

The situation which confronted the Confederate commander suggested no alternative to the costly one of assault. He therefore ordered the Sixth Virginia Cavalry, commanded by Lieutenant Colonel John Shac Green, to move forward and drive the Federals from their works. With the aid of sharpshooters from the Seventh and Eleventh Virginia regiments Colonel Green dismounted his men and attacked.[34]

The effort was a feeble one and the Federal fire was hot. The attack therefore failed. Further effort appeared suicidal and the Confederates made no other attempt. Finally, late in the afternoon they mounted and withdrew. Jones had received no word from Imboden, although he himself was within a single day's ride from Grafton. He regained the Northwestern Turnpike and again pointed his column west.

Events of comparative insignificance now passed in quick succession. Jones's squadrons arrived at Evansville in the forenoon of April 27. They spent much of the day destroying the small railroad bridges at Independence and both rolling stock and stationary railroad property at Newburg.[35] Jones tried to make contact with Imboden but his patrols gathered not a word concerning that general's whereabouts. Nor did they obtain more than rumor on the strength and disposition of the Federals. The Confederate commander however gave no heed to the uncertainty of the situation and again resumed march. This time he wheeled north; he reached Kingwood at night, tarried in the town but momentarily, then pushed out on the Morgantown-Kingwood Turnpike. He did not halt his command until midnight, which hour found both horse and rider too weary to proceed further. Although deep in enemy territory, the Confederate commander posted neither picket nor vidette.[36] All hands simply dismounted and fell upon the ground.

It was a short night. About four o'clock in the morning the Confederate camp was aroused by the approach of cavalry. It happily proved to be Harman's troops returning to join the main body.

This detachment had carried out its instructions to the letter. It had cut both railroad and telegraph at Altamont and Oakland, and demolished the railroad bridges and culverts at Cranberry Summit, now Terra Alta. But because of the delay at Greenland it had reached the railroad too late to capture a westbound train filled with Federal officers belonging to Colonel James A. Mulligan's command. It had however overrun much of the country to the Pennsylvania border and captured a number of isolated Union outposts.

Harman's force struck with a swiftness that baffled both soldier and civilian. At Oakland, Maryland, the surprise was complete. The Twelfth Virginia Cavalry entered the town about 11 A.M., April 26. Both soldier and citizen were on their way to church. Those in uniform were immediately made prisoners, then paroled.

This was not done without amusing incident. A Confederate officer relates that several Federal soldiers were taken on the streets as they accompanied their ladies to church. With the coolness of veterans they acquiesced to the fate that was upon them; but not so much can be said of their companions. It fell to the lot of a pious Confederate trooper to make prisoner the escort of one of the sharpest-tongued of the ladies. She protested vehemently. As the discomfited Confederate reported his prisoner, his comrades shook with laughter. "Please God," he retorted, "I have never heard a woman talk that way before." [37]

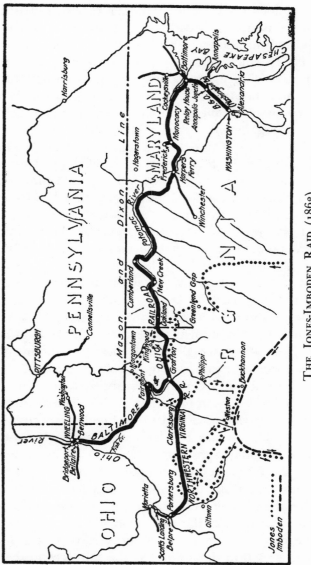

THE JONES-IMBODEN RAID (1863)

All was not fun and frolic. Harman carried instructions not only to destroy railroad property and to capture Federal soldiers but also to pick up all likely cavalry horses in his path. His command deployed widely and overran the greater part of Preston County from Kingwood to the Pennsylvania border. It also swept into the strongly pro-Union county of Monongalia and entered the county seat town of Morgantown.

All along the Confederates encountered the bushwhacker. Although this specie of combatant, Union or Confederate, was in most cases only a determined local partisan obsessed with opinions of patriotic self-sufficiency, he was sometimes the social scum of a community. His weapon was the rifle, and his cover was the woodland. He made no distinction between military foe and civilian enemy. He was detested by both the citizenry and the military; in the eyes of the latter his act was more criminal than espionage.

In the afternoon of April 27, 1863, as Harman's advance guard neared Morgantown three shots rang in rapid succession from the wooded hillside below. Captain W. I. Raisin's horse fell dead leaving its rider uninjured.

In a flash Raisin's comrades dropped their reins and dismounted. They soon came out of the woods with three captives, all of whom proved to be highly respected local citizens. Tradition has it that they were on a squirrel hunt that Monday afternoon and were led by sheer impulse to the fate that here ensnared them.

A drum court speedily passed sentence and a firing squad led the men off. A half dozen carbines sounded from a ravine nearby, and the gray troopers resumed march. But one of the doomed had a lucky star. At the lethal command he fell to the ground in the split second that intervened before the rifles crashed. Thinking their work well done, the Confederate executioners hurried away without discovering their mistake.[38]

Harman's men entered Morgantown within an hour after this event. There was only a civilian population to resent their coming, and it had been forewarned. Several hundred citizens had indeed armed themselves and had collected to offer resistance. But when summoned to disperse they surrendered unconditionally, deposited their muskets and sidearms in the courthouse, and retired to their homes.[39] United States Senator Waitman T. Willey, a native son, left town but a few hours previous to the arrival of the Confederates. Other citizens decamped to Pennsylvania with their horses, while some hastily concealed their horses and cattle in woodland pastures.

The Confederate occupation of the town comported with accepted military custom and usage. The United States flag in the courthouse square was of course hauled down and a Confederate flag raised in its stead. There was no general looting of private property. The nearest approach to ungentlemanly and unmilitary conduct was boisterousness caused by drinking the strong liquors which that day flowed freely across local bars. A Confederate officer writes that he had great difficulty in preventing two young men from fighting a duel over the affections of one of the town's more beautiful ladies.[40] Harman's squadrons tarried only until dark, then retraced their steps on the Morgantown-Kingwood pike. It was they who disturbed the repose of the main body in the early morning of April 28.

With a united command Jones marched now toward his next important objective. It was the long Baltimore and Ohio Railroad bridge which spanned the Monongahela

River at Fairmont. He did not hurry but again sent out small detachments to procure horses and to gather information.

The Confederates entered Morgantown a second time about noon, April 28, taking its population completely by surprise.[41] Many horses that had been hurried away on the previous day were now taken by the Confederates. Again the Southern soldiers tried to fit their behavior to the accepted military code; they bought freely at the stores using their own accepted medium of exchange, Confederate paper money; to forestall excessive conviviality the Confederate commander posted guards at the door of each saloon. With less regard for the amenities bands of his troopers meanwhile combed the countryside for new horses. Scarcely a village or hamlet within a radius of ten miles escaped their visits; Fayette and Greene counties, Pennsylvania, narrowly missed invasion.

The main body of Confederate cavalry left the immediate environs of Morgantown soon after nightfall and arrived on the northern outskirts of Fairmont at dawn, April 29. In a short time Jones's men had gained the opposite side of the town and closed the only avenue of Federal retreat south. They then charged pell-mell through the streets. Within an hour the Confederates were in complete control of the situation and work on the railroad bridge was begun.[42]

It was an iron structure of three spans, 615 feet long, said to be the most expensive bridge on the road. The superstructure was supported by tubular columns of cast iron resting on stone piers. Into these cannon-like tubes the Confederate pioneers poured powder. Although the Confederate officer in charge was a skilled pyrotechnician, his method proved faulty. Instead of catapulting the bridge into the river as expected, the explosives did no damage whatsoever. Other charges of powder also failed. General Jones then ordered the wooden parts of the bridge burned. After this order had been executed, the Confederates again tried powder. This time it proved effective and by nightfall the last span lay in the river.[43]

With this important task completed, Jones marched up the West Fork Branch of the Monongahela. He knew full well that he was moving straight into the muzzles of Federal rifles at Clarksburg but he did not change his course until he had contacted the enemy outguards. The Confederate raiders then made a detour and struck the Northwestern Virginia Railroad at Bridgeport, six miles east of Clarksburg. On April 30, 1863, they here captured a company of Federal soldiers, made sixteen civilian railroad employees prisoners, destroyed a train, and burned the bridges and trestles.[44]

The Southern cavalry then moved on. Already the troops were encumbered by the herds and droves which they had in custody. Consequently, upon reaching Philippi on May 1, Jones detached a part of Harman's command and sent it to Beverly with the horses and cattle. He then turned the remainder of his force westward with promise at last of effecting junction with Imboden.[45]

Imboden had left Shenandoah Mountain on April 20, a day before Jones's departure from Lacey Spring. By forced marches his army of 3,300, chiefly infantry,[46] had pressed forward on the Staunton and Parkersburg Turnpike to Beverly. There on April 24, 1863, the Confederates surprised a Federal force but failed to capture it.[47] Imboden had sent out cavalry reconnaissances to contact Jones's column but had not met with success.

Imboden next marched toward Buckhannon. At the end

of the first day however he received erroneous intelligence that Colonel James A. Mulligan's Federal force which was east of the Alleghenies but a few days previously had arrived at Philippi. Not unnaturally he guessed that Jones had failed to cut the railroad according to plan. At any rate Imboden believed that his army was in danger of being cut off, and he countermarched toward Beverly. Finally, on April 28, upon learning that Mulligan was at Grafton, he again moved forward and on April 29, entered Buckhannon.

He waited here for Jones to join him. Meanwhile detachments from his command raided the countryside gathering recruits, animals, rations, and forage.[48]

The Confederate leaders immediately agreed upon a common objective. They laid plans to capture Clarksburg. As a first step, on May 3, they shifted their forces to Weston. Imboden called in his raiders and Jones dispatched runners to Beverly to bring back Harman's convoy.

Both commands waited in comfort. So tranquil in fact was Weston on Sunday, May 4, 1863, that the invaders played ball upon the public grounds which there surrounded Virginia's hospital for the insane. But it was not long until Jones and Imboden received news of the arrival of Federal reinforcements at Clarksburg. This caused them to revise their plans. It was decided that Imboden should march south toward Summersville with his own wagon trains and livestock. Jones was to renew his operations against the Baltimore and Ohio.

This indefatigable soldier had all in readiness by May 6. Again he detached Harman. This time he sent him with two regiments and a battalion to break the Northwestern Virginia Railroad at West Union. Jones himself led the main body westward on the Staunton and Parkersburg pike with a view to striking the railroad near its western terminus at Parkersburg.

Harman captured some ninety members of the railroad guard at West Union and burned two railroad bridges in the vicinity.[49] Jones was even more successful. He captured the Federal guard at Cairo, burned three bridges, and so damaged a tunnel that it was unfit for use. He then led his men from the railroad and marched to Oiltown, the center of the Burning Springs oil field. There on May 9, 1863, his forces completely demolished the equipment and burned oil estimated at 150,000 barrels. In his report to General Robert E. Lee, Jones emphasized the picturesqueness of the scene which followed the explosions: "By dark the oil from the tanks on the burning creek had reached the river, and the whole stream became a sheet of fire. A burning river, carrying destruction to our merciless enemy, was a scene of magnificence that might well carry joy to every patriotic heart...."[50]

This act marked the end of Jones's operations in the vicinity of the Baltimore and Ohio Railroad. He moved south first to Glenville, then to Sutton, and finally joined Imboden at Summersville. The two armies withdrew leisurely across the Alleghenies, reaching the Valley about the middle of May.

While neither had achieved all that was intended, each had served the Confederacy well. In his report to General Lee, Jones stated that although his men had killed and wounded but few of the enemy they had captured nearly seven hundred with small arms and one piece of artillery; destroyed two railway trains, sixteen railroad bridges, a tunnel, a large amount of oil field equipment, and 150,000 barrels of oil. He also reported the procurement of 1,000 head of cattle and 1,200 horses,[51] all of which were sorely needed for the spring campaign. Imboden destroyed less enemy property but enlisted a few recruits and garnered a large amount of supplies, including horses, cattle, grain, and forage.[52] General Lee expressed belief that the ultimate effect of the raids would be to induce the United States "to keep troops to guard the railroad who might be otherwise employed against us."[53]

These movements had been prosecuted in the face of great odds and attendant uncertainties. In addition to General Benjamin F. Kelley's division of 10,000 men which was dispersed along the Baltimore and Ohio from Harpers Ferry to the Ohio River at the time Jones and Imboden left the Valley, there were approximately 3,000 Federals at Beverly and Buckhannon and perhaps an even greater number in the Great Kanawha Valley. Parts of Milroy's command at Winchester were detached and sent to Clarksburg as the raids reached high tide.[54] Major General Ambrose E. Burnside ordered such troops as he could spare from the Department of the Ohio to move by rail to Marietta and Bellaire.[55] He even obtained the cooperation of the navy and caused two gunboats to cruise speedily from the lower Ohio toward Parkersburg.[56] Militiamen were called to active duty in western Pennsylvania, northwestern Virginia, and eastern Ohio counties. Their main points of rendezvous were Pittsburgh, Uniontown, Wheeling, and Bellaire.[57] Some were quickly sent forward to Fairmont, Grafton, and Clarksburg.[58] In view of the fact that Major General Robert C. Schenck, commander of the Middle Department, had approximately 45,000 men available for duty when the raids began,[59] it is not improbable that by May 9, 1863, the day Jones left the railroad but twenty miles short of Parkersburg, the Federal forces in northwestern Virginia exceeded 25,000 men.

THE CONFEDERATES ATTACK

The strategy and tactics of the Confederates on the other hand caused such confusion and bewilderment that the United States forces shifted helplessly. By cutting the railroad and the telegraph at many points, Jones's men made Federal concentration slow and difficult; by dividing and scattering their own forces they magnified their real strength; and by threatening numerous points simultaneously they prevented the Federals from uniting against them. In short, they concealed their strength and their designs so successfully and moved with such skill and rapidity that their opponents were kept on the defensive throughout the campaign. For sheer boldness of strategy and audacity of execution the raids of Jones and Imboden rank high in Confederate annals; surely the accomplishments of Jones's cavalry in the face of tremendous odds compare favorably with more publicized achievements of the Civil War and deserve well at the hands of military historians.

Although the Baltimore and Ohio main stem had been cut at many places, it was reopened to through traffic on May 4, 1863.[60] Repairs were promptly made at Altamont, Oakland, Cranberry Summit, Newburg and Independence; but for weeks both passengers and freights were transferred by wagons and pontoon bridge at Fairmont. Repairs were likewise pushed on the Northwestern Virginia Railroad and on May 17, 1863, through traffic was resumed.[61] Aside from the stoppage of trains resulting from Confederate occupation during the Gettysburg campaign, which has already been related, the road was not again disturbed by a large force until the following winter.

The respite was broken by a mixed force under the command of the Confederacy's youngest brigadier general, Thomas L. Rosser. On February 2, 1864, with a part of his famous Laurel Brigade, Rosser moved against the main stem at the mouth of Pattersons Creek, eight miles east of Cumberland. He captured the railroad guard of forty men, destroyed the railway bridge, the water station, engine house, and cut the telegraph. Marching northward along the tracks he struck again and burned the North Branch bridge, six miles east of Cumberland.[62] Rosser's force then fell back rapidly and found safety in the wooded valleys that retreat so gently southwesterly from the parent Potomac.

Nine days later the Confederates struck again. This time it was that reckless partisan ranger, Major Harry Gilmor, whose name was already a synonym for daring on the border. A native of Baltimore he had joined the Confederate army at the beginning of the war; his leadership of cavalry bands was matched in picturesqueness and achievement by the exploits of but few of his contemporaries. In 1862, Gilmor had used his battalion of cavalry to good advantage against the "Jessie Scouts," sent out by the Federal commander Major General John C. Frémont. Attired in the gray uniform of the Southern soldier but wearing a distinguishing insignia, the "Jessie Scout" went forth singly and in detachments to mingle with Confederate pickets or unsuspecting Confederate civilians. Gilmor's vigilant horsemen brought swift retribution to many a Federal detailed on this perilous duty. It was Gilmor who penetrated the Federal lines north of Baltimore in July, 1864, and took from a Philadelphia, Wilmington and Baltimore Railroad passenger train the Union officer, Major General William B. Franklin.[63]

On the night of February 11-12, 1864, Major Gilmor chalked up a new entry in his logbook of hazardous deeds. With twenty men he penetrated the Union lines south of

THE CONFEDERATES ATTACK

Charles Town, moved silently through the darkness to Kearneysville, and halted upon the Baltimore and Ohio right of way. Here but eight miles east of Martinsburg he blockaded the tracks and sat down to wait for the first train.

Along came the Baltimore-Wheeling night express. Although it was making only scheduled time, the engineer could not save his train from crashing. The locomotive and tender were indeed wrecked but no lives were lost. Gilmor's men found the smoking car filled with Union troops who at the word of command stacked arms and surrendered to what they believed to be a superior force. Only a stubborn Irish cavalryman gave trouble. With the trooper's own revolver Gilmor subdued him with a blow on the head.

Not the least of the Confederate leader's aims was to appropriate a large amount of money which he believed was in the baggage car. In this he failed, for as the train grounded the baggageman escaped into the darkness, carrying with him the key to the heavy iron safe. Failing to obtain money from this source, the Confederates turned to robbing the passengers. They took watches, money, and other private property. Although the Confederate commander succeeded in stopping general pillage, some of his men undoubtedly carried off personal belongings. As a result the raiders were branded highwaymen in the Northern press, and Gilmor was arraigned before a Confederate court martial. He was however found not guilty of unmilitary conduct and restored to his command.[64]

If Gilmor's attack on the Baltimore and Ohio served no important military end, the sudden blow delivered against the road by another partisan ranger three months later was direct in its consequences. On May 5, 1864, Captain John

H. McNeill with sixty men reached the main stem at Bloomington. He destroyed a passenger train and two freight trains "heavily laden with commissary stores." He then marched east to Piedmont, where he burned the machine and paint shops, as well as sand-, oil-, and engine-houses. He also destroyed nine locomotives, burned twenty-two cars, and removed "about two thousand feet of track." He captured a detachment of Federal soldiers which he paroled.[65]

In actual accomplishments the McNeill raid seems inconsequential. But it produced immediate reaction in Washington. To strengthen railroad defenses the War Department immediately ordered reinforcements forward from Ohio. Fifteen new regiments of militia were assigned to the Department of West Virginia. Eleven of these were posted along the Baltimore and Ohio between Parkersburg and Harpers Ferry.[66]

Despite Sheridan's pre-eminence in the lower Shenandoah Valley in the autumn of 1864, Confederate detachments continued to molest the road to the very end of the war. That daring Confederate, Colonel John S. Mosby, was in this period a constant thorn in the Union flesh. On the night of October 13-14, 1864, occurred the "Greenback Raid," one of his most colorful exploits.

With a handful of men Mosby slipped through the Federal lines in the Charles Town neighborhood and fell upon the main stem at Quincy Siding, seven miles west of Harpers Ferry. Here he intercepted, looted, and destroyed a westbound passenger-express. It carried two Federal army paymasters who had in their possession money estimated at $173,000.[67] Mosby's men made off with the entire amount.

Mosby destroyed the train completely. The engine's

boiler exploded as it left the rails. He had only to burn the wooden coaches. One of these was filled with German immigrants who were on their way to take up cheap lands in the West. As the Confederates hustled all passengers from their seats, Mosby was surprised at the coolness of the Germans. They would not stir. Soon an interpreter came forward to explain. They had purchased through tickets, he reported, and were determined to remain aboard to the end of the line.

At this moment the eyes of the Confederate leader fell upon a stack of New York *Heralds* in a corner of the coach.[68] He ordered his men to scatter these newspapers in the aisle, then commanded them to "burn the d - - d Dutch up if they didn't disgorge and leave the car." [69] As the flames spread the astonished immigrants poured from both ends of the coach. The entire train consisting of eight cars was consumed on the spot as Mosby's band retreated swiftly up the Valley.

In the autumn of 1864, Rosser again raided the Baltimore and Ohio. His thrust was the last by a sizable Southern force. On November 28, he led fifteen hundred hungry Confederates to New Creek and Piedmont and captured a large quantity of military stores. He also took both civilian and military prisoners. Nor did his division overlook valuable railroad property. It destroyed the round houses, machine shops, rolling stock, and the telegraph.[70] Rosser's main motive was however the procurement of supplies; Sheridan had already completed his work of devastation in the middle Shenandoah Valley. His main concern was therefore to make off speedily with well-filled wagons. It was this haste which perhaps saved the Baltimore and Ohio thousands in money and enabled it to

THE BALTIMORE AND OHIO IN THE CIVIL WAR

close the breach within two days after the departure of the Confederates.

These operations undoubtedly fell short of the aims outlined in Confederate policy; but this is not to say that the constant hammering of the line did not accomplish important military ends. It often annoyed and sometimes inflicted damage on the enemy flanks and rear; in each year of the war, Confederate occupation and destruction together deprived the United States of a convenient line of communication and supply for a long period; and of greater military importance was the fact that the ever recurring attacks of the Southern forces compelled the Federal authorities to maintain an elaborate system of defense which required the presence of troops that might have been used elsewhere to advantage.

CHAPTER VII

The Federals Defend

PROTECTING the Baltimore and Ohio was a task for Hercules.[1] Federal military authorities were not only confronted with tactical and administrative problems not found in military manuals but they were harassed by an aggressive enemy aided and abetted by natural forces.

Their opponents in truth enjoyed most of the advantages inherent in Virginia geography. The main stem of the Baltimore and Ohio cut squarely across the lower Shenandoah Valley, and the lower Shenandoah was poorly fashioned for railroad defense. A glance at the map will convince the most indifferent observer of the defenseless nature of the terrain from Harpers Ferry to the top of the Alleghenies. The railroad not only paralleled the graceful curves of the serpentine Potomac but it also intersected at right angles the numerous tributaries that empty into that stream from the southwest. Each of these was the axis of a valley and each valley was traversed by a turnpike, a road, a trail or a bypath. From Winchester, from Romney, and from other convenient points of rendezvous in the lower Valley the road could be approached over a choice of many routes, and to add embarrassment to a problem already complicated, the railroad lay parallel to the Federal line of defense.

To offset these disadvantages the Federals must of necessity occupy the Shenandoah Valley as far south as Harrisonburg. But here again the geographical features seemed to favor the Confederates. It was in this very area that General Stonewall Jackson in 1862 played at the game of hide-and-seek behind the friendly Massanutten Mountains and with a meager force measured out swift punishment to three Federal armies. Divided longitudinally by high mountain ridges and sprangling forks of the Shenandoah River, the middle Valley region forms a topography eminently fitted for deceptive maneuver.[2] Certainly after the hard lessons of McDowell, Front Royal, Winchester, Cross Keys, and Port Republic, Union strategists quickly concluded that this area could not be successfully occupied by a force not large enough to repel attack by sheer weight of numbers.

Nor did the Valley of Virginia seem to lend itself to the conduct of the Federal offensive. It is true that the towering Blue Ridge screened the backdoor approaches to Richmond; and an invading army might debouch from its low gaps upon Gordonsville, a most important railway junction, then move against the Confederate capital from the north. Yet such a venture could not be carried out without grave danger to the Federal line of communication, for if the line of supply held fast in the mountain passes it seemed sure to snap on the Virginia Piedmont.[3]

If the military authorities of the United States ever seriously pondered such a movement against Richmond, the idea was abandoned after 1862. In fact it was an experiment too precarious to warrant serious consideration. From the Union point of view the Valley was a veritable *cul de sac* possessing little or no strategic value, and no determined effort was made by Union armies to hold it until the very close of the war. And this was done to starve Virginia rather than to strangle her. The Confederates were thus permitted to use the Shenandoah almost at will as an avenue of approach to Maryland and Pennsylvania and as a base for operations against the Baltimore and Ohio.

Throughout much of the war the military protection accorded the railroad reflected this negative policy. Although its purpose was definite, Union defense was indeed based on no clear conception of method. Strategically, it followed the mercurial lines of expediency; tactically, it pursued the more commendable course of experiment.

Experimentation began with the recovery of the main stem in March, 1862. An arrangement was then concluded which allocated the main line to respective military jurisdictions, the Mountain Department and the Department of the Potomac. Within these departments railroad districts were created and to each was assigned a subordinate officer charged specifically with railroad defense. General Benjamin F. Kelley was assigned to this special duty in the Mountain Department.[4] His district embraced that part of the Baltimore and Ohio which lay between the western boundary of Allegany County, Maryland, and the Ohio River. Colonel Dixon S. Miles was placed in command of the Cis-Allegheny railroad district.[5]

The virtues of the plan were obvious. The arrangement simply entrusted the defense of the Trans-Allegheny fraction of the railroad to the discretion of a commander whose base of operations and line of supply was the railroad itself; it placed the destinies of the eastern portion squarely in the hands of the defenders of the National Capital.

In practice however the plan fell short of perfection. Owing to the fact that the railroad districts remained under the jurisdiction of departmental commanders, the latter were under constant temptation to use railroad troops for reinforcement and replacement of their own armies. In fact, in May, 1862, General John C. Frémont, commanding the Mountain Department, was overborne by this temptation. Because of exigencies of his hapless Valley campaign against Jackson, he withdrew such a large part of the railroad guard that Kelley was constrained to inform the War Department that he had but two regiments to defend the road.[6] In the same period and for similar reasons, General Banks ordered so many of Colonel Miles's troops to the front that the railroad was left entirely without military protection at some of its most vulnerable points.[7]

These defects did not go unnoticed at Washington; and the surprising Federal defeats in the spring of 1862 were reflected in the administrative orders of the War Department. In order to consolidate the zone of defense around the capital as well as to relieve the commander of the Army of the Potomac of duties foreign to the capture of Richmond, the Secretary of War created a new military jurisdiction which absorbed a part of the Department of the Potomac.[8] Designated the Middle Department, it embraced Pennsylvania, Delaware, most of Maryland, and a small part of northeast Virginia.

The hour had also struck for a more effective railroad defense. Pressed with the necessity of providing a more workable scheme, the War Department decided to place the entire Baltimore and Ohio system in the hands of a single commander. On June 27, 1862, it delegated the responsibility of defending both main stem and branches to the aging veteran, Major General John E. Wool, who had but recently assumed command of the Middle Department. Wool was given exclusive control of all troops assigned to the defense of the road in both Mountain and Middle departments.[9]

This plan plainly secured unity of command. It did not in turn immediately remove conflicts of jurisdiction. That commanders operating at the front still regarded troops assigned to special duty on the railroad as an available reserve subject to their orders is evidenced by a protest which Wool dispatched to Secretary Edwin M. Stanton on July 16, 1862. He complained petulantly of repeated infringement of his prerogatives: [10]

> Since I have assumed command I have found myself embarrassed by orders from Major-Generals Banks and Sigel, who, disregarding me as the commander, have frequently given orders for the removal of officers and troops on the Baltimore and Ohio railroad without the slightest notice to myself; . . . This interference has compelled me to issue orders forbidding any officer on the roads placed under my charge from obeying any orders from any general without my sanction or approval, excepting supplies designed for the command of those generals and those for General Fremont. . . .

The upshot of this affair was a mixed result. The veteran Wool maintained his jurisdiction inviolate but his dourness killed effective co-operation with commanders in his front. To cure this rift in the Mountain Department, the Federal authorities placed General Kelley in command of strategic posts south of the railroad in northwestern Virginia; in the Cis-Allegheny they left the command of outposts and garrisons in the zone of operations to field commanders.[11]

Failure to accord Wool some tactical control in strategic territory adjacent to the road between New Creek and Harpers Ferry undoubtedly weakened his defense; certainly the ubiquitous human factor deprived him of the use of troops which might have been employed to great advantage in meeting enemy thrusts at the railroad. Fundamentally the plan was unsound. It owed its conception to the erroneous belief that the Baltimore and Ohio lay in the peaceful zone of the interior. The Federal authorities were only disabused of this opinion after the Confederates had taken heavy toll in the autumn of 1862.

The opportunity to make amends on the basis of experience came soon after the withdrawal of Lee's Second Corps under Jackson in October, 1862. On December 17, 1862, Wool was superseded by Major General Robert C. Schenck, a brave division commander but a general officer of untested worth, who had followed the listless leadership of both the indifferent Frémont and the incompetent Pope. The limits of the Middle Department were extended to include the lower Shenandoah Valley as far south as Winchester, the upper Potomac region as far north as Hancock, Maryland, and all of northwestern Virginia north of the Great Kanawha River.[12]

Schenck was charged with all the duties implicit in his rank and office. In addition, he was assigned the special duty of defending the Baltimore and Ohio from its eastern terminus to all its headpoints. This shift in organization and personnel was based on the true notion that the railroad was indispensable as a departmental line of supply and as a base for operations. Consequently, with the coming of spring campaign weather, it was strongly occupied. On March 27, 1863, Schenck assigned General Kelley to the command of a division containing six brigades and placed him in control of railroad defenses from Monocacy Junction to the Ohio River.[13]

On paper this organization fell but little short of perfection. Obviously it removed glaring incongruities that plagued the previous arrangement. But it soon became apparent that the new plan was by no means free from grave administrative defects.

General William E. Jones's dashing thrusts against the railroad in the spring of 1863 was its acid test. In the futile effort to catch him, it was forcefully demonstrated that troops charged with the defense of the Trans-Allegheny could not be successfully handled in times of crises by the mere issuance of orders from departmental headquarters in Baltimore. Explicit evidence of the difficulties which confronted Schenck during this affair was the embarrassing reminder sent him by the United States general in chief, Henry W. Halleck. On April 29, 1863, Halleck sent the commander of the Middle Department this caustic telegram: "The enemy's raid is variously estimated at from 1,500 to 4,000. You have 45,000 under your command. If you cannot concentrate enough to meet the enemy, it does not argue well for your military dispositions." [14] After the surprising successes of the Confederates, it was also apparent that reinforcements for the defense of the railroad west of the Cheat River bridge must of necessity be drawn from the West.[15] These conclusions impelled the War Department to turn once more to a new experiment.

The result was a new military jurisdiction. Created on June 24, 1863, four days after West Virginia had achieved statehood, it was designated the Department of West Virginia. It embraced the tier of Maryland and West Virginia counties penetrated by the Baltimore and Ohio west of Hancock, all of Trans-Allegheny West Virginia, and a chain of riparian Ohio counties extending along the entire western boundary of the new state. General Kelley was placed in command.[16] That part of the road lying east of Hancock remained under control of the officer commanding the Middle Department.

Despite the fact that this change was a return to the same system of regional control that had been unsuccessfully tried in 1862, the present scheme was different in important particulars. Under the old plan, military protection of the railroad was made secondary to offensive field operations which might extend far beyond departmental limits; under the new, campaigning by the two departmental commanders was implicitly restricted to departmental areas. From the standpoint of both administration and tactics, this arrangement held out many advantages. But the War Department was soon beset with embarrassment in maintaining it.

Because of frequent incursions of small bands of Confederates into the Department of West Virginia in the first months of 1864 and Kelley's repeated failures in thwarting them, that officer momentarily lost caste in the public favor. Since none of the raiders had reached the railroad west of the Alleghenies but had overrun most of the West Virginia counties south of it, the rumor soon passed that the departmental commander was more concerned with the defense of a corporation than with protection of the civilian population. It was even said that Kelley was incompetent to command. Although the charges were loose to the point of misrepresentation, they were repeated with some emphasis on the floor of the West Virginia legislature; [17] and pressure was exerted upon the administration at Washington to effect his removal.[18]

For those who fish for motives, this development will seem strangely timely; President Lincoln was in this preconvention season angling for the solid support of the German element in the approaching presidential campaign.

To him the exigency must have been welcome indeed because he wished for an opportunity to assign Major General Franz Sigel to important command. Suffice it to say, Kelley was relieved and the President of the United States risked another political appointment. Sigel assumed departmental duties on May 6, 1864, but not without stirring strong suspicion that the change had been made solely in the interest of political expediency.[19]

Military efficiency was however not completely sacrificed. Four days after Kelley had surrendered the departmental headship, he was placed in command of all troops guarding the railroad from Monocacy Junction to the Ohio River. His force was to operate as an independent unit, subject only to War Department orders.[20]

This action was no doubt prompted by a desire to relieve departmental commanders of duties incompatible with extensive aggressive movements which the United States now planned against the backdoor of Richmond. Certainly the Federal Secretary of War was not unmindful of the wisdom of placing the defense of the Baltimore and Ohio in the hands of an officer whose entire war experience was the war history of the railroad itself. That both the commander and the arrangement were satisfactory, if not entirely effective, is evidenced by the fact that the Federal authorities did not see fit to resort either to experiment or to change in the remaining eleven months of the conflict.

Questions of strategy and tactical employment of troops also pressed for answer during the greater part of the war. These problems like the one of organization and administration taxed the ingenuity of the Federals. The disposition of forces which followed the recovery of the road in March, 1862, contemplated the establishment of a system of defense which promised not only to meet incursions of enemy troops but also to forestall interference by civilians. The plan comprehended the retention of Winchester and strategic points in northwestern Virginia, the occupation of the South Branch Valley, and the employment of a substantial railroad guard.

Federal authorities acted promptly to comply with these requirements. The garrisons at Moorefield and Romney were strengthened and additional troops were concentrated at Relay House, Monocacy Bridge, Harpers Ferry, Martinsburg, Hancock, Cumberland, and New Creek,[21]—all important stations as well as strategic points on the Baltimore and Ohio main stem. Troop dispositions west of the Alleghenies followed the general pattern fashioned by General McClellan in 1861. Throughout the entire length of main line and branches, no effort, to all appearance, was spared to guard every yard of track. Detachments were drawn from central points and posted at important bridges and at all tunnels. It was said, perhaps with some exaggeration, that pickets patrolled every quarter mile of the road from its eastern end to its western terminals.[22]

This bristling line of defense with its numerous outposts dotting the landscape to the south and west was destined to remain intact for only a brief period. During May, 1862, when the Federals were confronted with the difficult task of holding the Confederates under Jackson in the middle Shenandoah Valley, Federal authorities, as before stated, withdrew the railroad guards in large numbers to support both Banks and Frémont. This act left the line practically without defenders in the danger zone which extended from Harpers Ferry to North Mountain. There was however some compensation for this disrup-

154

tion of well-laid plans. As the larger bodies of troops were ordered into the field, the dispersed pickets that had been wearily plodding their beats over long sections of track were called in and assigned to the more important duty of protecting tunnels and bridges.

Although this redistribution left a large mileage exposed to enemy caprice, it eventually disproved the need of maintaining sentinels at regular intervals along the tracks. Only vigilance was required and this was supplied by railroad employees in the pursuit of normal duties. In addition, time soon disclosed the fact that there was little likelihood of civilian sabotage; since isolated pickets of small strength were helpless against enemy raiders, it was soon apparent that troops could be employed to greater advantage elsewhere.

Although this arrangement afforded ample protection to the road during the summer of 1862, it was wholly inadequate during the first Confederate invasion of Maryland. Despite the fact that no system of defense, short of the employment of a large army could turn back the tide of major invasion, there was nevertheless strong belief after the withdrawal of Lee's forces in the autumn of 1862 that more effective measures should be adopted to protect the road.

It was however left to subordinate officers to shape working outlines. At least two of the plans submitted to higher authority came from men who possessed special knowledge of the subject. Both officers had witnessed the rise and fall of Baltimore and Ohio fortunes and both knew intimately the difficult topography it traversed.

Yet they did not see eye to eye on matters of railway defense. Brigadier General Benjamin F. Kelley, who was at the time commanding the railroad district west of

Cumberland, forwarded a recommendation to the War Department urging the occupation of Romney, Winchester, and Leesburg in force as the answer to Confederate thrusts against the line.[23] On the other hand from his vantage point at Camp Melvin, Cumberland, Lieutenant Colonel Gabriel E. Porter suggested that adequate protection would be accorded the road along the upper Potomac by the establishment of camps of instruction at strategic points in the railroad district between New Creek and Harpers Ferry.[24] He placed emphasis on the fact that concentration of troops in this area would provide training under actual war conditions, thereby giving the recruit practical as well as theoretical experience; he urged that training of troops there would result in appreciable savings to the Federal treasury because officers might well serve in the dual rôle of instructor and commander.

The Baltimore and Ohio Railroad never became an authorized training ground for Federal armies. The War Department turned a characteristic deaf ear to both proposals. Congress did become sufficiently interested in Porter's plan to entertain a resolution offered by Representative Francis Thomas of Maryland. It discloses the public interests that were at stake. The resolution was as follows: [25]

That the Committee on Military Affairs be instructed to inquire into the expediency of providing for the establishment of camps of military instruction at suitable points on or near the Baltimore and Ohio railroad, as an effectual means of protecting the Chesapeake and Ohio canal and the Baltimore and Ohio railroad, so that those public improvements may be safely used for the transportation of coal for the use of steam vessels of the United States Navy, and of supplies for the United States Army, while operating in Eastern Virginia, or on our Atlantic front.

1. Builders of the Baltimore and Ohio. From a painting by Francis B. Mayer (Courtesy of the Baltimore and Ohio Railroad Company)

2. Laying the first stone of the Baltimore and Ohio Railroad, July 4, 1828. Charles Carroll of Carrollton holds the spade. From a painting by Stanley M. Arthurs (Courtesy of the Baltimore and Ohio Railroad Company)

3. A composite view of B & O buildings and activity in Baltimore, MD. From James Taylor's Sketchbook. (Courtesy of The Western Reserve Historical Society, Cleveland, OH)

4. Camp Kelsey, near Annapolis Junction, MD. Co. F. (LLI), 10th ME Reg. From an early engraving. (Courtesy MC/MOLLUS & USAMHI)

5. Annapolis Junction, Washington Branch of the B & O, ca 1870. From "Photographic Views of the Baltimore and Ohio and Its Branches". (Courtesy B & O Museum)

6. Abraham Lincoln arriving at the Baltimore & Ohio Station in Washington, February 23, 1861. From a painting by H. D. Stitt (Courtesy of the Baltimore and Ohio Railroad Company)

7. Relay House at Washington Junction in Baltimore County, MD. From "Photographic Views of the Baltimore and Ohio and Its Branches". (Courtesy B & O Museum)

8. The Relay House at the junction of the B & O Railroad & and the Washington Branch, nine miles from Baltimore. From a stereoview by New York Stereoscopic Co. (Courtesy Dan Toomey Collection)

9. Union soldiers waiting to search westbound trains in front of the Relay House. From a stereoview by E. & H.T. Anthony & Co. (Courtesy Dan Toomey Collection)

10. The Relay House at the Washington Junction of the Baltimore and Ohio Railroad in Baltimore County, MD. From James Taylor's Sketchbook. (Courtesy of the Western Reserve Historical Society, Cleveland, OH)

11. Relay House, MD. From a photograph. (Courtesy MC/MOLLUS & USAMHI)

12. The Winan's Steam Gun, captured by General Butler's Command near The Relay House, MD. From Harper's Weekly. (Courtesy Battles & Commanders of the CW)

13. The Thomas Viaduct at Relay, Maryland. View from Relay House with Howard County in the background. From "Photographic Views of the Baltimore and Ohio and Its Branches". (Courtesy B & O Museum)

14. The Thomas Viaduct at Relay Junction, looking south. From a stereoview. (Courtesy Dan Toomey Collection)

15. Members of Cook's Boston Light Artillery posed in front of the Thomas Viaduct at Relay Junction. From a stereoview by E. & H.T. Anthony & Co. (Courtesy Dan Toomey Collection)

16. Co. J., 8th Massachusetts Infantry, Relay House, MD. 1861. From a photograph. (Courtesy MC/MOLLUS & USAMHI)

17. View of Cook's Artillery Battery and gun emplacements overlooking the Thomas Viaduct and the Patapsco River at Relay Junction. From a stereoview by E. & H.T. Anthony & Co. (Courtesy Dan Toomey Collection)

18. The Boston Battery, commanding the Viaduct over the Patapsco River, on the Baltimore & Ohio Railroad near The Relay House. From Frank Leslie's Illustrated Newspaper. (Courtesy Battles & Commanders of the CW)

19. Union troops at Elkridge, near the Relay House, commanding the Washington Branch of the Baltimore and Ohio Railroad. From Harper's Weekly. (Courtesy Battles & Commanders of the CW)

20. Colonel Schoonmaker keeps the line open. From a painting by H. D. Stitt. (Courtesy of the Baltimore and Ohio Railroad Company)

21. Town of Alberton, Elysville Station, Howard County, Maryland, ca 1870. From "Photographic Views of the Baltimore & Ohio Railroad and Its Branches". (Courtesy B & O Museum)

22. Frederick Junction at the Monocacy Battlefield, Frederick, MD. From "Photographic Views of the Baltimore & Ohio Railroad and Its Branches". (Courtesy B & O Museum)

23. The historic meeting between Generals Grant and Sheridan at Frederick Junction, August 6, 1864. From James Taylor's Sketchbook. (Courtesy Western Reserve Historical Society, Cleveland, OH)

24. General Lew Wallace's Headquarters on the Monocacy Battlefield (Frederick Junction in distant rear). From a photograph. (Courtesy Frederick County Historical Society, Frederick, Maryland)

25. The Railroad Bridge over the Monocacy River at Frederick Junction. From "Photographic Views of the Baltimore & Ohio Railroad and Its Branches". (Courtesy B & O Museum)

26. The scene of General Lew Wallace's battle with General Early on the Monocacy River, July 9, 1864. (Frederick Junction in the left rear. From James Taylor's Sketchbook. (Courtesy the Western Reserve Historical Society, Cleveland, OH)

27. Bridge and battlefield at the Monocacy River in Frederick, MD. From "Photographic Views of the Baltimore & Ohio Railroad and Its Branches". (Courtesy B & O Museum)

28. View of the Monocacy Battlefield with B & O Bridge and General Lew Wallace's Headquarters in the distance. From a photograph. (Courtesy Frederick County Historical Society)

29. Scene at Frederick City Station on the corner of All Saints and South Market Streets. From James Taylor's Sketchbook. (Courtesy Western Reserve Historical Society, Cleveland, OH)

30. Point of Rocks, MD, the Southern terminus of the Catoctin Spur of the B & O Railroad. This scene shows a canal boat of the C & O Canal moving up the Potomac River. From James Taylor's Sketchbook. (Courtesy the Western Reserve Historical Society)

31. Harper's Ferry from the Maryland side of the Potomac River. From James Taylor's Sketchbook. (Courtesy the Western Reserve Historical Society, Cleveland, OH)

32. Harper's Ferry at the beginning of the Civil War. From a contemporary sketch by A. Weidenbach. (Courtesy of the Baltimore and Ohio Railroad Company)

33. Destruction of the railroad bridge at Harper's Ferry, June 15, 1861. From a contemporary drawing in Harper's Weekly.

34. Maryland Heights from Harper's Ferry showing the C & O Canal and Potomac River. From "Photographic Views of the Baltimore & Ohio Railroad and Its Branches". (Courtesy B & O Museum)

35. Harper's Ferry at the time of its capture, 1862. From a contemporary photograph.

36. Confederate Battery overlooking Harper's Ferry. From Frank Leslie's

Illustrated Newspaper. (Courtesy The Soldier in our Civil War)

37. The Federal Camp on Bolivar Heights, 1862. From a photograph.

38. Duffield Station on the Baltimore and Ohio, six miles from Harpers Ferry. From James Taylor's Sketchbook. (Courtesy the Western Reserve Historical Society, Cleveland, OH)

39. Stockades such as this one were constructed much faster than the preferred blockhouses as a means of defending the railroad lines. From James Taylor's Sketchbook. (Courtesy the Western Reserve Historical Society, Cleveland, OH)

40. Kerneysville Station, 5 miles east of Martinsburg, WV, view looking east. From James Taylor's Sketchbook. (Courtesy the Western Historical Society, Cleveland, OH)

41. Stephenson's Depot, 6 miles north of Winchester, where the leaves of the Army were supplied with Quartermaster and Commissary Stores. From James Taylor's Sketchbook. (Courtesy the Western Reserve Historical Society, Cleveland, OH)

42. General Jackson's Headquarters at Winchester, Virginia, 1861-1862. From a recent photograph.

43. The Tray Run Viaduct at Rowlesburg. From William Prescott Smith, "Great Railway Celebrations of 1857".

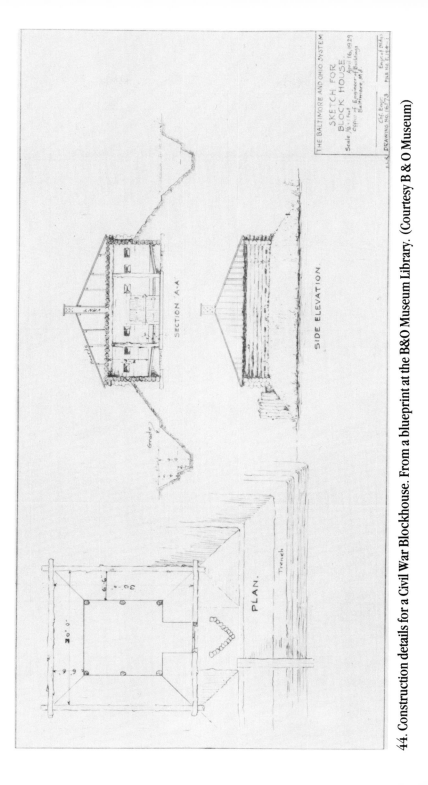

THE BALTIMORE AND OHIO SYSTEM

SKETCH FOR
BLOCK HOUSE
Scale ½ = foot   April 16, 1929
Office of Engineer of Buildings
Baltimore, M.

Ch'f. Eng'r.   Eng'r of B'ld's
DRAWING No. 16,773   File No. E-394-1

SECTION 'A-A'

SIDE ELEVATION.

PLAN.

Trench

30'0"

16'0"

9'6"

44. Construction details for a Civil War Blockhouse. From a blueprint at the B&O Museum Library. (Courtesy B & O Museum)

45. Trestlework near Rowlesburg, West Virginia with a Blockhouse in the background - upper view. From "Photographic Views of the Baltimore and Ohio and Its Branches". (Courtesy B & O Museum)

46. Trestlework near Rowlesburg, West Virginia with a blockhouse in the background - under view. From "Photographic Views of the Baltimore and Ohio and Its Branches". (Courtesy B & O Museum)

47. The Battle of Philippi, June 3, 1861. From a contemporary drawing in Harper's Weekly.

48. Bridge #112 over the Monongahela River, Fairmont, West Virginia, built 1852. From a photograph.

49. The 16th Ohio Volunteers, under Colonel Irwine, crossing the Tray Run Viaduct, near Cheat River on the Baltimore and Ohio Railroad. From Frank Leslie's Illustrated Newspaper.

50. Cavalry's method of destroying railroads. The ties were lighted and rails heated until of their weight they bent out of shape. From a photograph. (Courtesy MC/MOLLUS & USAMHI)

51. Twisting the rails. From a contemporary drawing in Harper's Weekly.

52. A powder car of Civil War days. From a recent photograph. (Courtesy of the Baltimore and Ohio Railroad Company)

53. A railroad battery, 1863. From Harper's Weekly Newspaper. (Courtesy of the Baltimore and Ohio Railroad Company)

54. Confederate Cavalryman Harry Gilmor shown helping a Federal Cavalryman to disembark from the train. From James Taylor's Sketchbook. (Courtesy the Western Reserve Historical Society, Cleveland, OH)

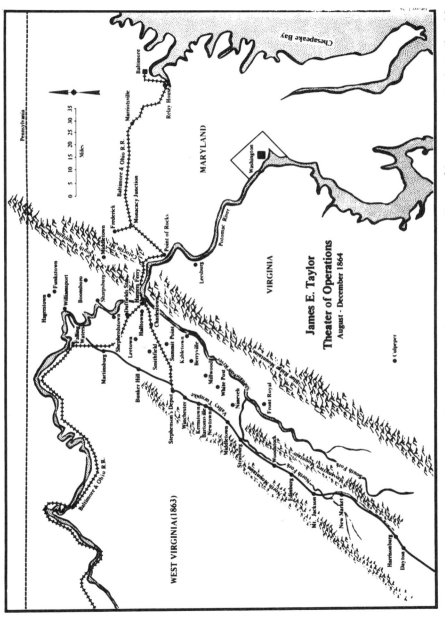

55. Theater of Operations of James Taylor, Sheridan's artist, from August to December 1864. From James Taylor's Sketchbook. (Courtesy the Western Reserve Historical Society, Cleveland, OH)

THE FEDERALS DEFEND

The peak of interest in the proposal was reached in this resolution; no further step, it appears, was taken to carry it into effect. The War Department was thus left a free hand to devise ways and means for the military protection of the Baltimore and Ohio.

As the Federals gradually extended their protecting arm over the road in the closing weeks of 1862, it was again plain that they regarded their work little more than a police function. Troops were again posted at vulnerable points along the line between Harpers Ferry and Hancock; Harpers Ferry once more became an armed camp; and the military posts at Cumberland and New Creek again bristled with bayonets and cannon.[26]

It was in this season too that Federal military authorities introduced innovations,—new not only to railroad defense but to modern warfare. The first was a blockhouse which United States military engineers designed to shelter the smaller detachments that guarded the larger bridges and tunnels at widely separated points between the Potomac and the Ohio. They were crude forerunners of Yankee pillboxes of another day. The following description was written by a Federal officer who saw them daily: [27]

... They were barns, constructed out of the largest and longest logs that could be obtained, each barn being from forty to fifty feet square and ten to twelve feet in height. They were timbered on the top to keep the shells out and were notched through the sides for the purpose of shooting through above the earthwork. In building them stone is first piled around the proposed foundation, about four feet high, then a deep ditch, four or five feet wide, is dug around the stone pile, the earth from the ditch being thrown upon the stones to a height of six or seven feet to protect the inmates of the house from shot and shell. The whole is surrounded with an abattis; we had no barbed wire in those days and the entrance to the building was made in a zigzag fashion. . . .

The order directing the construction of these unique fortifications was issued in March, 1863,[28] and the first structure was located at Rowlesburg. Others were constructed in that year while a few did not see completion until the spring of 1864.

Finally as a fitting complement to these miniature forts, armored cars were designed and put in general use in 1863. They were box cars covered or lined with thick iron sheeting and equipped with ordinary service cannon.[29] Although they were helpless in the face of artillery, they were sufficiently strong to withstand the fire of small arms. Like the blockhouses they were a distinct novelty. Their main functions were to patrol the road in times of threatening danger and to strengthen the defenses at bridges and tunnels.[30]

The success or failure of Union defense of the Baltimore and Ohio finds some explanation in the human element. The troops on railroad guard duty were as a whole an indifferent lot. This is not to say that the men were of inferior quality. The plain fact is that most units stationed on the road were raw militia placed there for seasoning; many excellent regiments of the Union army saw service on the Baltimore and Ohio before marching southward to more arduous service.

Some units, however, spent their entire period of organized existence on railroad guard duty, the dullest kind of police work. Composed of men who had entered the army to see active service, these organizations contained many who never smelled battle powder. In fact whole companies went through the war without firing a shot at a visible enemy. Naturally the men lost heart; they found consolation in fishing in the mountain streams or hunting on the forested Allegheny slopes.

They often lacked both discipline and *esprit de corps.* The measure of these frustrated regiments may well be taken from a singular incident that occurred in 1863.

The valiant stand of a detachment of the Sixth (West) Virginia Infantry at the Cheat River bridge was not tarnished by the fact that it was made with every advantage of position. Two days after the event, however, the Federals became completely demoralized and beat a rapid retreat north. The grim humor in the situation was the fact that they fancied they were flying from the enemy when in reality they were actually following him; for, on April 28, 1863, the last Confederate horseman had hardly disappeared behind the green hills that overlook Morgantown from the west when this Union detachment entered the town.

The Federals were not stayed by knowledge that danger had passed. Under the command of Major John H. Showalter, they pushed rapidly on to Uniontown and thence to Pittsburgh, where they took boats to Wheeling. With adequate supplies, sufficient ammunition, unsurpassed shelter, and the recent success to bolster their morale, they had simply been stampeded by the deep solitudes of the Cheat River canyon. The only sound explanation advanced by their commander was the plausible one that supplies were low.[31]

Yet Major Showalter's superiors could bring him to account with but poor grace; in the same week that this shameful episode marred the record of a few brave men, a Federal brigadier, Benjamin S. Roberts, held his force of 4,000 men in Clarksburg while 2,500 Confederates leisurely occupied the neighboring town of Bridgeport, six miles away, cut the Union line of communication with the east, and drove off livestock with impunity. When the Federal garrison had been swelled to 6,000 bayonets the same officer made no effort to move, although for days the Confederates remained in striking distance at Weston.

In fact the list of general officers who commanded in the Baltimore and Ohio zone is adorned by few names of distinguished soldiers. Most were of inferior stamp. It is true that both McClellan and Sheridan cleared the road of the enemy and kept it free in their respective jurisdictions over long periods,—the former in the beginning, the latter in the closing months of the war. For the most part however the commanders assigned to duty in the railroad district and the protecting areas south of it were selected for reasons foreign to military efficiency.

Generals Robert Patterson and John W. Wool were veterans too old for hard service; General Robert C. Schenck was sent wounded to the rear after Second Manassas and given high command, it seems probable, because of his prominence in Ohio Republican politics; General John C. Frémont's appointment to the command of the Mountain Department in 1862 was in all probability a strategic political shift to bring him under closer surveillance of Washington; General Franz Sigel gained favor in 1864 from the operation of obvious political motives; and even the efficient General Kelley's first tour of railroad duty ran concurrently with his convalescence from a painful chest wound received at the battle of Philippi.

The effectiveness of measures adopted for the military protection of the Baltimore and Ohio Railroad was unquestionably minimized by the unique geographical location of the line and the peculiarities of adjacent topography; the handicaps imposed by nature were heightened by the employment of raw troops and of officers without reputation or promise; but in the final analysis the destiny of the road was in the hands of Union forces at the front. In view of the inability of the latter to hold the middle and the lower Shenandoah Valley, the South Branch basin, and the mountain passes into northwestern Virginia, it is not strange that the line suffered severely from Confederate attacks.

Yet for long periods the entire main stem was kept open. It was more than a convenient trunk line railroad or a supplementary line in the service of supply. It proved also to be a helpful agency in Union strategy and as such was a determining factor in the conduct of important operations.

CHAPTER VIII

Strategic Use

I T is wholly superfluous to remark at this point that the railroad played a decisive rôle in the Civil War. It made possible not only the speedy transportation of troops but of their equipment and supplies as well. For many months after April, 1861, however, the value of any railroad as a logistical agency was but little appreciated. It is true that its function in wartime had already been strongly suggested. In the Austro-Sardinian War, by way of illustration, two French corps were carried from the outskirts of Paris to the Italian border in forty-eight hours.[1] But the best of strategists were slow to learn the lessons involved. In fact, military experts of Europe continued to speculate on the potential value of the railway in operations. It was left indeed to the leaders of the War between the States to stumble, as it were, upon irrefutable proof of its tactical utility.

Because of its nearness to the Eastern theater of the war, the Baltimore and Ohio acted a leading part in this demonstration. In fact its timely aid to Union arms gave it prior claim to many first honors. In McClellan's dash upon Grafton, (West) Virginia, near the end of May, 1861, the world saw for the first time a railroad used as a convenient agency for actual invasion; the surprise of the Confederate forces at Philippi which followed within the week was effected by an unprecedented strategic movement based on deceptive use of the railroad; and the part

STRATEGIC USE

acted by the Washington Branch of the Baltimore and Ohio in 1861 in making Washington secure bears further witness to its providential aid.

This employment of the railroad however resulted more from circumstance than from policy. Despite the possibilities suggested by successful use at home and equally skillful employment at the South, Federal military authorities did not fully comprehend the potentialities of mechanized transport until the conflict had almost passed. It was indeed left to the impact of crises to emphasize the really important advantages of railway transportation; even then the lessons taught did not find lodgment in the military mind until experimentation had dissipated all misgivings.

The first noteworthy experiment was conducted on the Baltimore and Ohio in the second year of the war. On August 8, 1862, an order was issued directing Brigadier General Jacob D. Cox, commanding Federal forces in the Great Kanawha Valley, to march posthaste cross country and join Major General John Pope's Army of Virginia, already launched upon its ill-fated campaign against Richmond.[2] Characteristic of Pope's planning, the order exhibited an unwarranted optimism. It directed Cox to move all available troops in his command, at best not two full divisions, by way of Lewisburg, Covington, Warm Springs, Augusta Springs, and Harrisonburg, and thence by the most direct roads to Charlottesville. There he might expect to effect a junction with the main army.

The entire route was a tortuous and dangerous path. It not only penetrated two hundred miles of difficult country but it also lay entirely in enemy territory. Directness was the single feature recommending it.

Cox immediately took steps to execute the order, although he doubted its wisdom. His troops were stationed

163

at Princeton, Raleigh Court House, Fayetteville, Gauley Bridge and other widely scattered posts. His own head-quarters were at Raleigh Court House. The arrangements preliminary to the march was the work of days. Concentration of troops had scarcely begun however when Cox submitted a proposition to Pope.[3]

He recommended that the movement be made by rail. Although the nearest railroad was the Baltimore and Ohio, two hundred miles north, the recommendation was promptly approved by General Halleck, and Pope gave his assent. The suspicion is strong however that official acceptance was based more on the thought of safety to the troops than to conviction that movement by rail would be more expeditious.

Cox was directed to leave 5,000 men to hold the region already occupied south of the Great Kanawha River and to march the remainder of his force to Parkersburg, the western terminus of the Northwestern Virginia Railroad.[4] The moving column included 5,000 men, 1,100 horses, 12 pieces of artillery, 270 wagons and camp equipage.[5]

The distance to be traversed was approximately two hundred miles. The route crossed the Great Kanawha at Kanawha Falls and followed the north bank of that stream to Camp Piatt, thirteen miles east of Charleston. Steamboats waited there. The march overland was without incident, but the men all but recoiled from the choking dust of the roads and the blistering heat of the August sun. The Ohio River was at low stage and the larger draft steamers covered the distance from Point Pleasant to Parkersburg with difficulty.[6] Nevertheless, the leading elements of the division reached Parkersburg on August 21, 1862.

Then came demonstration of what careful planning

could do. While the division was moving up, Baltimore and Ohio officials and employees worked overtime to complete preparations to expedite the movement east. On the ground at Parkersburg was Peter H. Watson, Assistant Secretary of War, who played the part of co-ordinator. Approximately four hundred cars with the necessary complement of locomotives were assembled and held in readiness. In fact the first regiments moved out on August 21. Next day others entrained and these were followed on August 23 by the last units of the division. By the end of that day, all of Cox's command, except animals and wagons, had reached the railroad and was pushing toward Washington.[7]

Each day trains steamed out of the Parkersburg yards within sight of each other. Of necessity their speed was abnormally slow. Nevertheless, each traversed the distance of four hundred miles in approximately forty hours.[8] Cox's leading regiments joined Pope in time to participate in the second battle of Manassas; others were employed in strengthening the defenses of Washington; [9] and all were with McClellan on the Antietam.

Cox's lone division without doubt rendered helpful service in a period of national emergency. It is perhaps not too much to say that 5,000 men tipped the scales from inevitable disaster to orderly retreat. But the real significance of the feat lies in the probability that it was made the basis of calculation for a more extensive strategic movement in the following year.

The transportation of two Federal corps with arms and equipment from the line of the Rappahannock to the Tennessee in the early autumn of 1863 was the accomplishment par excellence in Civil War logistics.

This movement too was executed under the stress of

emergency. On September 19-20, 1863, the Army of the Cumberland under Major General William S. Rosecrans was routed at Chickamauga, Georgia, and all but cut to pieces, but it had successfully fallen back and had taken refuge in Chattanooga. Shattered, demoralized, and confronted with General Braxton Bragg's victorious Confederate forces, it was here facing starvation and capture. Grant had been ordered to send reinforcements from Vicksburg before the fateful battle; but because of shallowness of water in the Mississippi and the bad condition of the railroads leading east from Memphis he had been unable to comply.[10]

There was no immediate aid in prospect from that quarter and the situation was alarming. General Rosecrans, his chief of staff, Major General James A. Garfield, and Charles A. Dana, an Assistant Secretary of War then with the Army of the Cumberland, all brought this fact to the attention of the War Department. Their telegrams called plaintively for reinforcements.[11] They expressed opinion that the army could hold out ten days, but not much longer.

Dana's message barely concealed the sender's defeatism: "No time should be lost in rushing twenty to twenty-five thousand efficient troops to Bridgeport [Alabama]. If such re-enforcements can be got there in season everything is safe, and this place indispensable alike to the defense of Tennessee and as base for future operations in Georgia will remain ours." [12] This dispatch was received at Washington in the evening of September 23, 1861.

The Secretary of War was not slow in comprehending its full import. Summoning General Henry W. Halleck, Stanton hurriedly sent messengers for the President and

166

certain cabinet members. All met in conclave at Stanton's War Department office.[13]

The plight of Rosecrans's army was the subject of a long conference. None could deny the military necessity of sending reinforcements. The ways and means however became a correlative issue. President Lincoln recommended that the necessary troops be detached from Major General Ambrose E. Burnside's army in eastern Tennessee. General Halleck seconded this view and gave his opinion that 20,000 of Burnside's men could reach Bridgeport by forced marches within ten days.[14]

Secretary Stanton expressed sharp dissent to this proposal; he was opposed to interfering with operations in eastern Tennessee; and with a surprising turn he proposed instead to send 30,000 men from the Army of the Potomac. "There is no reason to expect that General Meade will attack Lee although greatly superior in force," he stated, "and his great numbers where they are, are useless." He concluded his statement with the electrifying prophecy that within five days a force of 30,000 could be transported by rail from Meade's army to Chattanooga.[15]

To this President Lincoln replied: "I will bet that if the order is given tonight the troops could not be got to Washington in five days." [16]

Stanton stood firm on his conviction. He answered: "On such a subject I don't feel inclined to bet; but the matter has been carefully investigated, and it is certain that 30,000 bales of cotton could be sent in that time by taking possession of the railroads and excluding all other business, and I do not see why 30,000 men cannot be sent as well. But if 30,000 cannot be sent, let 20,000 go." [17]

The President was reluctant to weaken Meade's force, and much discussion followed. Secretaries Salmon P.

Chase and William H. Seward supported Stanton's contentions, while General Halleck continued to stand with the President.

But the Secretary of War was tenacious and had his way. A compromise agreement was reached about midnight. It was that the Eleventh and Twelfth Corps of the Army of the Potomac should be sent without delay to Rosecrans, provided that Meade was not preparing for an early advance against Lee.[18] To Halleck fell the task of ascertaining Meade's intentions.

Stanton's first act was to forestall Meade's judgment. This he did by taking positive steps toward carrying his own plan into effect before Meade had been heard from; for before Halleck had received the latter's answer he dispatched telegrams to John W. Garrett, president of the Baltimore and Ohio Railroad, Samuel M. Felton, president of the Philadelphia, Wilmington and Baltimore, and Thomas A. Scott, vice-president of the Pennsylvania Central, requesting each to come immediately to Washington.[19]

Accompanied by William P. Smith, master of transportation, the president of the Baltimore and Ohio reached Stanton's office about the middle of the forenoon of September 24. Felton and Scott arrived in the capital at noon. Meade's answer had comported with War Department wishes, but Halleck sent him a second telegram to clarify the point that the Eleventh and Twelfth Corps were to be detached at once.[20]

The framework of a plan was quickly fabricated. It was decided that the movement should be made entirely by rail over a single route. Beginning at Culpepper Court House, Virginia, on the Rappahannock River and ending at Bridgeport, Alabama, on the Tennessee, this all-rail route passed through Washington, Bellaire, Columbus, Indianapolis, Jeffersonville, Louisville, and Nashville. It was approximately twelve hundred miles in length. Colonel Daniel C. McCallum, director of military railroads, was assigned responsibility of the movement from Culpepper Court House to Washington; John W. Garrett, of the Baltimore and Ohio, from Washington to Jeffersonville, Indiana; and Thomas A. Scott, of the Pennsylvania Central, from Jeffersonville to Bridgeport. Garrett and Scott were clothed with military powers already possessed by McCallum. Each was commissioned to suspend all other traffic and to commandeer rolling stock and machinery, both along the route and on connecting lines.[21]

Armed with this authority, Garrett hastened to perfect arrangements for the movement from Washington to Jeffersonville. He leaned heavily on his own staff of able subordinates. He made William P. Smith, Baltimore and Ohio master of transportation, accountable for the concentration of cars in the Washington yards and delivery to the Orange and Alexandria Railroad; sent John L. Wilson, master of road, to Benwood to provide adequate means for the transfer of troops and equipment across the Ohio River; dispatched Alexander Diffey, general supervisor of trains, to Bellaire to assist in the concentration, loading, and forwarding of cars on the west bank of the Ohio; and, finally, assigned to another trusted subordinate, Lewis M. Cole, general ticket agent, the important task of supervising the movement from Indianapolis to Jeffersonville.[22] He also ordered additional watchmen to be posted along the line and directed that operators remain on duty in the telegraph offices day and night until the movement was completed.[23]

In the meantime Garrett telegraphed instructions to

THE BALTIMORE AND OHIO IN THE CIVIL WAR

Hugh J. Jewett, president of the Central Ohio Railroad, directing him "to concentrate, by 10 P.M. of Saturday the 26th inst—175 cars—125 for passengers and 50 for baggage, freight, horses, artillery &c..." and "to have the same quantity of cars additionally, each by 10 P.M. Sunday and 10 P.M. Monday for the conveyance of 15,000 troops, and artillery, equipments &c that will reach Bellaire at or about the respective dates and hours stated, say about one third at each period." [24]

The Baltimore and Ohio president sent similar instructions to Dillard Ricketts, president of the Jeffersonville Railroad, directing him to forward cars and locomotives to Indianapolis.[25] Officials of connecting lines were in like fashion invested with details of the plan and ordered to co-operate with those directly charged with carrying it out.[26]

The troop movement began promptly. The leading elements of the Eleventh Corps reached Washington about mid-afternoon of September 25, 1863. They were quickly sent west over the Baltimore and Ohio. For seventy-two hours a veritable stream of Federals passed through Washington; during this period Baltimore and Ohio officials concentrated approximately six hundred troop and stock cars in their Washington railroad yards and sent them over the Long Bridge. All other business on the road was kept at a standstill. Most of the rolling stock was supplied by the Baltimore and Ohio itself but a small fraction came from the United States military railroads in Virginia. Other cars were furnished by the Northern Central and the Philadelphia, Wilmington and Baltimore railroads.[27]

The first threat to orderly progress of the movement had been foreseen. As already observed, the connection between the terminus of the Central Ohio Railroad and the Baltimore and Ohio was maintained by the employment of a ferry steamer between Bellaire and Benwood. Garrett had relied on this ferry as the means of crossing the Ohio. Contrary to expectations John L. Wilson, master of road, found the river low and falling rapidly when he reached his post at Benwood. His discovery led Garrett to order the construction of a pontoon bridge.[28]

Under Wilson's direction a "superior bridge of scows and barges strongly connected" was built in less than two days.[29] At Jeffersonville, Indiana, where the river was deeper at low stages, a steamboat ferry supplemented by additional craft waited to carry the column promptly to the southern bank of the Ohio at Louisville, Kentucky.[30]

The movement of trains from Washington to Benwood was slow but at a uniform rate. For example, on September 26, 1863, William P. Smith reported that trains were passing through Martinsburg, West Virginia, at intervals of fifteen minutes. The first train arrived at Benwood, 412 miles from Washington, at 11:00 A.M. on September 27, 1863, forty-two hours after its departure from the capital. Smith had assured the Secretary of War that the run could be made in forty-four hours.[31]

Despite constant effort by Garrett and his managers, they met difficulty in supplying rolling stock to the Orange and Alexandria Railroad. In the early afternoon of September 26, 1863, McCallum sent a mild complaint to the War Department stating that the Twelfth Corps was at Bealeton, Virginia, delayed for want of cars.[32] He was careful to explain however that hearty co-operation of officers had enabled him "to rush matters forward more rapidly than originally contemplated either by Messrs. Garrett & Smith or myself." In turn Smith reminded

171

McCallum that "you have loaded troops faster than arranged at Department and that is why cars enough have not gone down although we have sent them faster than the understanding which was 140 per day for three days. Up to dusk yesterday [September 25, 1863]," he stated, "we had delivered you 390 cars besides those for horses though we have a whole day yet in which to deliver the 420 for troops per arrangement." [33]

It need only be explained that the requirements of the movement exceeded the first estimates by a considerable margin. Preparations were made for 15,000 men with equipment, artillery, and horses but more than 20,000 men with a proportionate increase in *materiel* were actually loaded in Virginia.[34]

It would have been phenomenal indeed if the transfer of such a large force over such a distance should have been effected without friction. Major General Carl Schurz, commanding the third division of the Eleventh Corps, fretted under the disorganization that prevailed in his command; as train passed train and the column seemed inextricably confused, he could not control his military instincts.

Before his own train had yet passed the Alleghenies, he dispatched a telegram to the Baltimore and Ohio agent at Grafton ordering him to hold the third division until its commander arrived. The Grafton agent ignored the order. The officious but well-meaning Schurz was soon on the ground at Grafton fuming at the presumptuous conduct of the station agent. Only with great skill and tact was the latter able to frustrate Schurz's plan of taking possession of an engine "and running on after the trains to try to stop them." [35] Schurz did dispatch a telegram to Fairmont instructing the station agent there to hold his command until he arrived. This message too went unheeded and no delay resulted.

Baltimore and Ohio authorities met this interference with prompt decision. Upon receipt of notice of Schurz's first act, William P. Smith transmitted the information to the War Department; in the same message he informed Secretary Stanton that the Baltimore and Ohio had instructed its agents pointedly not to stop or hold any train without direct War Department sanction.[36]

Stanton gave emphatic approval to this action with a curt order to report to him "any officer that presumes to interfere with you. . . ." [37] Within an hour after this assurance was received Smith dispatched explicit instructions to his agents directing them upon authority of the Secretary of War and General Hooker "that under no circumstances for any pretext must any train of troops or stores be stopped on the route unless by accident, or other necessity without their own order." [38]

Schurz did not escape reprimand. Late in the evening of September 27, the bristling Stanton notified him that "Major General Hooker has the orders of this Department to relieve you from command and put under arrest any officer who undertakes to delay or interfere with the orders and regulations of the Rail Road officers in charge of the transportation of troops." [39] To William P. Smith who had catered to Schurz's whims by making up a special train for him at Grafton, Stanton confided: "You need not have furnished him an extra but let him and any other officers who lag behind get along the best way they can." [40]

An exchange of telegrams closed the affair. In the forenoon of September 28, Schurz wired the irate Secretary of War this inquiry from Benwood: "Am I to understand from your dispatch that I am relieved from command?" [41]

He then stated reasons for his action on the preceding day, emphasizing the fact that trains had so displaced each other in the schedule that the whole column was a jumble. He strengthened his argument by calling sharply to attention the fact that confusion in the column was causing great inconvenience at Benwood where the troops were then detraining and marching to the Ohio shore.

The Secretary of War seems to have had the last word, and his reply to Schurz's question bore scant trace of tolerance. The full text of Stanton's terse telegram was: [42]

Genl Hooker is authorized to relieve from command any officer who interferes with or hinders transportation of troops in the present movement.

Whether you have done so and whether he has relieved you from command ought to be known to yourself. The order will certainly be enforced against any officer whatever his rank may be who delays or endangers transportation of troops.

The rear regiment of the Twelfth Corps was loaded about noon on September 28, 1863; the last troop train reached Benwood on September 30; and before that day had passed Hooker's entire force, except a residue of horses, mules, and wagons had crossed the Ohio. In five days the Baltimore and Ohio had loaded, forwarded, and transported over 412 miles of its road approximately 20,000 soldiers and much of their equipment. The movement required the use of thirty trains of approximately twenty cars each. Excepting only minor annoyances incident to loading, transfer, and feeding of men and animals, there was negligible delay in the movement east of the Ohio.

Progress through Ohio and Indiana was scarcely less satisfactory. The first trains passed through Columbus at 3 A.M. on September 28; before daybreak "over 8,000 men besides several batteries," had left Bellaire.[43] It is true that the War Department showed anxiety as the troops moved further west. But this feeling was due more to remissness of managers in making reports than to actual delay. Nevertheless, despite the fact that Stanton had received assurance that all was proceeding according to plan, he wired Smith in the evening of September 28 that he "would be better assured if you or Mr. Garrett could now go on to Indianapolis and see the movement through and prevent any hitch in the consummation of what has been so ably managed." [44]

Smith replied that neither Garrett nor himself could conveniently leave Baltimore because there was "so much yet in progress on our road," [45] and both needed rest. He then declared that the Baltimore and Ohio was not unmindful of its engagement to supervise the movement as far as Jeffersonville. "Our Captain Cole has been repeatedly instructed & strengthened by telegrams urging energy, foresight, order, distinctness & firmness of will, the elements that will insure continued success." Smith promised that "If any difficulty occurs, as soon as the movement is safely effected over our line we will follow up west in person or with some of our first class officers."

There were no difficulties that might have been obviated by different personnel. Beyond Benwood there were two points of transfer between railroads where delay was inevitable. At Indianapolis the column must needs detrain from the Indiana Central Railroad, a line of 4 feet 10 inches gauge, and change to the Jeffersonville Railroad, a road of narrower dimension. The second gap in the route was at Jeffersonville, Indiana, where the troops must alight from trains and cross the Ohio to the Kentucky side. It was these transfers which gave Stanton concern.

It was not long until his apprehension was dispelled. Displaying the same brand of skill in organization that had characterized Smith's work east of the Ohio, Captain Lewis M. Cole, who served in the dual rôle of Garrett's agent and Hooker's aide, anticipated major requirements of the undertaking and passed both men and material through Indianapolis with a minimum of delay. It is true that precious time was lost by marching troops from the railroad station to Soldier's House to be fed, and railroad officials on at least one of the co-operating lines did not heed Cole's requisition for cars, compelling him to impress them. Smith however estimated the delay at Indianapolis at but six hours, explaining it in these words to Stanton: [46]

The change of cars at Indianapolis with the march of over a mile across the town has been very tedious & difficult because there was no track room or other facility for such an occasion. Nor were they familiar in that quarter with the details of such things on such a scale. Under all the circumstances however wonders have been achieved even there.

The head of the column detrained at Jeffersonville early in the morning of September 29, 1863.[47] As indicated above, ferry steamers here bridged the second gap between railroads.

The military authorities had in fact made careful preparations in advance for all stages of the movement south of Jeffersonville. On September 24, 1863, Secretary Stanton had directed Brigadier General Jeremiah T. Boyle, commanding at Louisville, to summon the managers of the Louisville and Nashville, the Kentucky Central, and the Nashville and Chattanooga railroads to come to Louis-

176

ville before noon of Saturday, September 26. There they were to confer with Thomas A. Scott who was being sent by the War Department to direct the movement from Louisville south.[48] As a result of this conference all conveniently available locomotives and cars of proper gauge were ordered concentrated at Louisville. Scott and his assistants, both civilian and military, had all in readiness when advance elements arrived at the Louisville station.

The troops did not tarry long in the city. Scott reported to Stanton about mid-forenoon of September 29, as follows: "First train arrived at Louisville Depot 4 A.M. Got rations & left at 5:30 A.M. Second train 7 A.M., third train 10 A.M. Men for next train just landing." [49]

The intervals between arrivals and departures during the remainder of that day averaged one and a half hours. Scott informed Stanton that his dispatchers could have forwarded troops at even shorter intervals had there not been delay north of Jeffersonville. So rapid indeed was progress on the last leg of the journey that Scott notified Stanton late in the evening of September 30, just five days after the first contingent had entrained on the Orange and Alexandria Railroad, that "the first four trains have arrived" at Bridgeport, Alabama, and "the trains have been returned north." [50]

Two days later, October 1, 1863, Scott wired the Secretary of War that he had "sent south 21 trains with 13,615 men and 4 batteries of artillery" and again stated that the facilities at his command were not employed to full capacity because of delays north of Jeffersonville. Yet before dusk had fallen on October 5, 1863, the last infantry regiment passed Louisville; next day "Everything belonging to the Eleventh and Twelfth Corps" went forward from that point "except one battery and about four hundred

(400) horses that they have held over at Indianapolis to feed." [51] In truth most of Hooker's force negotiated the distance of some 1,200 miles in the short period of nine days; [52] the whole column of personnel completed the movement in 11½ days.[53]

It remained now for the co-operating railroads to rush forward the impedimenta. Baltimore and Ohio officials were again confronted with a sizable task, the requirements of which passed beyond the limits of their road; for as in the troop movement the War Department placed its main reliance upon the managerial supervision of Garrett and his staff.

Collecting all available stock cars on the road and borrowing others from the Northern Central Railroad, Garrett and his subordinates started on October 4, 1863, a second procession of trains toward the Ohio. Again the Baltimore and Ohio president sent instructions to co-operating lines and to his own officers on duty west of the Ohio River, urging them to "concentrate requisite machinery at the proper points and do all that is possible to ensure prompt and successful movement." [54]

For almost a week a steady stream of trains containing wagons, animals, and equipage, moved across the Long Bridge at Washington to the tracks of the Washington Branch Railroad. Once more section after section steamed north to Relay House, thence west over the main stem to Benwood.

Both at Benwood and at Bellaire platforms were erected to facilitate transfer to the Central Ohio Railroad. From Bellaire to Indianapolis the route lay open to through trains; at the latter point, as already noted, the change in gauge required a change of cars. Many of the difficulties of transfer at this point experienced during the preceding

STRATEGIC USE

week had however been obliterated. Additional sidetracks had here been hastily constructed in order that cars might be loaded alongside.[55]

The movement nevertheless lost momentum at Indianapolis and Garrett sent Smith to that point to give it acceleration. He arrived on October 11 and found that efficiency had not lagged for want of intelligent direction. Captain Cole was still on the ground and was using all facilities to capacity. Delays were due chiefly to the scarcity of stock cars on the Jeffersonville Railroad, to the difficulties of unloading and reloading of property, particularly mules which could not be loaded easily at night, and to the feeding of animals.[56]

Despite unforeseen causes, the last train load reached Indianapolis early on October 13, 1863, and arrived at Jeffersonville two days later. From Louisville south progress was slower; just when Scott was reporting that his schedule of trains was working in perfect order the enemy appeared.

The Federal authorities had exercised due vigilance in screening the movement. On September 26, 1863, Halleck wired Meade that "It is all important that the military railroad in Virginia should be strictly guarded during the movement of troops over it;" [57] already on September 24, he had sent emphatic directions of like nature to General Benjamin F. Kelley whose forces were guarding the Baltimore and Ohio; and as an afterthought he had enjoined Kelley in a second telegram to strengthen the guard at Benwood and "to close all drinking saloons at the principal stations." [58] In fact at the East the Confederates seem to have had no definite knowledge of what was occurring until Hooker's entire column had crossed the Alleghenies.[59]

179

In the West however the enemy threatened to disrupt plans before the last troop train had departed from Louisville. On October 4, 1863, Confederate cavalry cut the Nashville and Chattanooga Railroad near Murfreesboro, Tennessee; next day a band of enemy raiders entered Glasgow, Kentucky, a village within striking distance of the Louisville and Nashville Railroad at Cave City.[60] The second division of the Twelfth Corps was actually cut off and badly used as a Confederate force jabbed the Union line of communication between Bridgeport and Stevenson, Alabama.[61] It appears that prompt action by Hooker saved the day until proper dispositions were made, and with the arrival of General Ulysses S. Grant on October 23, 1863, the last remedial step was taken to safeguard Chattanooga. As a result both the city and Rosecrans's army were saved.

The transfer of the Eleventh and Twelfth corps from the Rappahannock to the Tennessee however served more than immediate military ends. The feat all but broke down the averseness of the military mind to mechanized movement; it set a new record in logistics. Never before had such a body of troops moved over such distance on land in such a brief period.[62] This accomplishment removed many doubts concerning the effectiveness of the railroad as an agency in war; it proved conclusively that the railway had strategic value.[63]

While these results speak praise for the teamwork of soldier and civilian, chief credit for the inauguration and success of the movement must be assigned to the foresight and skill of the latter. In truth the experiment was set in motion by civilian initiative in the face of military disapproval; it narrowly missed disaster on the rock of general staff ineptitude. On the other hand the record could

STRATEGIC USE

not have been written without quick response and punctual performance by both officers and men of the army. Once committed to the undertaking, they spared no effort to make it a success. It was indeed only at the inception of the plan that high command showed unwillingness to execute it; this reluctance perhaps finds explanation more in military psychology than in personal incapacity.

CHAPTER IX

Virginia Unredeemed

THE Baltimore and Ohio helped the politician as well as the soldier.

Of the permanent results of the Civil War the establishment of the State of West Virginia was one of the most conspicuous. In fact the dismemberment of Virginia afforded the single instance of territorial change in the war period. In no other state were the boundary lines disturbed by the conflict. Disruption took heavy toll of the mother of commonwealths. She not only lost her Trans-Allegheny jurisdiction; she also saw six of her cismontane counties crumble under Baltimore and Ohio Railroad influence and become integral parts of a new Virginia.

The crest of the Alleghenies was a natural line of cleavage; social and economic differences completed the estrangement foreshadowed by nature. East of the mountains, plantation owners lived in comparative ease on the fruits of Negro slavery and dominated a society of feudal proportions; between the Allegheny Mountains and the Ohio River a different people drew sustenance from the small farm, the mine, the forest, and the factory.

Remote from and inaccessible to cismontane Virginia, the Trans-Allegheny was viewed by the dominant planter class of the east as a mere adjunct of the state proper. In turn northwest Virginians were bound by ties that identified them with the people of bordering states. The editor of the Morgantown *Star* called up this fact in the summer

VIRGINIA UNREDEEMED

of 1861. "Now while the boundary lines of Virginia held us with Eastern Virginia," he declared, "our intercourse has been principally with the people of Pennsylvania, Maryland and Ohio; and we know but little of the people of Eastern and the Valley of Virginia from personal intercourse, and they knew so little of us that they never have properly appreciated our interests." [1]

Politically, the sections were constantly at loggerheads over domestic relations that reflected this incompatibility. In the Trans-Allegheny the embers of political discontent had long smouldered. The fuel that kept them alive was glaring discriminations in taxation and marked inequalities in representation, all of which the Tidewater slavocracy had incorporated in the basic law of the commonwealth in its own interests. These grievances were sharpened by belief that the state government had not returned an equitable fraction of the revenues for expenditure in the northwestern counties.

The guardians of northwest Virginia had indeed pursued a niggardly policy. They had established few state institutions west of the Alleghenies and they had given scant encouragement to transmontane public improvements.[2] Of the $20,000,000 which the commonwealth had invested in railroads before 1860, not one dollar was expended west of the Alleghenies.[3] This fact alone went far to sustain the contention that the dominant eastern section was indifferent to the welfare of the northwest. The transmontane policy of Virginia statesmen prior to the war of secession was at best shortsighted; certainly it lacked those elements of fairness and consideration that insure maternal attachment and filial respect.

Preliminary fencing over secession further weakened the frail chords of political union. Then came the fate-

ful ordinance of April 17, 1861, which attempted to cut
Virginia adrift from the old confederacy for a new. Whatever hopes the inhabitants of the Trans-Allegheny entertained in the direction of further adherence to the Old
Dominion were by this act dissipated. The truth was, the
northwest counties were situated between the scissor-
blade states of Pennsylvania and Ohio and were in imminent danger of Federal invasion. This fact alone was
sufficient to make loyalty spontaneous in the Trans-Allegheny; it explains much of the precipitate haste which
characterized the new state movement.

Once committed to the serious task of state-making
northwest Virginians early showed a disposition to ignore
the boundaries that nature had established for them. On
August 8, 1861, John S. Carlile, a leading exponent of the
division movement, introduced a resolution in the Second
Wheeling Convention providing for the formation of a
separate state "out of, and to be composed of" thirty-eight
western Virginia counties, five of which were the cismontane counties of Jefferson, Berkeley, Morgan, Hampshire,
and Hardy.[4]

Although this resolution failed to weather the opposition of the convention, which objected to the inclusion of
Cis-Allegheny counties on the ground that they were out
of step on the issues of secession and slavery, and could
not in any event be defended from Confederate attack,
the ordinance which passed on August 20, 1861, left the
matter open for future settlement. While the ordinance
specifically named thirty-nine northwest counties as the
nucleus of the new state, it also extended implicit invitations to others, including Hampshire, Hardy, Morgan,
Berkeley, and Jefferson, to participate in an election to be
held on October 24, 1861, to authorize the formation of a

new state and to choose delegates to a constitutional convention. The ordinance empowered the constituent assembly to change the boundaries so as to include any of
the counties invited, provided only that they or "either of
them" should "declare their wish to form part of the proposed State, and . . . elect delegates to the said convention." [5]

On the appointed day thirty-five Trans-Allegheny counties balloted, but only two counties east of the mountains
took part in the plebiscite. These were Hampshire and
Hardy, both of which held elections under the aegis of
Federal guns. In the former the ordinance was approved
by a vote of 195 out of a total vote of 213, while the latter
reflected military intimidation to a greater degree by reporting 150 votes for and none against.[6] Both counties
sent delegates to the constitutional convention which assembled at Wheeling on November 26, 1861.

A considerable bloc in the convention was quick to
show dissatisfaction over the failure of other eastern
counties to join the new state movement. They contended
that these counties were under Confederate military dom-
inance at the time the election was held and consequently
should be given an opportunity to ballot in such season
and under such conditions as would insure a fair and free
poll. As a result the question of boundaries became an
important issue.

On November 28, 1861, the president of the convention appointed a special committee to make a study of the
question and to submit a report. The committee drafted
its recommendations within the week. It proposed that
in addition to the inclusion of certain Trans-Allegheny
counties that had not participated in the election of October 24, 1861, a chain of contiguous Valley of Virginia
counties should be privileged to vote on the propriety of

joining the proposed state. These were Wise, Buchanan, Scott, Lee, Tazewell, Bland, Giles, Craig, Alleghany, Bath, Highland, Pendleton, Hardy, Hampshire, Frederick, Jefferson, Berkeley, and Morgan.[7]

For days the convention debated the expediency of accepting the committee's recommendations; day after day saw that body strike out county after county until it had reached the map of the lower Valley. Here it stopped abruptly and made provisions for the inclusion of seven counties—Pendleton, Hardy, Hampshire, Frederick, Jefferson, Berkeley, and Morgan. The reason for this action is the burden of this chapter.

As political units these counties were bound to the east by social and cultural ties, while their geographical location and economic life made them one with the Valley. The population of all presented a strange contrast to the heterogeneity of peoples in the Trans-Allegheny. Although largely of non-English colonial Virginia stock, they fused the traditions of the Piedmont and the Tidewater with their own; they hallowed the ground which was Virginia. In 1860, Jefferson County contained 3,960 slaves [8] and that county alone supplied approximately 1,600 recruits for the Confederate army.[9] It is true that pro-Union fires burned brightly on the hills of Morgan County, and they were never extinguished in the upland sections of Hampshire and Hardy. But in none except Morgan, did the daily life of the majority of inhabitants belie the ideals of caste and the canons of taste of the dominant East.

Despite apparent social and cultural contrasts, statemakers in the Trans-Allegheny were not without claim to kinship with Virginians of the lower Valley. The sections were joined in the bonds of economic union. Through both ran the Baltimore and Ohio, a common outlet to

Eastern markets. It was this fact that gave point to the convention's plan to include the seven eastern counties. The Baltimore and Ohio was the most important commercial highway in western Virginia. It furnished a convenient inlet and outlet both to the lower Valley and to

WEST VIRGINIA'S EASTERN PANHANDLE

the greater part of the Trans-Allegheny. It "is the great artery that feeds our country," said Waitman T. Willey in 1861. "It conveys into our center, or by its ramifications of necessity infuses through the entire body politic of this new State the life blood of its existence. We cannot do without it." [10]

THE BALTIMORE AND OHIO IN THE CIVIL WAR

The first weeks of the war not only saw the severance of this channel of communication but also the closing of the Mississippi. As a result trade was paralyzed in northwest Virginia. It was estimated that nine-tenths of the farmers there were unable to move any produce whatever after the Baltimore and Ohio was closed.[11] Mercantile, manufacturing, and mining interests experienced similar embarrassment. This generated strong sentiment locally in favor of the immediate opening of the Baltimore and Ohio main stem and the employment of adequate military forces for its protection.[12]

The desire to see this done was accompanied by a determination to remove the road entirely from the jurisdiction of Virginia. Partly because of Virginia's traditional dislike of the Baltimore and Ohio, there was an undercurrent of feeling in the West Virginia constitutional convention that following the close of the war, regardless of the outcome of the conflict, Virginia would burden the road with statutory restrictions; [13] it was equally clear that if the Confederacy should succeed a large part of West Virginia's single outlet to the seaboard would lie on foreign soil.

These considerations carried great weight with new state artificers. The result was the erection of a corridor commonly called the Eastern Panhandle.

The decision of the constitutional convention to pass over the summit of the Alleghenies and fix the eastern boundary of West Virginia on the Potomac River was not reached without careful deliberation and prolonged debate. The report of its Special Committee on Boundary contained a resolution which placed the issue squarely before the convention. Designated "Schedule C," this resolution was as follows: [14]

VIRGINIA UNREDEEMED

Resolved, that the district comprising the counties of Frederick, Jefferson, Berkeley, Morgan, Hampshire, Hardy, Pendleton, Highland, Bath and Alleghany shall also be included in and constitute part of the proposed new State, provided a majority of the votes cast within the said district, at elections to be held for the purpose on the third Thursday in April, in the year 1862, and a majority of the said counties are in favor of the adoption of the Constitution to be submitted by this Convention.

Chapman J. Stuart of Doddridge County was the first to speak at length in favor of the resolution. He took special pains to explain that Hampshire and Hardy counties had been included in the resolution solely because their interests were identical with certain other contiguous Cis-Allegheny counties. He then hinted strongly that although both had approved the new state idea, neither would adhere to the new state without the inclusion of its neighbors. While he urged that these Valley counties were all pro-Union and anxious to sever political connections with Tidewater Virginia, he placed main emphasis on the community of interest afforded by the Baltimore and Ohio Railroad. All of them, including Hampshire and Hardy, he said in effect, were actually or potentially bound to northwest Virginia by the iron bands of this railway. While some were not penetrated by the Baltimore and Ohio, he admitted, "their interests are so identified and inter-locked with the counties bordering on the Road that it is almost impossible to separate them." [15]

It was Stuart who first sounded warning of the danger of leaving a large part of the main line of the Baltimore and Ohio under Virginia jurisdiction. "It is well known that in a majority of our northwestern counties all of our trade and commerce, and very near all our travel, is over the Baltimore and Ohio Railroad," he stated. "Now, sir, unless we have the control of that road what is to become of us? Do you not see? The eastern portion of our State has always been disposed to unfriendly legislation towards us; and now when this excitement is up, and we are forming a new State, and cutting ourselves loose from the old State,—I appeal to the members of this Convention, what they think will be the legislation of Eastern Virginia towards us in regard to this great improvement, to which every vital interest we have is second...." [16] He emphasized his belief that the new state could not grow and prosper without uninterrupted use of this important channel; in closing he intimated that he for one would be willing to annex Jefferson, Berkeley, and Morgan without their consent, in case they should vote adversely.

Thomas R. Carskadon of Hampshire County added weight to Stuart's argument. He too emphasized identical interests which held the lower Valley together and said that both Hampshire and Hardy were opposed to joining the new state unless invitations were extended to their contiguous neighbors. He summarized his points in a nutshell: [17]

We lie there together. We have a community of interest; and if we are to be taken in without those other counties having the privilege of coming in, it as far as I am conversant with the views of the people, met with their disapprobation. They wish to go to the Blue Ridge or not go at all. We live together in a common interest, and the Baltimore and Ohio Railroad is our outlet to market, and if we are cut off there with but two counties, we know that then we can get no internal improvements from the government of West Virginia. ... I believe the constituency which I represent would rather be out than in unless those counties lying along the Baltimore and Ohio Railroad and contiguous would have an opportunity to vote on the question.

VIRGINIA UNREDEEMED

Carskadon went farther afield. He sounded warning that if these cismontane counties were not given an opportunity to vote on the question of joining the new Virginia, they would formally petition Congress to postpone admission until the question had been submitted to them.

Despite forceful speeches by Stuart and Carskadon, strong sentiment raised its head in opposition. Gordon Battelle of Ohio County wished to incorporate in the new state only the four counties penetrated by the Baltimore and Ohio Railroad, and of the non-railroad counties only Hardy. Of the Baltimore and Ohio itself he expressed desire "to have every rod of that great improvement within the limits of this new State." [18]

Taking a cue from Battelle's remark, Waitman T. Willey introduced an amendment striking out Alleghany County. He urged that this county was more closely connected with eastern Virginia than with the Trans-Alleghany. He explained too that its inclusion would saddle the new state with a heavy debt that had been contracted locally for internal improvements. [19]

The Willey amendment evoked hot debate but it was adopted by the convention. [20]

The result of the balloting gave new heart to the strong antislavery bloc of delegates. Among these was James Hervey of Brooke County who seized the occasion to offer a resolution striking out all Valley counties, save Hampshire and Hardy. [21]

In urging the adoption of this motion, its author found an able ally in Joseph Pomeroy of Hancock County. Both Pomeroy and Hervey were willing to include Hampshire and Hardy because these counties had already voted affirmatively on the new state question; they opposed the annexation of the remaining counties on the ground that

191

THE BALTIMORE AND OHIO IN THE CIVIL WAR

they were proslavery and prosecessionist. The Hervey resolution ushered the railroad question to the center of the
convention stage.

It is worthy of note that those who now rushed forward
to save these alleged proslavery counties to the new state
were one with Hervey and Pomeroy in their dislike of
human bondage. Peter G. Van Winkle and William E.
Stevenson, both of Wood County, and Waitman T. Willey of Monongalia, were all of the stuff of which abolition-
ists were made, although Willey had once owned slaves.

Willey spoke twice. In his first address he stressed the
importance of the Baltimore and Ohio as an outlet for the
farming and industrial interests of northwest Virginia and
emphasized the necessity of removing the line from the
jurisdiction of the Old Dominion. "You might as well
sever an artery in the human body as to cripple and cut
off this great artery of trade and expect our bodies to live
as expect this State to live and flourish unless we include
in our boundary this Baltimore and Ohio Railroad," [22] he
said. His second speech contained the pertinent suggestion
that the incorporation of the Baltimore and Ohio counties
in the new Virginia would insure the support of public
opinion in Baltimore and the votes of the entire Maryland
delegation when the enabling act should claim the attention of Congress. "If we exclude these counties," he declared, Marylanders "will not care anything about the new
State." [23]

William E. Stevenson spoke with equal force, although
he frankly stated that he had not made up his mind on the
propriety of including Bath, Frederick, Highland, and
Pendleton. On the question of adding the four railroad
counties—Jefferson, Berkeley, Morgan, and Hampshire—
he went straight to the point. Here was territory, he de-

192

clared, that was more essential to the prosperity of West Virginia than the Trans-Allegheny counties of Pocahontas, Monroe, Mercer, McDowell, and Greenbrier, which the convention had annexed by arbitrary action; if the railroad counties could not be obtained in any other manner he would be willing to annex them without their consent.[24]

Peter G. Van Winkle merely added emphasis to arguments already presented. As president of the Northwestern Virginia Railroad, he seems to have served as official spokesman for the Baltimore and Ohio company on the floor of the convention. Yet his arguments were carefully shaped to reflect only concern for the public welfare. He too stressed the necessity of removing the railroad entirely from Virginia and gave the stock reasons. He also emphasized the importance of the Baltimore and Ohio in the commercial, industrial, and agricultural development of the region it served. Few sections of the new state, he said, had missed the benefits conferred by the road.

Van Winkle waived the slavery issue with disdain. To him the existence of Negro servitude in the railroad counties presented no valid objection to their adherence to West Virginia. ". . . the objection, however formidable it may have appeared in the beginning, vanishes and becomes nothing," he stated, when viewed in the light of material advantages which would ensue as a result of the free and uninterrupted use of the state's single trunk line railroad.[25]

The Hervey motion was defeated by a vote of 11 to 34. Pomeroy of Hancock then moved to strike Bath County from the main resolution. After short debate his motion was adopted.[26]

As debate was resumed only eight counties remained in

the main resolution. These soon drew heavy fire from Granville Parker, a delegate from Cabell County, whose position on all questions of boundary not only mirrored the antislavery attitudes of the Massachusetts man that he was but also revealed his high regard for the democratic processes. He had opposed the annexation of Pocahontas, Greenbrier, Monroe, and Mercer because he disliked consanguinity with slave counties and the arbitrary method employed.[27]

Of all the delegates who participated in this debate Parker seems to have been the least variable on the slavery issue, and naturally he was obstinate in his opposition to the inclusion of Valley counties. He gave two practical reasons: (1) their people did not wish to be a part of West Virginia; and (2) they could not be defended in wartime.

Parker buttressed his contention with pertinent military considerations: he emphasized the fact that a boundary following the crest of the Alleghenies from the southeast corner of Highland County to the Fairfax Stone would not exceed fifty miles while the distance between the same points around the outer limits of Frederick, Jefferson, Berkeley, Morgan, Hampshire, and Hardy counties was approximately six times that distance. Nor did these counties desire separation from the mother state. ". . . they are identified with the East however they were twenty years ago," he declared. "I admit then they were with the West, but since then the East has covered the whole Valley with internal improvements—with railroads and turnpikes. They have won them to themselves and broken them off from us. . . . Their railroads, their trade, their every interest is there beyond." [28]

Parker maintained that these considerations outweighed the arguments of expediency based on the al-

194

VIRGINIA UNREDEEMED

leged necessity of controlling the Baltimore and Ohio Railroad. He did what he could to minimize the prospective importance of the road in West Virginia's development; he intimated strongly, but perhaps too emphatically, that the whole scheme to incorporate the railroad counties was the handiwork of the Baltimore and Ohio Railroad Company itself.[29]

His remarks were not without effect. Immediately Gustavus F. Taylor of Braxton County offered a motion striking out Highland County, and it was adopted.[30] Lewis Ruffner of Kanawha County then moved to eliminate Pendleton.[31] It was now apparent that the opposition hoped to gain by attrition and piecemeal what it had failed to obtain at a single stroke. Ruffner's proposal evoked stirring speeches from Ephraim B. Hall of Marion County and Thomas R. Carskadon of Hampshire who, as already noted, had shouldered heavy burdens in the debate.

Carskadon rested his argument on the statement that however remote Pendleton was from the Baltimore and Ohio, that county like Hampshire depended on its facilities for contact with the seaboard.[32]

Hall struck the Ruffner amendment only by indirection. Like others who had preceded him he pointed his guns at Virginia's traditional hostility toward the Baltimore and Ohio and urged the annexation of the railroad counties. In support of his position he offered the new argument that the inclusion of these political units would cement the support of delegations in Congress from Midwestern states which were much interested in placing the Baltimore and Ohio entirely in Union territory. So necessary was this consummation, he concluded, that if these

195

counties refused to join the new state, he too was ready to turn to coercion and "take them *nolens volens.*" [33]

The motion to strike out Pendleton was rejected and the antislavery offensive was checked. Stuart of Doddridge then led a counterattack. He introduced an amendment providing that all words after *State* should be struck from the main resolution.[34] Acceptance of this motion meant simply the annexation of the counties of Hardy, Hampshire, Morgan, Berkeley, Jefferson, Frederick, and Pendleton by convention fiat.

Stuart's friends however would not permit his amendment to be put to test immediately. Soon after debate had opened Daniel Lamb of Ohio County offered a substitute providing that the clause "or at such later day as the Legislature of Virginia may appoint" should be inserted in the main resolution following the words "third Thursday in April in the year, 1862." [35] Adoption of this motion would serve the double purpose of holding open the gates of opportunity until all counties should see fit to ballot on adhesion; it kept up appearance of religious regard for the principle of self-determination.

Despite the good intentions of Lamb, his motion was lost and Stuart again came forward with the resolution to annex the counties *nolens volens.*[36] The discussion which followed was marked by stinging comment from both friend and foe; there were those who hoped to secure adherence of the railroad counties but whose democratic instincts balked at the employment of arbitrary methods.

Robert Irvine of Lewis County was one of the few who favored the proposal with reservations. He stated his position as follows: [37]

... It seems clear to my mind ... that we have no authority to include within this boundary any counties beyond the line prescribed by the ordinance of the Convention, unless we place it on the ground of absolute necessity. I am in favor of including Morgan, Berkeley and Jefferson. I place this upon the ground that it is absolutely necessary that we should have those three counties in addition to the two counties of Hampshire and Hardy; because without those three counties, unfavorable legislation on the part of Virginia might mar the prosperity of the New State as well as of the State of Ohio and of some other States. I think then it can be justified on the ground of necessity, and I place it upon the ground of necessity—that we must have those three counties. . . . But I do not think that the counties of Pendleton and Frederick ought to stand on the same footing. We cannot contend that it is absolutely necessary for the welfare of the New State that the counties of Pendleton and Frederick should be annexed to the New State. I do not think we possess the power to annex them. I think we can make the other three counties an exception to the general principle on the ground of absolute necessity. . . .

No less a student of international law, Hall of Marion based his remarks on equally practical considerations. His main contention was that if the lower Valley counties, particularly the railroad counties, were not annexed the constitution would be defeated in other railroad counties. He prophesied that his own constituents would vote against it if the convention made no provisions to include all counties penetrated by the Baltimore and Ohio. "Why? Because you are cutting us off from Maryland; *you* are destroying this great artery that contributes more than any other to our prosperity and the very means by which our industrial interests and resources are made valuable to us; . . ." [38]

Nor did Stuart speak with less emphasis in support of the motion. "I would not give one cent, sir, for the State and deny to my people the very right to travel over the

Baltimore and Ohio Railroad. Our every interest and hope of future prosperity are connected with it." [39]

Blinded by enthusiasm the sponsors of arbitrary annexation had overlooked a factor of great potential danger, namely, the fact that although these eastern counties might be annexed against their will each would nevertheless be entitled to vote on the new constitution. Since the pro-Southern proclivities of the inhabitants of the lower Valley were well-known, it was clear that pro-Southern voters might swarm to the polls and defeat the constitution. William E. Stevenson sighted this danger early in the debate and gave it this turn: [40]

I am just as anxious to include the Baltimore and Ohio Railroad as any man in this convention can be; and yet I would not be willing to run even the risk of sacrificing this whole movement after what we have done for the sake of getting either these counties or that part of the railroad which runs through them.

Although Waitman T. Willey ardently wished the inclusion of this debatable area, he too raised strong objections to annexation by simple decree. Basing his opposition on principle rather than expediency he declared that Stuart's amendment contemplated the annexation of people who had had "no opportunity of being heard here on this floor in the formation and ordination of the fundamental law under which they are to live." [41]

Others spoke for and against the motion. Then Stuart called for the yeas and nays. The amendment was lost by the decisive vote of 9 to 37.[42] The convention was now ready for the next move.

It was promptly made by Willey. In order to preserve to the people of the lower Valley counties their sacred rights of self-determination and at the same time disperse their collective voting strength, he offered five resolutions which proposed to allow the seven eastern counties to come into West Virginia separately or in contiguous groups as they ratified the constitution.

The first resolution provided for the admission of a district composed of Pendleton, Hardy, and Hampshire; the second, Morgan, but on condition that Pendleton, Hardy, and Hampshire should vote to come in; the third, Berkeley, provided, however, that Pendleton, Hardy, Hampshire, and Morgan should ratify the constitution; the fourth, that Jefferson should be admitted provided that Pendleton, Hardy, Hampshire, Morgan, and Berkeley should vote favorably; and fifth, that Frederick should be admitted on condition of the adherence of the other six counties.[43]

Willey's plan was more ingenious than it was practical. Almost immediately members of the convention put their fingers on the weak link of the Willey chain. It was Pendleton County. Simply by concentrating their vote in this county, anti-new staters could deprive West Virginia of the seven. The Willey proposals seemed too precarious, and they were rejected.[44]

On the same day, however, the convention reached a conclusion. It was left to the statesmanlike touch of Peter G. Van Winkle to strike the harmonious chord. On December 12, 1861, he introduced an amendment providing that the qualifying clauses "or, if from any cause such elections are not held on that day, then on such other day as the Legislature of Virginia may appoint," should be inserted in the main resolution immediately following the words "on the third Thursday in April, in the year 1862."[45] It was the Lamb amendment in new clothes.

This proposal found immediate favor among the delegates. Although it left the Cis-Allegheny counties hanging on a slender thread, it empowered the legislature of the reorganized government of Virginia to postpone the plebiscite to a favorable day. Practically considered, the success of Van Winkle's plan was conditional on the success of Union armies in the lower Valley. It was adopted by a vote of 25 to 19.[46]

The main resolution was then approved. Next day, December 13, 1861, it was amended. Delegate Ephraim B. Hall of Marion asked the convention to accept this addition: "But if a majority of the votes in the said counties of Pendleton, Hampshire, Hardy, Morgan, Jefferson, Berkeley and Frederick be not in favor of forming a part of the new State, but a majority of the votes in the counties of Pendleton, Hampshire, Hardy and Morgan be in favor of forming a part of the New State, then that the four last named counties be included." [47] This provision was agreed to.

It proved to be a timely afterthought. Of the counties listed in the main resolution only those named in this amendment held elections on the appointed day, April 3, 1862. Because of the unsettled military situation in the Shenandoah Valley, no elections were held in Frederick, Jefferson, and Berkeley counties. Nor did the opportunity to ballot on the West Virginia constitution appear there until more than a year had passed. Meantime West Virginia was admitted to the Union and its geographical limits provisionally defined.

There was still room for the remaining railroad counties of Jefferson and Berkeley. On January 31, 1863, the general assembly of reorganized Virginia sitting at Wheeling passed an act providing that the polls should be opened in Berkeley on the fourth Thursday of May,

VIRGINIA UNREDEEMED

1863, for the purpose of taking the sense of the qualified voters on the question of joining West Virginia.[48] On February 4, 1863, the assembly authorized Jefferson County to do likewise on the same day.[49]

These elections were held under the protection of armed Federal forces but three weeks before Lee's Confederate army swept down the Valley toward the Susquehanna. The results were certified to the West Virginia legislature under the seal of the Alexandria government; on August 5, 1863, Berkeley County was declared to be a part of West Virginia;[50] on November 2, 1863, Jefferson County was also incorporated in the new state by legislative act;[51] on March 10, 1866, the Thirty-Ninth Congress authorized these transfers by joint resolution;[52] and finally in March, 1871, the Supreme Court of the United States approved the whole proceeding.[53]

Thus did West Virginia obtain the adherence of six of Virginia's lower Valley counties. That the desire to remove the Baltimore and Ohio Railroad entirely from the jurisdiction of Virginia was a prime consideration in the acquisition of at least four of them can hardly be doubted; and it appears equally plain that the other two cast their lot with their neighbors under the compulsion of identical economic interests.

Whether the policy which brought these results was the work of sound statesmanship or the fabrication of a Baltimore and Ohio Railroad lobby are questions that must be answered with caution. The railroad management undoubtedly looked with favor on the program and in an unobtrusive way exerted influence upon makers of West Virginia's first organic law. On the other hand the debates of the convention show convincingly that the same conclusions might well have been reached, even though the railroad company had stood in opposition. Certainly the decision to fix the eastern boundary of West Virginia at the Potomac River was politically salutary in wartime; the act itself was clothed with legal respectability by a decision of the United States Supreme Court; but whether the method was morally justifiable even in the light of circumstances is a question for honest doubt.

CHAPTER X

Influence on National Railroad Policy

IN addition to its strategic location, the Baltimore and Ohio enjoyed a pre-eminence of situation that was denied all other railroads. The Washington Branch was the only line entering Washington from the North. Over its tracks moved much of the freight that sustained the National Capital and the tented cities on its outskirts. Indeed for four years this important arm was seemingly the busiest railway in America, and by the same token it appeared to be the most prosperous.

Its supremacy, however, did not go unchallenged. Despite strong endeavor, the company was at times unequal to its task. Often it was simply impossible to handle traffic with customary promptness and dispatch. The result was anxiety that the army and the capital would suffer; agitation soon spread which urged the building of a second line of railroad between Baltimore and Washington.

While immediate public necessity was the mainspring of this movement, it was borne along by current belief that there was great need for a competing railroad between the two cities. There were those who held that the southbound traffic of the Northern Central and the Philadelphia, Wilmington and Baltimore railroads, which converged at Baltimore, could not flow without interruption into Washington over a single-track railroad. Moreover, the prevailing tariffs on both freights and passengers on the Washington Branch were commonly held to be iniquitous and burdensome; the capitation tax assessed on passenger travel by the State of Maryland was considered mischievous and oppressive.[1] Poignant objections to this tax were that it raised passenger charges to an unreasonable level and that it was a tax on travel to the capital of the nation. Because of these opinions and lingering belief that high officials of the company were Southern sympathizers, there was strong sentiment, particularly in Washington, favorable to destroying the Baltimore and Ohio monopoly.

Owing to the fact that Maryland held a vested interest in the Washington Branch Railroad, it was unthinkable that her legislature would countenance such action. There was, however, strong belief that Congress had power to construct railroads within the states. Early in the war a situation arose which put Congress in a mood to exercise this authority.

In October, 1861, the Confederates erected batteries on the right bank of the Potomac at Quantico Creek, Cockpit Point, and Shipping Point, effectively cutting off water communication between Washington and the Atlantic.[2] As a result heavy tonnage that had come to Washington by sea was shunted up Chesapeake Bay to Baltimore, thence overland across the single-track Washington Branch of the Baltimore and Ohio. ". . . one hundred cargoes were thrown from the mouth of that [Potomac] river to Baltimore;" and the daily freight business of the Washington Branch which averaged from six to ten cars a day before, and not more than twenty cars during the first months of the war, now "swelled to four hundred and fifty cars per day."[3]

Two months later a new burden was added. As already noted, in December, 1861, the Confederates cut the Chesapeake and Ohio Canal near Williamsport, thereby closing the single channel of trade which entered the District of Columbia from the northwest.[4] In January, 1862, both canal and river froze over and gave permanence to the blockade; for two months the Washington Branch Railroad was the sole means of supplying the Army of the Potomac and Washington's civilian population.

In coping with this situation the Baltimore and Ohio company displayed consummate energy. It was stated that railroad officials went to extremities to utilize every available resource. In "furnishing the requisite additional facilities" they expended "a quarter of a million dollars." Much of this money defrayed the cost of repairs on the overworked main road and the construction of new sidetracks; and after the Chesapeake and Ohio Canal was closed and the fuel supply for Washington thrown upon, the Washington Branch Railroad, "the Baltimore and Ohio Company transported from Baltimore to Washington, draymen, together with their horses and drays, free of charge," to relieve congestion in the Washington yards. As a direct result of this action, so stated John W. Garrett before the Committee on Military Affairs of the House of Representatives, the price of coal in the city was reduced from $10 to $3 or $4 per ton.[5]

Meanwhile Congress examined a proposal which contemplated the construction of a competing railroad. On November 13, 1861, the Metropolitan Railroad Company, a corporation created by the State of Maryland in 1856 to build a railroad from Washington to Hagerstown, addressed a memorial to Congress. It asked for authority to build a line from Washington to points on the Northern Central and the Philadelphia, Wilmington and Baltimore railroads. The petitioners contemplated the establishment of a route to the capital which, sweeping northwesterly around Baltimore from the Philadelphia, Wilmington and Baltimore railroad, tapped that city's only railroad arteries from the north and isolated it.

Their request was buttressed by argument that seemed unanswerable. They emphasized the point that the proposed road would insure uninterrupted and rapid transit between the nation and its capital; relieve chronic congestion of traffic at Baltimore; obliterate the discomforts of transfer in that city; save millions in money to the Federal treasury; and, not least, place a friendly railroad at the disposal of the government. In calling up the inadequacy of the Washington Branch, the petitioners rested their case on weaker ground. They subscribed to this admixture of fact and opinion: [6]

In a rebellion, we have seen *the single* means of approach so interrupted as to delay relief, endanger the capital, and strike a panic into the heart of the country. Had there been two or three good railroads from the west and north into Washington, troops and munitions would have poured in so rapidly as to have driven the rebellion backward in its earliest stage—the disasters of Bull Run could not have occurred, and the millions of dollars thereby lost would still be a resource to the treasury.

They concluded with the following high-sounding phrases:

... Wisdom, imperative necessity, the maintenance of a government, the integrity of the country, the support of the troops, alike demand that early steps should be taken to afford all the necessary means of connecting the capital with the nation at large in such reliable manner that the government may be respected, and protected by the people who have intrusted its welfare to the hands of the present administration.

All this was prologue to a simple plan based on contemplated government support. It proposed that the

United States should lend its credit to the Metropolitan company to the extent of two million dollars and be indemnified with first mortgage bonds of the railroad; that the Metropolitan should have thirty-six years to redeem its bonds; and that for the duration of the war the United States should enjoy preferential rates on troops, military supplies, and other government property.[7]

Secretary of War Simon Cameron favored the proposition and urged its acceptance upon President Lincoln.[8] But it failed to find immediate support in Congress. It was placed in the hands of the House Committee on Roads and Canals but that committee decided to take no immediate action.[9]

When the matter next came up for legislative consideration, it bore the marks of evolutionary change; the plan now contained a new element which contemplated the construction of a continuous, independent line from Washington to New York. The sponsors of the Metropolitan proposition obviously expected aid from critics of the Camden and Amboy, a New Jersey railroad, that enjoyed a virtual transportation monopoly between New York and Philadelphia and whose record of exploitation of the public had often been a subject of comment.

On January 15, 1862, the House of Representatives passed a resolution directing the Secretary of War to ascertain and report what arrangements could be made with the railroad corporations "on the line between Washington and New York, by the way of Baltimore and Philadelphia, for the construction of a side track ... from Back River to the Relay House, in Maryland, through West Baltimore; and also for the construction of another track between the Relay House and Washington, so as to form and open a speedy and direct communication" [10] between New

York and Washington. That body also directed the Secretary of War "to invite propositions for the construction of a distinct and direct road from New York to Washington."

Secretary Cameron addressed communications to the presidents of the constituent railroads.[11] John W. Garrett was one of the first to return an answer. On February 9, 1862, he sent his reply to Edwin M. Stanton, Cameron's successor as War Department head.[12] It was long and bore the marks of careful preparation. Garrett disclosed with emphasis his determination not only to oppose the projection of a competing line across Maryland but also any connecting lines which would result in the deflection of traffic from Baltimore.

He pronounced the proposal to build a "side track" from Back River to Relay House an aberration. The scheme was impracticable, and the road itself would be unnecessary. He then called attention to the fact that a convenient water connection between the Philadelphia, Wilmington and Baltimore and the Washington Branch railroads was soon to be put in operation at Baltimore; that the Baltimore and Ohio company itself was laying tracks in the city streets to close the gap between the Northern Central Railroad and its own Washington Branch, thereby enabling troops and supplies using these roads to pass through Baltimore without a change of engines and cars.[13]

Firmly set in his opposition to the proposed through railroad between New York and Washington, Garrett stated his objections to it in pointed language. He wrote with emphasis how palpably unfair the building of such a competing railroad would be to existing lines, especially to those in his own state. ". . . those who urge it," he declared, "mean only to make the *war* the means and occasion of building up, under the authority of Congress, lines of railroad within the State of Maryland, which, costing many millions of public money, are not needed for the war, but will serve when *peace* comes *as a means of commercial rivalry with our Maryland lines.*" [14]

Garrett admitted that the collection of a capitation tax on the Washington Branch was a sharp weapon in the hands of proponents of a second road but he defended its incidence on the ground that Maryland had expended millions on her railroads and for years had received little from her investment. He therefore expressed hope that Congress would refuse sanction and support to any scheme of Federal works or private enterprise that contemplated the laying of competing lines on Maryland soil and the isolation of Baltimore.

In presenting this part of his argument Garrett did not pass over the opportunity to declare that the proposed line between New York and Washington was, like the proposed "side track" north of Baltimore, an impractical conception of a railroad and unnecessary under the circumstances. He called attention to the parallel lines of the Baltimore and Ohio main stem and the Washington Branch, which formed a double-track route between Baltimore and Relay House; he asserted that the single track between the latter point and Washington was adequate for all exigencies. To give substance to this statement he reminded Stanton that the Washington Branch had already proved its capacity and efficiency. It had "not only demonstrated that its means were sufficient to send forward, without delay, the numbers constituting the great army now upon the Potomac, but it also made itself capable of furnishing an ample channel for the supply of that army with provisions and military stores when the use of the Potomac river as a means of communication was abandoned." [15]

He contended that existing lines between Washington and New York afforded the most direct route that could

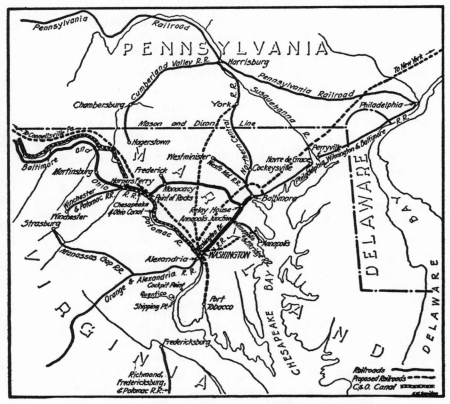

PROPOSED COMPETING RAILROADS (1861-1865)

be built. Any other, he maintained, would be circuitous and require expenditures out of proportion to the benefits derived.

Nor did Garrett overlook larger aspects of the question.

INFLUENCE ON NATIONAL RAILROAD POLICY

He expressed belief that the fundamental cause of the demand for an additional seaboard line was congestion of traffic on the New York Central, the New York and Erie, and the Pennsylvania railroads. "This plethora of business for the northern lines," he stated, "does not result from the increase of business in the sections of the country from which their trade is naturally drawn, but from the fact that the traffic and travel, which ordinarily find their way to the seaboard over the Baltimore and Ohio railroad, have been by the closing of that road forced to find an outlet to the ocean and the seat of war by such routes." [16] With strong insinuation that his own Washington Branch had succeeded where the Northern Central and the Philadelphia, Wilmington and Baltimore railroads had failed, he urged that the immediate opening of the Baltimore and Ohio main line which had been closed since May 23, 1861, was the cure for the ills that seemed to threaten the nation's capital and its main army.

Stripped of its local application and perhaps some bluster, Garrett's protest reflected the uneasiness of railway executives in many parts of the country. Certainly many in the Border states were on needles and pins because of the uncertain attitude of both the President and Congress toward public control and public ownership. The disturbing element was that President Lincoln favored some scheme of governmental regulation which would place all railroads under the supervision of the War Department for the duration of the war; it was commonly believed among railroad men that the President would not hesitate to use his war powers to construct new lines. His advocacy of a plan to build a railroad in eastern Tennessee and western North Carolina at government expense seemed to give railroad officials adequate ground for their apprehension.[17]

The truth is, the darkest dreams of the railway owners had all but come true. On January 21, 1862, a measure providing for government operation of railroads was introduced in the Senate.[18] The bill authorized the President to seize any and all railway and telegraph lines within the United States and to subject their officers, agents, and employees to military authority under the articles of war; it gave to the Secretary of War and his agents power to supervise the transportation of all troops and military supplies on the railroads; and it provided for a board of three commissioners to determine damages that might ensue to the railway and telegraph companies as a result of the application of the act.

Senator James A. Pearce of Maryland immediately attacked the bill. He declared with force that the measure had been spitefully framed by the Baltimore and Ohio's rivals and enemies of its management, and he rhetorically defended the railroad by holding up to light its record of loyalty and service. In replying to allegations of disloyalty that had been lodged against company officials, he answered that the charges were simply preposterous. The company had handled the traffic between Baltimore and Washington "with the most perfect devotion to the interests of the country,"—it had put the needs of the government first; it had postponed its commercial tonnage and substituted government freight and passengers.[19]

Pearce stated his objections to the bill in summary form. He prophesied that the assumption of government control over existing lines, then in excellent working condition, would result in a loss of efficiency in operation; he foresaw trouble for the government when it attempted to handle the complex financial arrangements of the railroad companies.[20]

Despite the protests of Pearce, who was defending a Maryland interest, and the opposition of others who opposed government control on principle, the bill passed and became law. A majority of Congress had been led to believe that the express powers granted in the act were necessary to enable the executive branch of the government to prosecute the war with vigor. A few of this number also favored the measure because it appeared to be a step in the direction of government ownership.[21]

Under authority of the statute the Secretary of War, by order of the President, placed the Baltimore and Ohio Railroad under War Department control on May 25, 1862.[22] He did this however with the tacit understanding that the road would be permitted to operate as a private line so long as it satisfactorily met the demands of the government.

The Baltimore and Ohio had won suspended judgment and was now on probation. The presumption is strong that this change of status gave new verve to the company's loyalty, certainly to its efficiency; its desire to retain control of its lines goes far to explain its unvarying support of the Union and co-operation thereafter in the conduct of the war. That the management was entirely successful in its effort is indicated by the fact that the company was permitted to operate its road without government supervision and with a minimum of government interference to the end of hostilities.[23]

This relationship between government and the railroads had not yet been formally defined when the Metropolitan proposition again put in appearance. On April 10, 1862, Representative Hendrick B. Wright of Pennsyl-

213

vania, chairman of the Committee on Military Affairs, introduced a bill providing for the acceptance of the Metropolitan plan which, as before stated, contemplated the construction of a railroad from Washington to points near Baltimore on the Northern Central and the Philadelphia, Wilmington and Baltimore railroads; it also contained a provision authorizing the Metropolitan Railroad Company to construct between Washington and the points of junction a double track "upon the line of any railway, when the Secretary of War shall so direct." [24] This provision was obviously inserted in the bill to enable the Metropolitan company to locate its line closely parallel to the Washington Branch Railroad. The Secretary of the Treasury was authorized to issue bonds to assist in building the new road. The bill was read twice, ordered to be printed, then returned to the Committee on Military Affairs.[25]

This measure soon sent Garrett scurrying to Washington. On April 25, 1862, he appeared before the committee and gave testimony. He emphasized his belief that the proposed road could not be built under the authority of its charter. He next repeated arguments that he had earlier employed against the proposal in his formal reply to the Secretary of War: that there was no need for it; and that the construction of the proposed line would be "a most extraordinary and unjust attack upon the interests of Maryland, which are so largely identified with these works of public improvement." Garrett closed with a statement at once tactful and decisive. If "any adverse action to her system of internal improvements be taken by Congress, without any absolute military necessity," he said, it would "unquestionably be regarded as a matter of

great and grave importance to the State of Maryland, and
as an almost fatal stab at her financial interests." [26]

All that Garrett intended to convey in this statement is
not clear. Certainly Maryland's course in the war was still
problematical. He undoubtedly wished to invoke attention to this fact with its probable effect on Maryland public opinion.

Garrett's testimony was not without weight in the committee. Chairman Wright in particular showed readiness
to share his views, and the committee failed to report the
measure back to the House. This ended the matter. Aside
from perfunctory consideration of a bill contemplating
the extension of the Pittsburgh and Connellsville Railroad
from Connellsville, Pennsylvania, to Cumberland, Maryland, no further effort was made during that session to
project railroads in Maryland.

Yet a new danger threatened in the next. Early in 1863,
the Columbia and Reading Railroad Company, a Pennsylvania corporation, presented a memorial to both houses
asking Federal authorization to build a railroad from
Washington to New York. Signed by S. P. Case, the petition was commonly known as the "Case Memorial."

It too emphasized the inadequacy of existing means of
transportation between Washington and New York; called
attention to the uncertainties and inconveniences of connections at Baltimore and Philadelphia; and dwelt at
length upon the special taxes on railroad travel collected
by New Jersey, Delaware, and Maryland. The memorial
struck hard at the Baltimore and Ohio. In its list of allegations was a declaration that the company charged extor-
tionate rates on passengers, coal, and even the United
States mails.[27]

The petition however fell flat. In the Senate it narrowly

missed being ignored entirely. On February 7, 1863, a bill authorizing the construction of the proposed line was introduced in that body, but it was promptly referred to the Committee on Military Affairs and the Militia,[28] from which it never emerged.

In the House of Representatives the memorial met a similar fate. On January 14, 1863, Representative Reuben E. Fenton of New York introduced a measure which granted to the Columbia and Reading company the right to construct a military and postal railway between Washington and New York. The bill was read twice and referred to a special committee.[29]

Four separate attempts were made to report the bill. Each effort recoiled before objections by representatives from Maryland, Delaware, or New Jersey, or by their close allies. Finally, on March 3, 1863, a motion was made to suspend the rules, but this step too was abortive.[30] The bill remained in the hands of the committee until the end of the session.

Nor was the Case proposal the single concern of the Baltimore and Ohio management during that session. Concurrently, a second movement equally derogatory of the company's interests began ominously in another quarter. Late in January, 1863, the Corporation of the City of Washington, acting through its so-called mayor, placed a memorial in the hands of the Senate Committee on Military Affairs and the Militia.[31] It contained the outlines of a plan for the construction of a continuous line of railroad from Port Tobacco to Washington and thence to Point of Rocks, Maryland, from which point it would traverse the most practicable route to Connellsville, Pennsylvania. There it would connect with the Pittsburgh and Connellsville Railroad. To all appearance the proposed road would

216

parallel the main stem of the Baltimore and Ohio from Point of Rocks to Cumberland.

The proponents of this line were not without reasons in showing why it should be built at once. They urged that it would facilitate connection with the proposed Pacific Railway at Pittsburgh, thereby providing a more direct route to the Northwest. They pointed out that the road would shorten the distance by rail between Washington and Pittsburgh a hundred and ten miles. They epitomized their argument with an appeal to national pride. "... the Capital of no other great nation in the civilized world is so nearly isolated from its sources of reliance," ran the concluding paragraph, "London having ten railroads extending outward as means of support and military protection, Paris seven, Berlin five, Vienna four, and Richmond, the rebel capital has five, and these have been extended under the pressure of a defensive war, and without one tithe of the vast resources of our legitimate government." [32]

The Senate turned a deaf ear to this plea. It is true that a bill was framed to give form to the proposal.[33] But like others of its kind, it perished in committee.

All the while the Baltimore and Ohio management had recognized the need of a second track between Relay House and Washington, although Garrett had been reluctant to admit that it was pressing. In the summer of 1862 he took steps to build it but, as already noted, his company was compelled to forego plans because of Confederate activity. Materials collected for the second track were diverted to rebuild the main line north of Harpers Ferry. For the same reason the laying of new track was deferred in the summer of 1863 and again in the summer of 1864. But following the expulsion of the Confederates from the upper Potomac in September, 1864, work on the Washington Branch was resumed and on December 14, 1864, the new line was opened.[34]

If this act removed immediate danger of competition between Baltimore and Washington, the Baltimore and

Baltimore and Ohio Railroad

TELEGRAM,

From Wash.___ *July* 5 1864

Received, Baltimore, ___ o'clock, 50 min. ___ P.

To J. W. Garrett

You say telegraphic communication is re-established with Sandy Hook Well what does Sandy Hook say about Operations of enemy of Sigel doing today

A. Lincoln

Photograph of a telegram recently discovered in B & O archives. The great Civil War President was often dependent upon railroad wires for news of the enemy

Ohio still faced a running fight in western Maryland. After the failure of the Corporation of Washington to obtain a charter to build a competing line toward the northwest, the Baltimore and Ohio company made ready to assist the Pittsburgh and Connellsville Railroad in extending its tracks from Connellsville to Cumberland. Closing of the gap between these points would complete a railroad triangle, the vertices of which were Washing-

ton, Harrisburg, and Pittsburgh. Since the Baltimore and
Ohio would be the base of this figure, the sides of which
were the Northern Central and the Pennsylvania Central
railroads, the proposed extension would enable the Baltimore and Ohio to divert traffic from its rivals at Pittsburgh.

But the Pennsylvania Central did not stand idle while

Baltimore and Ohio Railroad
TELEGRAM,

First news to President Lincoln of the Battle of Monocacy evidently came to him
from the B & O

its traffic territory was about to be invaded. As a result of
its influence, the Pennsylvania legislature repealed the
law which authorized the extension of the Pittsburgh and
Connellsville line to the Maryland border.[35] The Pennsylvania Railroad Company then advanced a plan of its own
for meeting the demand for a more direct route between
Washington and Pittsburgh. It asked Congress to authorize the construction of a railway from Washington to a
convenient point on the Northern Central Railroad.

THE BALTIMORE AND OHIO IN THE CIVIL WAR

On February 18, 1865, Representative John F. Farnsworth of Illinois introduced a bill in the House of Representatives authorizing the construction of this road.[36] The bill granted to the Northern Central Railroad Company the right to build its line from the District of Columbia to York, Pennsylvania. Sponsors of the measure urged its enactment on the ground that the road would provide a short and convenient route between Washington and Pittsburgh and a more direct line of travel between Washington and New York.

Like the Metropolitan proposition this bill was a direct threat to Baltimore and Ohio supremacy in Maryland; because the proposed road would lie almost entirely on Maryland soil, its passage promised to nullify all that remained of Maryland's claim to reserved rights to construct her own public improvements. This result was clearly foreseen, and it evoked a strong negative speech from Representative Francis Thomas of Maryland.[37]

Thomas contended that the provisions of the measure were unconstitutional because they contemplated the creation of a corporation within the states and infringed the reserved rights of a state. He thundered that the measure was a plan of attack upon the Baltimore and Ohio Railroad and other Maryland interests; that the single motive behind the scheme was the well-known desire of the Pennsylvania Railroad to encroach upon the traffic territory of its traditional rival. Then straining oratorically he demanded in the name of justice that the State of Maryland be reimbursed for all her losses, if Congress approved the Pennsylvania Railroad program.

Nor did the pending measure go without notice at Annapolis. Early in February, 1865, the Maryland general assembly entered formal protest. In a joint resolution it remonstrated against "the granting by Congress of any charter to build a railroad from the Northern Central Railroad to Washington City;" [38] and on February 27, 1865, the House of Delegates emphasized its interest in the matter in a resolution requesting the attorney general of the state to proceed to Washington "in conjunction with a committee of three members from the House." [39]

Garrett also entered formal protest. On February 28, 1865, he dispatched a long communication to the Speaker of the House of Representatives. He held up to light the alleged mischievous purpose of the Pennsylvania Railroad Company to cripple the Baltimore and Ohio; emphasized the point that the need for an additional line of railroad across Maryland had been supplied by the completion of the second track on the Washington Branch Railroad; and called up the fact that the proposed route to Pittsburgh was long and circuitous. He suggested instead the propriety of building a spur from a convenient point on his own main stem between Monocacy Junction and Harpers Ferry to Washington, and of closing the break between Cumberland and Connellsville. These improvements, he stated, would provide a more direct route between Washington and Pittsburgh than the one contemplated in the Pennsylvania Railroad Bill. With an air of optimism Garrett announced his intention to build these connecting lines in the not too distant future; he urged that "if the power of Congress is to be invoked at all in favor of any route, it would seem that the direct route to the capital from the Northwest via Pittsburgh, Connellsville, and Cumberland ought to have a superior claim to the exercise of such authority." [40]

Again the defenders of the Baltimore and Ohio were victorious. The measure did not weather opposition in the House and died with the session. No other bill of like character appeared to trouble Baltimore and Ohio councils.

When the Civil War ended in April, 1865, the Baltimore and Ohio Railroad still held a monopoly on travel to the capital of the nation. It had successfully opposed the schemes of other railroads to encroach upon its territory; it had held high the right to private operation in a period when government control threatened; and, despite strained capacity of its Washington Branch, it had exerted strong influence on the makers of national railroad policy. In achieving these ends the company found a willing ally in the State of Maryland with her vested interests and her sovereign claims. But it was the railroad management that mapped the strategy and led the attack.

In the larger field of governmental policy the road was a determining factor in situations which more directly affected the public interest. Not only was it instrumental in making secure the National Capital in 1861, when the safety of Washington lay in the lap of the gods, but it subsequently saved that city and the protecting Union army from great discomfort when the lower Potomac River was closed and communication on the Chesapeake and Ohio Canal was broken. Throughout the conflict, the Washington Branch stood out conspicuously as the only railroad which joined the capital and the loyal states. Whether concerned with routine civilian travel or a military emergency, this line served the North as did no other railroad. During four uncertain years the Washington Branch rendered incalculable service to the Union.

The value of the road, however, did not stem altogether from the forty miles of inanimate iron that connected Baltimore and Washington. Because of its unique geographical location and of its fiscal and administrative dependence upon Maryland and Baltimore, it was strategically situated to turn the course of public opinion in that pro-Southern city and to shape public policy in the state at large. Because it kept trains moving and always acted the passive rôle of an endangered public work, the company was not without influence in the pacification of Maryland.

Of no less significance was the Baltimore and Ohio main line, with its 379 miles of track connecting Chesapeake Bay and the Ohio River. Joined west of the Alleghenies by an important auxiliary, the road possessed two terminals on the Ohio at widely separated points. It branched on the map like a river nearing the sea and made a broad inland delta of transmontane territory which it penetrated. The railroad also put a new face on that part of Virginia which jutted north almost to the Great Lakes. In fact, it clothed northwest Virginia with new strategic importance. To widen the east-west corridor which this section almost closed, the Federal government found the Baltimore and Ohio to be a convenient agency. With the railroad in their hands, Union troops moved with ease against secession in Virginia's northwest counties. It was no accident that General McClellan seized this indispensable area in 1861 with an alacrity that he seldom displayed as a military commander. Once this region was taken, the United States held it, and held it tenaciously; and when the inhabitants organized the occupied territory for statehood they took great care that not one foot of the railroad between the Potomac and the Ohio should lie on possible "foreign" soil. West Virginia's quick admission as a state was accelerated by her military importance; for the duration of the war she was in truth along with western Pennsylvania and northeastern Ohio the geographical keystone of the new Union.

The proximity of the Baltimore and Ohio Railroad to the eastern theater of the war and the connections which it maintained with Eastern and Western lines enhanced its military value. Its general utility, however, was not always fully appreciated by Federal high command which seemed at times to regard it only as a welcome convenience. The Confederates on the other hand clearly recognized its value to the United States and seldom overlooked an opportunity to damage it. The toll which they took during each year of the conflict amounted to millions, but after each thrust the Federal government repeatedly extended its protecting arm. This practice necessitated the employment of many troops but the government never seemed to count the cost. As a result, Union forces used the road to advantage during long periods. With the railroad as their base, they defended with confidence the crest of the Alleghenies from the Kentucky to the Maryland border. From the railroad, Union armies also constantly threatened Virginia's fullest granary, the Shenandoah Valley. Union strategists made spectacular use of the line in 1863, when with the help of co-operating roads, they rapidly transported 20,000 men from the Rappahannock to the Tennessee. By a single stroke Federal military authorities effected the relief of Chattanooga and dispelled the last doubt about the reliability of the railroad as a tactical agency.

The Baltimore and Ohio was the first railroad to play a leading part in the drama of war; no other railway rendered more important service to the United States during the Civil War. The founders spoke prophetically when they dedicated it to the nation's use. The Baltimore and Ohio did "contribute to the permanence of the union of the United States."

NOTES

CHAPTER I

1. *The Mayor and City Council of Baltimore* vs. *The Baltimore and Ohio Rail-Road Company*, 6 Gill, 296 (Maryland Reports).

2. Milton Reizenstein, *The Economic History of the Baltimore and Ohio Railroad, 1827-1853*, pp. 9-11; James Morton Callahan, *Semi-Centennial History of West Virginia*, p. 110; John Moody, *The Railroad Builders*, pp. 96-97; J. L. Ringwalt, *Development of Transportation Systems in the United States*, p. 152.

3. *Acts of the General Assembly of Virginia* (1826-1827), p. 84.

4. William P. Smith, *The Book of the Great Railway Celebrations of 1857*, pp. 36, 40; *Acts of the General Assembly of Virginia* (1844-1845), pp. 69-73.

5. *Acts of the General Assembly of Virginia* (1846-1847), p. 86.

6. *Thirty-Fourth Annual Report of the President and Directors to the Stockholders of the Baltimore and Ohio Railroad Company*, p. 16; John Ashcroft, (comp.), *Railway Directory for 1862*, p. 104.

7. *Report of the Finance Committee of the Baltimore and Ohio Railroad Company, In Opposition to the Payment to the State of Maryland of the Capitation Tax upon Passengers Travelling over the Washington Branch Road*, p. 7.

8. See *Journal of the Proceedings of the Senate of Maryland* (January Session, 1864), pp. 384-399, for a complete list of stockholders. Of the 632 stockholders listed in 1864, 545 were residents of Maryland. This report shows also that all of those holding more than 1,500 shares, excepting only the City of Wheeling, which held 5,970, were Marylanders. That such was

227

the case in 1861 is strongly implied in United States *House Executive Documents* (1861-1862), No. 79, p. 6.

9. *Twenty-Ninth Annual Report*, pp. 12, 18, 29; Edward Hungerford, *The Story of the Baltimore and Ohio Railroad*, Vol. I, p. 323.

10. Charles Henry Ambler, *A History of Transportation in the Ohio Valley*, p. 197.

"Travel by the River is too slow, and too uncertain; and the indications are unmistakable that those splendid floating palaces now filled with their hundreds of passengers, will soon be remembered as a comfortable but antiquated contrivance for killing time..." (John H. Done to William G. Harrison, June 12, 1854, *The Papers of Robert Garrett and Sons*).

11. Jacob H. Hollander, *The Financial History of Baltimore*, p. 191; Baltimore *Sun*, January 21, 1862.

12. *Reports of the Majority and Minority of the Committee on Western Connections of the Baltimore and Ohio Railroad*, p. 5; Hungerford, *op. cit.*, Vol. I, pp. 293-294; Hollander, *op. cit.*, p. 191.

13. John H. Done to William G. Harrison, June 12, 1854, *Garrett Papers*.

14. This was a loan of $400,000 of the bonds of the Northwestern Virginia Railroad Company [*Baltimore and Ohio Railroad Company* vs. *City of Wheeling*, p. 13; 13 Grattan, 45, 52 (Virginia Reports); *Reports of the Majority and Minority of the Special Committee of the Baltimore and Ohio Railroad Company Appointed to Investigate Its Financial Condition*, p. 25].

15. 13 Grattan, 48.

16. *Twenty-Ninth Annual Report*, p. 8; 13 Grattan, 77. Wheeling claimed that the connection at Benwood was in violation of an act of the Virginia assembly passed March 6, 1847, which designated that city as a terminus of the road. She based her right to take legal action on the fact that she owned $500,000 of the stocks of the company (13 Grattan, 42-43).

17. *Reports of the Majority and Minority of the Special Committee of the Baltimore and Ohio Railroad Co. Appointed to Investigate Its Financial Condition*, p. 8.

NOTES

18. The city council of Baltimore guaranteed $1,500,000 of the bonds of the Northwestern Virginia Railroad in 1853 (Hollander, *op. cit.*, p. 191).

19. *Reports of Special Committee Appointed to Investigate Financial Condition*, p. 9.

20. *Ibid.*, p. 9. This criticism was directed inferentially at Johns Hopkins and John W. Garrett, members of the board of directors, who had served on the Committee on Western Connections and had been prominent in the negotiations. Both were interested in the bonds of the Central Ohio Railroad at the time and it was not unreasonable to suspect that each had not pushed a close bargain in the interest of the Northwestern Virginia route to Cincinnati (*See* J. Thomas Scharf, *History of Western Maryland*, Vol. II, p. 1512).

21. Baltimore *Sun*, February 11, 1860; Hollander, *op. cit.*, p. 192.

22. *Twenty-Ninth Annual Report*, pp. 8-9.

23. *Ibid.*, pp. 12, 18, 29; *Thirtieth Annual Report*, pp. 3, 4, 6; *Thirty-First Annual Report*, pp. 5, 6, 9, 10, 23. See also Hungerford, *op. cit.*, Vol. I, pp. 323-326.

24. *Baltimore and Ohio R. R. Company Extra Dividend Case. Statement Made by the President to the Board of Directors at their Meeting on the 12th September, 1860*, p. 10.

25. Baltimore *American and Commercial Advertiser*, March 27, 1863.

26. *Reports of Special Committee Appointed to Investigate Financial Condition*, p. 5.

27. *Ibid.*, p. 5; *Thirty-First Annual Report*, pp. 5-6; *Thirty-Second Annual Report*, pp. 6, 15.

28. *Reports of Special Committee Appointed to Investigate Financial Condition*, pp. 5-11.

29. *Ibid.*, pp. 17-30.

30. Scharf, *op. cit.*, Vol. II, pp. 1512-1514.

31. *Hunt's Merchants' Magazine and Commercial Review*, Vol. XXXIX, p. 750 (December, 1858) and Vol. XLV, p. 135 (August, 1861); Baltimore *Sun*, January 14, 1859.

32. *Letter of H. J. Jewett, President of the Central Ohio Railroad Company to the President and Directors of the Balti-*

THE BALTIMORE AND OHIO IN THE CIVIL WAR

more and Ohio Railroad Company in Regard to the Connection Between the Two Roads, pp. 7-8.

33. *Thirty-First Annual Report,* pp. 5-6, 9-10, 23; *Thirty-Second Annual Report,* pp. 6, 8, 9.

CHAPTER II

1. Wheeling *Intelligencer,* October 15, 1887.

2. *Thirty-Second Annual Report,* pp. 6, 8, 9; *Thirty-Third Annual Report,* pp. 6, 9, 11; Scharf, *op. cit.,* Vol. II, p. 1514.

3. *Thirty-Third Annual Report,* p. 22.

4. Baltimore *Sun,* April 5, 1859.

5. *Reports of Special Committee Appointed to Investigate Financial Condition,* p. 21.

6. Baltimore *Sun,* February 10, 1859.

7. "Report of a Select Committee of the House of Delegates of Maryland Relative to Charges of James E. Tyson Against the Baltimore and Ohio Railroad Company," in *Maryland House Documents* (BB, 1860), pp. 3-6.

8. *Objections to Yielding to Northerners the Control of the Baltimore and Ohio Railroad,* p. 11.

9. Baltimore *Sun,* May 12, 1859.

10. Quotation from Baltimore *Daily Exchange* in Baltimore *Sun,* September 12, 1860.

11. *See* Baltimore *Sun,* February 26, 1859, and September 12, 1860.

12. *Journal of the Proceedings of the Senate of Maryland* (January Session, 1860), pp. 44, 97, 299-300.

13. *Journal of the Proceedings of the House of Delegates of the State of Maryland* (January Session, 1860), pp. 158-160. Formal charges were filed against the company in the House of Delegates by James E. Tyson and a special committee was appointed to make an investigation. During the hearing it fell out that the company had not only discriminated against Baltimore and in favor of Philadelphia and New York but had also changed its rates at will. The committee apparently accepted Garrett's explanation of these practices. Nevertheless, at the close of the inquiry it voted a mild censure of the Baltimore and Ohio for its indifference to the interests

NOTES

of local shippers. On the other hand the committee commended the company for favorable rates granted on westbound traffic from Baltimore which, it asserted, increased business transactions of the merchants of the city [*Maryland House Documents* (BB, 1860), pp. 3-4].

14. *Maryland House Journal* (January Session, 1860), p. 160.
15. Baltimore *Sun*, January 14, 1859.
16. *Ibid.*, January 18, 1859.
17. *Ibid.*
18. Richmond *Daily Enquirer*, March 15, 1860; Ambler, *Transportation*, p. 229.
19. Richmond *Daily Enquirer*, March 14, 1860.
20. *Ibid.* See also Ambler, *Transportation*, pp. 228-229.
21. Richmond *Daily Enquirer*, March 15, 1860.
22. Wheeling *Intelligencer*, April 4, 1860; Richmond *Daily Enquirer*, March 15, 1860. The provisions of these acts went far to substantiate charges that Wheeling had driven a shrewd and stiff bargain. The most important restrictions and conditions were: (1) no work was permitted to be done on either the Holliday's Cove Railroad or the Steubenville bridge until $200,000 should have been subscribed to the capital stock of a bridge company at Wheeling; (2) beyond building the abutments and piers to a height of six feet above low water mark, no work was permitted to be done on either the railroad or the bridge until the railroad bridge at Wheeling was chartered and its piers and abutments likewise raised to a height of six feet above low water mark; (3) following the erection of the piers and abutments to the designated height, work on the two structures was to proceed *pari-passu* to completion; (4) neither the Steubenville bridge nor the Holliday's Cove Railroad was to be opened for use until a railroad route should have been completed from Pittsburgh to Wheeling either by way of the Chartier's Valley and Hempfield railroads or by way of the Pittsburgh and Steubenville Railroad and the Holliday's Cove line, extended to Wheeling; and (5) neither the Holliday's Cove Railroad nor the Steubenville bridge might be opened for the use of through traffic until the Wheeling bridge had been in operation for thirty days [*Acts of the Gen*

eral Assembly of Virginia (1859-1860), Ch. 126, Secs. 3, 7, 8, 9, 11, 13; Ch. 127, Sec. 14].

23. *Acts of the Virginia Assembly* (1859-1860), Ch. 20; Wheeling *Intelligencer*, February 9, 1860; Richmond *Daily Enquirer*, March 19, 1860; Charles H. Ambler, *Sectionalism in Virginia from 1776 to 1861*, pp. 315, 318.

24. Peter G. Van Winkle, president of the Northwestern Virginia Railroad Company, was on hand as a lobbyist during a part of the session of 1859-1860 and worked to prevent the passage of so-called inimical legislation [*Debates and Proceedings of the West Virginia Constitutional Convention*, 1861-1863 (MS), December 11, 1861].

25. *Acts of the Virginia Assembly* (1859-1860), Ch. 127, Sec. 4.

26. *Ibid.*, Sec. 16. Garrett spoke unfavorably of these measures in his annual report of September 30, 1860 ["Annual Reports of the Rail Road Companies of the State of Virginia for Year Ending September 30, 1860," *Virginia Documents* (1861-1862), Part 3, p. 526].

27. Henry S. Garrett to John W. Garrett, August 24, 1859, *Garrett Papers;* Scharf, *op. cit.,* Vol. II, pp. 1512-1514.

28. Baltimore *Sun*, February 11, 14, 1860; *Objections to Yielding to Northerners the Control of the Baltimore and Ohio Railroad*, p. 3.

29. Baltimore *Sun*, February 11, 1860.

30. *Ibid.*, March 9, 1860.

31. *Ibid.*, March 2, 1860.

32. *Ibid.*, February 13, 1860; Baltimore *Daily Exchange*, March 5, 1860; *Objections to Yielding to Northerners the Control of the Baltimore and Ohio Railroad*, pp. 7-10.

33. Baltimore *Sun*, February 13, 1860. The president of the Baltimore and Ohio was described as "by far the most powerful individual in the Commonwealth, and by far more powerful, for good or evil, than was the President of the United States Bank" (*Objections to Yielding to Northerners the Control of the Baltimore and Ohio Railroad*, p. 9).

34. *A Statement Showing the Effect That Might be Produced Against the State of Maryland and City of Baltimore by the Proposed Increase of the Stockholder Directors in the*

NOTES

Baltimore and Ohio R. R. Company, by a Marylander, p. 4; *Objections to Yielding to Northerners the Control of the Baltimore and Ohio Railroad,* pp. 15-18. It is noteworthy that it was alleged that the real motive behind the movement was the desire of Garrett and other large stockholders to make their stocks more speculative. It was intimated that persons high in official positions of the company were primarily concerned with the protection of large interests held in the Central Ohio Railroad Company; and it was consequently believed that there was a design on foot to bend the policies of the Baltimore and Ohio to promote these interests (Baltimore *Sun,* March 9, 1860; *Objections to Yielding to Northerners the Control of the Baltimore and Ohio Railroad,* p. 19; *A Statement Showing the Effect That Might be Produced Against the State of Maryland and City of Baltimore,* pp. 4, 5).

35. Following the failure of the Central Ohio, a meeting was held at Coshocton, Ohio, July 6, 1860, for the purpose of consolidating the Central Ohio and the Pittsburgh, Columbus and Cincinnati railroads. Thomas A. Scott, vice-president of the Pennsylvania Central, was present (quotation from Columbus (Ohio) *Journal* in Baltimore *Sun,* July 14, 1860).

36. F. A. Lane to J. W. Garrett, November 30, 1860, and January 2, 1861; Jas. Snyder to Messrs. Garrett & Son, October 12, 1860; Campbell Graham to Henry S. Garrett, August 3, 1860, *Garrett Papers.*

37. *Congressional Globe,* April 5, 1860, p. 1546.

38. *Ibid.,* p. 1547.

39. *Ibid.,* May 19, 1860, pp. 2196-2197.

40. Memorandum, 1860, *The Papers of Simon Cameron;* Ashcroft, *op. cit.,* p. 106.

41. The Pennsylvania Central acquired controlling interest in the Northern Central Railroad during the monetary depression which followed Abraham Lincoln's election (William B. Wilson, *History of the Pennsylvania Railroad,* Vol. I, p. 243; H. W. Schotter, *The Growth and Development of the Pennsylvania Railroad Company,* p. 85).

42. *Congressional Globe,* May 19, 1860, p. 2196.

43. *Ibid.,* December 21, 1860, p. 179.

44. *Ibid.,* p. 180.

THE BALTIMORE AND OHIO IN THE CIVIL WAR

45. Thomas A. Scott to Simon Cameron, December 24, 1860, *Cameron Papers.*

46. *Letter of the President of the Baltimore and Ohio R. R. Co. to the Chairman of the House Committee on the District of Columbia,* pp. 3-7.

47. *Virginia Documents* (1861-1862), Part 3, pp. 526-527, 529.

48. William Dennison to John W. Garrett, January 14, 1861; "Statement of the Liabilities and Assets of the Baltimore and Ohio Railroad Company on March 31, 1861," *Garrett Papers; American Railroad Journal,* January 26, 1861; Baltimore *Sun,* March 14, 1861; Moody, *op. cit.,* p. 101; *Thirty-Fourth Annual Report,* pp. 6, 10.

49. *Baltimore and Ohio R. R. Company Extra Dividend Case,* pp. 11, 12, 25; quotation from Chicago *Tribune* in Wheeling *Intelligencer,* October 17, 1887; Moody, *op. cit.,* p. 107.

50. Moody, *op. cit.,* p. 101.

51. *Thirty-Fourth Annual Report,* p. 33.

52. *Ibid.,* pp. 167, 172.

53. Wheeling *Intelligencer,* April 27, 1861.

CHAPTER III

1. R. Garrett and Sons to J. B. Floyd, October 19, 1859, *Garrett Papers; Calendar of Virginia State Papers,* Vol. XI, pp. 74, 85; William P. Smith to J. M. Bennett, March 27, 1860, *Papers of Jonathan M. Bennett.* For its assistance in effecting the capture of Brown and his companions the Baltimore and Ohio was voted the formal thanks of Virginia [*Acts of General Assembly* (1859-1860), p. 700].

2. Newspaper clipping, 1860, *Garrett Papers. See* also Richmond *Daily Enquirer,* February 28, 1860.

3. Baltimore *American and Commercial Advertiser,* January 26, 1861.

4. J. W. Garrett to S. L. Blaine, March 15, 1861, *Garrett Papers.*

5. New York *Herald,* January 28, 1861.

6. Baltimore *Sun,* February 7, 1861.

NOTES

7. Quotation from New York *Herald* in Baltimore *American and Commercial Advertiser,* January 22, 1861.

8. *Report of Committees of the House of Representatives,* 2d Sess. 37th Cong., Vol. 2, pp. 614, 615.

9. *Ibid.,* p. 619. "Dispatches from our western agents and connections say no fr't can be obtained to go east via B. & O. Route while present excitement continues. This fact is not attributable only to a fear of loss or detention to property or to misrepresentations of rival lines but is the general public sentiment consequent upon the attitude of Va." (D. S. Gray to John King, April 17, 1861, *Garrett Papers*).

10. *Report of Committees,* 2d Sess. 37th Cong., Vol. 2, p. 615.

11. W. P. Smith to J. H. Sullivan, April 16, 1861, and J. W. G. to Mas. T., April 16, 1861, *Garrett Papers.*

12. J. W. Garrett to Governor W. Dennison, April 17, 1861, *ibid.; Report of Committees,* 2d Sess. 37th Cong., Vol. 2, p. 618. See *American Railroad Journal,* August 16, 1862. The number of Ohio troops did not exceed 800 men (H. J. Jewett to D. S. Gray, April 17, 1861, *Garrett Papers*). W. P. Smith at a later date stated there were only 500 (*Report of Committees,* 2d Sess. 37th Cong., Vol. 2, p. 620).

13. Dennison sent the following dispatch to the Secretary of War on April 18: "We had made arrangements with the Baltimore and Ohio road to transport troops, and Mr. Garrett was anxious to take them until late last night, when he declined on the alleged ground that the Washington Branch will employ all his empty cars in transportation of troops. This looks ominous. We hope Harper's Ferry is safe" (*Official Records,* III, Vol. I, p. 84). William P. Smith offered the following explanation for the lack of preparation for such a contingency: "It was understood and expected by our company that the great majority of the troops from the northern States would proceed to Washington by water in steamers from the eastern ports by sea up the Potomac river" (*Report of Committees,* 2d Sess. 37th Cong., Vol. 2, p. 617).

14. *Ibid.,* pp. 617-618.

15. *Official Records,* I, Vol. LI, pt. 1, p. 327. Thomson was placed in charge of troop transportation from Philadelphia

THE BALTIMORE AND OHIO IN THE CIVIL WAR

to Washington on April 17 (Simon Cameron to J. Edgar Thomson, April 17, 1861, "Military Book," XLIII, *Files of the Secretary of War*).

16. *Report of Committees*, 2d Sess. 37th Cong., Vol. 2, pp. 619-620.

17. B. Despard to John W. Garrett, April 18, 1861, *Garrett Papers*.

18. Hungerford, *op. cit.*, Vol. I, p. 359; Philadelphia *Inquirer*, April 20, 1861; Baltimore *Daily Exchange*, April 19, 1861; Horace Greeley, *The American Conflict*, Vol. I, p. 462. Hungerford states that Garrett refused the guarantees (Hungerford, *op. cit.*, Vol. I, p. 359). Colonel Angus McDonald had been sent from Winchester to Baltimore on a similar mission on April 16th. He brought a petition signed by sixty residents of Frederick County urging Garrett to prevent the removal of arms from the arsenal at Harpers Ferry (W. S. Clark to J. W. Garrett, April 16, 1861, *Garrett Papers*).

19. *Thirty-Fifth Annual Report*, p. 46; G. M. Lauman to J. W. Garrett, April 18, 1861, *Garrett Papers; Report of Committees*, 2d Sess. 37th Cong., Vol. 2, p. 620. The movement from the Ohio River was expected to begin in the evening of April 18 or on the following morning (*Report of Committees*, p. 617). The Ohio troops would have encountered the Virginians at Harpers Ferry.

20. *Report of Committees*, 2d Sess. 37th Cong., Vol. 2, p. 617.

21. Philadelphia *Inquirer*, April 19, 1861; Hungerford, *op. cit.*, Vol. I, p. 358.

22. Hungerford, *op. cit.*, Vol. I, pp. 359-364.

23. Thos. H. Hicks, Geo. Wm. Brown, and Charles Howard to John W. Garrett, April 19, 1861, *Garrett Papers; National Intelligencer*, April 22, 1861.

24. John W. Garrett to Thomas H. Hicks, Geo. William Brown, and Charles Howard, April 19, 1861, *Garrett Papers; National Intelligencer*, April 22, 1861; Baltimore *South*, April 22, 1861; Greeley, *op. cit.*, Vol. I, p. 465. On April 20, 1861, the Baltimore *Sun* stated that the Baltimore and Ohio company had sent "an official communication to the Northern Central Railroad informing them that they would pass no

NOTES

more troops to Washington that should reach that city by that route."

25. John G. Nicolay and John Hay, *Abraham Lincoln; A History*, Vol. IV, pp. 120-121; Hungerford, *op. cit.*, Vol. I, p. 366.

26. *Report of Committees*, 2d Sess. 37th Cong., Vol. 2, p. 621.

27. Baltimore *Evening Patriot*, April 19, 1861.

28. *Ibid.* A. Diffey, supervisor of trains, accompanied the Sixth Massachusetts from Baltimore to Washington. Three hours and fifty minutes were required to make the run from Relay House to Washington, a distance of thirty-one miles. Diffey described the difficulties encountered on the road between Baltimore and Relay House as follows: "We were detained at Spence's Crossing (two miles from Baltimore) by track being obstructed with rails, cross-ties, and stones. At Jackson's Bridge the track was torn up.... We found stones and railroad chairs on the track west of the bridge" (*Report of Committees*, 2d Sess. 37th Cong., Vol. 2, p. 621n).

29. "The Secretary" to John Garrett, Esq., Friday M, April 19, 1861, *Garrett Papers*.

30. Hungerford, *op. cit.*, Vol. I, p. 369.

31. Wheeling *Intelligencer*, April 22, 1861.

32. "The telegraph says that you have declared against the passage of any more troops to Washington.... Excitement intense if so nothing can prevent the movement of five hundred thousand men from the West alone to clear any obstructions in reaching the federal capital please answer" (A. Stone, Jr., and L. M. Hubby to John W. Garrett, April 20, 1861, *Garrett Papers*. *See* also quotation from Cincinnati *Gazette* in Wheeling *Intelligencer*, May 11, 1861).

33. Philadelphia *Inquirer*, April 20, 1861.

34. *Official Records*, I, Vol. LI, pt. 2, p. 21.

35. *Ibid.*, I, Vol. II, p. 578.

36. J. W. Garrett to Geo. Wm. Brown, and Geo. Wm. Brown to J. W. Garrett, April 21, 1861, *Garrett Papers*; J. Thomas Scharf, *The Chronicles of Baltimore*, p. 602.

37. Simon Cameron, Sec. of War, to "The Officer in com-

mand of the United States troops now on the way from Harrisburg to Baltimore," April 21, 1861, *Cameron Papers*.

38. "Report of the Secretary of War, Washington, July 1, 1861," in *Senate Executive Documents*, 1st Sess. 37th Cong., No. 1, p. 25; Thos. H. Hicks to Frederick W. Lander, April 24, 1861, *The Papers of Frederick W. Lander*.

39. Baltimore *American and Commercial Advertiser*, April 24, 1861; Baltimore *South*, April 24, 1861; Baltimore *Daily Exchange*, April 24, 1861.

40. "Military Book," Vol. XLIV, p. 238, *Files of the Secretary of War; Official Records*, I, Vol. II, p. 603; *The National Cyclopedia of American Biography*, Vol. XIII, p. 335.

41. Thomas A. Scott to Simon Cameron, April 28, 1861, *Cameron Papers*.

42. Baltimore *American and Commercial Advertiser*, April 24, 1861.

43. Baltimore *Sun*, May 2, 1861. The company was however permitted to run a passenger train from Baltimore to Washington on Saturday afternoon, April 27. This train returned to Baltimore next day, and brought a large number of women and children (Baltimore *Sun*, April 29, 1861). From April 27 to May 5 the company ran passenger trains from Baltimore to Annapolis Junction. After the occupation of Relay House on May 5, passenger and freight trains were permitted to run between Baltimore and Washington on a schedule arranged by the Federal authorities (Baltimore *Sun*, May 7, 9, 1861).

44. *Official Records*, I, Vol. II, p. 617. In making his application to Cameron, Garrett stated: "For more than ten years past we have run four regular passenger trains daily each way between Baltimore and Washington, and at least one freight train. We now ask the privilege of running two passenger and mail trains and one freight train each way daily, subject to such supervision as you may deem desirable, and not to interfere with the movements of Government trains. The interests and convenience of numerous parties in Washington and Baltimore, and we hope of the Government, can be greatly served if you can gratify these requests" (*ibid.*, p. 615).

45. Kenton Harper to John W. Garrett, April 19, 1861,

NOTES

Garrett Papers; John W. Garrett to Kenton Harper, ——, 1861, *ibid.;* C. J. M. Gwinn, counsel for the Baltimore and Ohio company, made several visits to Harpers Ferry and carried on the negotiations for Garrett *(ibid.;* Baltimore *American and Commercial Advertiser,* August 26, 1865).

46. Baltimore *American and Commercial Advertiser,* April 26, 1861.

47. Baltimore *South,* April 23, 1861; Baltimore *Sun,* April 24, 1861. Harper was succeeded in command by Colonel Thomas J. Jackson on April 27.

48. Callahan, *op. cit.,* p. 142.

49. Wheeling *Intelligencer,* April 20, 1861. *See* also quotation from *United States Railroad and Mining Register* in *ibid.,* April 2, 1861.

50. Wheeling *Intelligencer,* April 27, 1861.

51. *Official Records,* I, Vol. II, p. 597.

52. Theodore F. Lang in *Loyal West Virginia from 1861 to 1865* takes the point of view that Thomson was actuated solely by the desire to eliminate a powerful rival. He says: "A rivalry that would assail a competing corporation at such a time, and under such circumstances, can be contemplated with feelings of genuine condemnation" (p. 150).

53. *Official Records,* I, Vol. II, p. 609.

54. *Ibid.*

55. Baltimore *American and Commercial Advertiser,* May 6, 7, 1861; Baltimore *South,* May 6, 1861; Bradley T. Johnson, "Maryland," in *Confederate Military History,* Vol. II, p. 29.

56. *Official Records,* I, Vol. II, p. 629.

57. *Ibid.*

58. Baltimore *Sun,* May 9, 1861.

59. *Ibid.;* Johnson, *op. cit.,* p. 29.

60. *Official Records,* I, Vol. LI, pt. 2, p. 78.

61. Frank Moore, *Rebellion Record,* Vol. I, p. 37.

62. *Official Records,* I, Vol. II, p. 635. These roads were repaired under War Department direction and supervision *(Official Records,* I, Vol. II, p. 604; "Military Book," Vol. XLIII, p. 255, in *Files of the Secretary of War).* Public sentiment in Baltimore was strong for the reopening of these railroads. A petition containing the names of two hundred Balti-

more business men and business firms was presented to the Maryland legislature in session at Frederick requesting that steps be taken to secure the opening of these lines. It was declared that their closing had had disastrous effects on business (Baltimore *American and Commercial Advertiser*, May 6, 1861).

63. Baltimore *Sun*, May 18, 1861.

64. *Ibid.*, May 8, 1861. On May 3, 1861, Governor Letcher wrote Governor Hicks: "I desire to cultivate amicable relations with the people of Maryland, and with this view will give instructions to Col. Jackson to restrain those under his command from all acts of violence and lawlessness" (Baltimore *Sun*, May 10, 1861).

65. G. F. R. Henderson, *Stonewall Jackson and the American Civil War*, Vol. I, p. 121; John D. Imboden, "Jackson at Harper's Ferry in 1861," in *Battles and Leaders of the Civil War*, Vol. I, p. 123.

CHAPTER IV

1. *Official Records*, I, Vol. LI, pt. 2, p. 50.

2. This account is reconstructed from Imboden, *op. cit.*, pp. 122-123; Baltimore *American and Commercial Advertiser*, May 28, 1861; *Thirty-Fifth Annual Report*, p. 46; Hungerford, *op. cit.*, Vol. II, pp. 6-8; Henderson, *op. cit.*, pp. 121-122.

3. *Official Records*, I, Vol. LI, pt. 2, p. 25.

4. *Ibid.*, p. 29.

5. *Ibid.*, pp. 31-32. There was however some difference of opinion in regard to the expediency of putting the northwestern counties in a state of defense. Upon learning of the plans of Major General Thomas S. Haymond to occupy Wheeling and defend it with arms, Judge George W. Thompson of the twelfth judicial circuit made this appeal to Governor John Letcher: "We are at peace, and such a procedure will only bring upon our people the bitterness of intestine feud and the military occupation of the northwest by the forces of the surrounding States under the authority of the Union, and if resistance is made it will make us the theater of civil war and predatory warfare, with the inability of the

NOTES

State or of the entire South to protect us. A glance at the map will satisfy you of our exposed and defenseless position, and just now we feel and are satisfied that our weakness is our strength, and our people desire to be left in that condition . . ." (*ibid.,* pp. 39-40).

6. *Official Records,* I, Vol. II, p. 788.

7. *Ibid.,* pp. 790-791.

8. *Ibid.,* pp. 802-803; Robert E. Lee to George A. Porterfield, May 4, 1861, *The Papers of George B. McClellan.*

9. *Official Records,* I, Vol. II, p. 860.

10. *Ibid.,* pp. 827, 855; Richmond *Daily Examiner,* June 11, 1861; Wheeling *Intelligencer,* May 13, 1861; Robert White, "West Virginia," in *Confederate Military History,* Vol. II, p. 8.

11. *Official Records,* I, Vol. II, p. 827; White, *op. cit.,* p. 8.

12. *Official Records,* I, Vol. II, p. 827.

13. *Ibid.,* p. 830; Lang, *op. cit.,* p. 25; White, *op. cit.,* p. 8.

14. *Official Records,* I, Vol. II, p. 843.

15. *Ibid.,* p. 855.

16. White, *op. cit.,* p. 9.

17. Thomas S. Haymond to William J. Willey, May 25, 1861, *McClellan Papers.*

18. Memorandum, 1861, in *ibid.;* George B. McClellan, *McClellan's Own Story,* p. 51.

19. George M. Hagans to G. B. McClellan, May 13, 1861, *McClellan Papers.*

20. William Dennison to Winfield Scott, May 20, 1861, *ibid.*

21. Winfield Scott to William Dennison, May 20, 1861, *ibid.*

22. William Dennison to George B. McClellan, May 20, 1861, *ibid.*

23. George B. McClellan to Simon Cameron, May 20, 1861, *ibid.*

24. Winfield Scott to George B. McClellan, May 21, 1861, *ibid.*

25. H. B. Carrington to Salmon P. Chase, June 16, 1861, *The Papers of Salmon P. Chase;* George B. McClellan to B. F. Kelley, May 26, 1861, *McClellan Papers;* Jacob D. Cox, *Military Reminiscences of the Civil War,* Vol. I, p. 42; Baltimore *Sun,* May 22, 1861.

26. Granville D. Hall, *The Rending of Virginia*, p. 287; White, *op. cit.*, p. 14.

27. George A. Porterfield to William J. Willey, May 25, 1861, *McClellan Papers*. A dispatch from Governor John Letcher to Porterfield dated May 25 indicates that the latter had merely anticipated the governor's wishes: "When you get matters in proper condition at Grafton, take the train some night, run up to Wheeling and seize and carry away the arms sent recently to that place by Cameron, the U. S. Secretary of War, and use them in arming such men as may rally to your camp. . . . It is advisable to cut off telegraphic communication between Wheeling and Washington, so that the disaffected at the former place cannot communicate with their allies at headquarters. . . . If troops from Ohio and Pennsylvania shall be attempted to be passed on the railroad, do not hesitate to obstruct their passage by all means in your power, even to the destruction of the road and bridges" (Richmond *Daily Examiner*, June 11, 1861).

28. *Official Records*, I, Vol. II, pp. 51-52; *Thirty-Fifth Annual Report*, pp. 46, 48; Wheeling *Intelligencer*, May 27, 1861; W. E. Porter, "Keeping the Baltimore and Ohio in Repair in War Time was a Task for Hercules," in *Book of the Royal Blue*, X, (July, 1907), p. 17. A bridge over Simpsons Creek was also destroyed but it was promptly repaired by the company.

29. Geo. B. McClellan to Benjamin F. Kelley, May 26, 1861, *McClellan Papers*; Geo. B. McClellan to Col. E. D. Townsend, May 26, 1861, *ibid.*; *Official Records*, I, Vol. II, pp. 44-47; McClellan, *op. cit.*, p. 50.

30. Geo. B. McClellan to Col. J. Irvine, May 26, 1861, *McClellan Papers*.

31. *Official Records*, I, Vol. II, pp. 44-47. McClellan claims entire responsibility and credit for this movement (McClellan, *Own Story*, p. 50). On the other hand Whitelaw Reid who excoriates McClellan at every turn gives all credit to Governor Dennison and War Department officials. *See* Whitelaw Reid, *Ohio in the War: Her Statesmen, Her Generals, and Soldiers*, Vol. I, p. 811. A dispatch from General Winfield Scott to McClellan dated May 24, 1861, lends support to the view that the latter did not act entirely on his own initiative. In this

NOTES

telegram Scott said: "We have certain intelligence that at least two companies of Virginia troops have reached Grafton, evidently with the purpose of overawing the friends of the Union in Western Virginia. Can you counteract the influence of that detachment? Act promptly, and Major Oakes, at Wheeling, may give you valuable assistance" (*Official Records*, I, Vol. II, p. 648). See also *ibid.*, p. 44.

32. *Official Records*, I, Vol. II, pp. 45, 49; W. H. H. Showacre to Francis H. Pierpont, April 4, 1862, *The Papers of Francis H. Pierpont;* Lang, *op. cit.*, p. 29. Kelley also sent a detachment forward to protect the railroad bridge across the Monongahela River at Fairmont (*Official Records*, I, Vol. II, p. 49).

33. *Official Records*, I, Vol. II, p. 52.

34. *Ibid.*, pp. 46, 49; George B. McClellan to Benjamin F. Kelley, May 26, 1861, *McClellan Papers;* George B. McClellan to Thomas A. Morris, May 28, 1861, *ibid.;* White, *op. cit.*, p. 15; Lang, *op. cit.*, p. 29.

35. George B. McClellan to Frederick W. Lander, May 27, 1861, *Lander Papers*.

36. *Official Records*, I, Vol. II, pp. 45, 46, 47.

37. George B. McClellan to Frederick W. Lander, May 27, 1861, *Lander Papers*. Similar instructions had been telegraphed to Kelley on May 26 (*Official Records*, I, Vol. II, pp. 45-46).

38. J. B. Steedman to F. W. Lander, 5 P.M., May 30, 1861, *Lander Papers*.

39. Statement of P. W. Shipley, Engineman, Engine No. 150, June 4, 1861, *ibid.;* F. W. Lander to G. B. McClellan, 7 P.M., May 30, 1861, 12:00 M. and 1:30 P.M., May 31, 1861, *ibid.*

40. J. B. Steedman to F. W. Lander, May 31, 1861, and 8:25 P.M., May 31, 1861, *ibid.*

41. J. B. Steedman to F. W. Lander, 4:15 A.M., June 1, 1861, *ibid.*

42. F. W. Lander to G. B. McClellan, June 8, 1861, *McClellan Papers*.

43. *Official Records*, I, Vol. II, p. 66.

44. Lang, *op. cit.*, p. 29.

45. *Official Records,* I, Vol. II, pp. 66-67; White, *op. cit.,* p. 16.

46. *Official Records,* I, Vol. II, p. 67.

47. The Confederate pickets were asleep and failed to give the alarm. (*Official Records,* I, Vol. II, pp. 69, 72.)

48. White, *op. cit.,* p. 16; Lang, *op. cit.,* pp. 31-32. Kelley was severely wounded in this engagement.

49. Reid, *op. cit.,* Vol. I, pp. 281, 281n.

50. Memorandum showing distribution of troops along the railroad in June, 1861; Thomas A. Morris to George B. Mc-Clellan, June 24, 1861, *McClellan Papers.*

51. Wheeling *Intelligencer,* June 20, 1861.

52. Frederick W. Lander to George B. McClellan, June 8, 1861; J. B. Steedman to George B. McClellan, July 3, 1861; J. W. Garrett to McClellan, June, 1861, *McClellan Papers;* statement of P. W. Shipley, Engineman, June 4, 1861, *Lander Papers.*

53. *Official Records,* I, Vol. LI, pt. 2, p. 124.

54. *Ibid.,* I, Vol. II, p. 239.

55. *Ibid.,* p. 237.

56. *McClellan Papers.*

57. G. B. McClellan to T. A. Morris, June 20, 1861, *ibid.*

58. *Official Records,* I, Vol. II, pp. 194, 195; George B. Mc-Clellan to William S. Rosecrans, June 22, 1861; *McClellan Papers;* George B. McClellan to Colonel E. D. Townsend, June 22, 1861, *ibid.*

59. Quoted in Reid, *op. cit.,* Vol. I, p. 811.

60. Not to be confused with West Union, the county seat of Doddridge County, (W.) Va.

61. *Official Records,* I, Vol. II, p. 224.

62. *Ibid.,* p. 195. *See* also Cox, *op. cit.,* Vol. I, p. 50.

63. *Official Records,* I, Vol. II, pp. 212, 213; Cox, *op. cit.,* Vol. I, p. 50.

64. *Official Records,* I, Vol. II, pp. 200, 201.

65. *Ibid.,* pp. 205-207; Cox, *op. cit.,* Vol. I, pp. 51-53.

66. *Official Records,* I, Vol. II, p. 204. McClellan did not occupy Beverly until the afternoon of July 12 (Cox, *op. cit.,* Vol. I, pp. 53-54).

67. *Official Records,* I, Vol. II, pp. 219, 220, 222, 223.

NOTES

68. *Ibid.,* pp. 224-225.
69. *Ibid.,* p. 225; Cox, *op. cit.,* Vol. I, p. 54.
70. *Official Records,* I, Vol. II, pp. 226, 233.
71. *Ibid.,* pp. 225, 226.
72. *Ibid.,* pp. 230, 231.
73. *Ibid.,* p. 228.
74. *Ibid.,* pp. 228, 232.

CHAPTER V

1. *Official Records,* I, Vol. II, p. 924; Nicolay and Hay, *op. cit.,* Vol. IV, pp. 317-318.
2. *Official Records,* I, Vol. II, p. 814.
3. *Ibid.,* p. 471.
4. *Ibid.,* Joseph E. Johnston, *Narrative of Military Operations,* p. 19.
5. *Official Records,* I, Vol. II, pp. 883, 904, 910.
6. Will H. Lowdermilk, *History of Cumberland,* p. 398.
7. Johnston, *op. cit.,* p. 22.
8. *Ibid.,* p. 23.
9. *Thirty-Fifth Annual Report,* p. 47.
10. *Official Records,* I, Vol. II, p. 471; Johnston, *op. cit.,* p. 23. On June 19, 1861, a detachment of Hill's command struck the Baltimore and Ohio at New Creek and destroyed the railroad bridge at that point (*Official Records,* I, Vol. II, p. 131).
11. *Ibid.,* pp. 904, 952. McDonald left Winchester, June 18, 1861. See Mrs. Cornelia McDonald, *A Diary with Reminiscences of the War and Refugee Life in the Shenandoah Valley, 1860-1865,* pp. 21, 21n.
12. *Official Records,* I, Vol. II, p. 472.
13. See *ibid.,* pp. 922, 949.
14. Johnston, *op. cit.,* p. 27.
15. *Official Records,* I, Vol. II, p. 949.
16. See above, p. 67.
17. *National Intelligencer,* July 12, 1861.
18. Baltimore *American and Commercial Advertiser,* June 26, 1861.
19. Wheeling *Intelligencer,* July 1, 1861.

THE BALTIMORE AND OHIO IN THE CIVIL WAR

20. Quotation from New York *Commercial Advertiser* in *National Intelligencer*, July 3, 1861.

21. *National Intelligencer*, June 28, 1861.

22. Baltimore *Exchange*, June 26, 1861. *See* also Baltimore *South*, June 25, 1861; Baltimore *Sun*, June 25, 1861.

23. Baltimore *Exchange*, June 26, 1861.

24. *Official Records*, I, Vol. II, p. 945.

25. *Ibid.*, pp. 472, 473.

26. *Statement of John W. Garrett, President of the Baltimore and Ohio Railroad Company, Made before the Committee on Military Affairs of the House of Representatives, On the 25th of April, 1862*, p. 9.

27. *Thirty-Fifth Annual Report*, p. 48; Baltimore *American and Commercial Advertiser*, July 22, 1861.

28. Wheeling *Intelligencer*, August 26, 1861.

29. *Diary of Sarah Morgan McKown*, August 22, 1861.

30. Hungerford, *op. cit.*, Vol. II, p. 14.

31. Quotation from Cincinnati *Gazette* in Baltimore *Sun*, October 4, 1861.

32. John A. Gano, Secretary, Merchants Exchange, Cincinnati, to Hon. Simon Cameron, Secretary of War, October 9, 1861, *Correspondence of the Secretary of War* (Adjutant General's Office).

33. Wheeling *Intelligencer*, October 9, 1861.

34. Quotation from Wheeling *Press* in Baltimore *American and Commercial Advertiser*, October 15, 1861.

35. Baltimore *Evening Patriot*, October 15, 1861.

36. Baltimore *American and Commercial Advertiser*, October 3, 1861. The reference is to McClellan.

37. John A. Gano, Secretary, Merchants Exchange, Cincinnati, to Hon. Simon Cameron, Secretary of War, October 9, 1861, *Correspondence of the Secretary of War* (Adjutant General's Office); J. R. Swan to S. P. Chase, October 19, 1861, *Chase Papers;* Baltimore *Sun*, October 14, 1861.

38. Baltimore *Evening Patriot*, October 28, 1861.

39. Quotation from New York *Evening Post* in *ibid.*, October 9, 1861.

40. S. M. Felton to Simon Cameron, December 21, 1861, *Cameron Papers*.

NOTES

41. *Reports of Committees of the House of Representatives,* 2d Sess. 37th Cong., Vol. II, p. 632.
42. *Ibid.,* p. 1373.
43. *Ibid.,* pp. xv, 632.
44. *Ibid.,* p. 629.
45. Baltimore *Evening Patriot,* October 28, 1861.
46. *Official Records,* I, Vol. V, pp. 338, 625.
47. *Ibid.,* pp. 379-380, 644.
48. *Thirty-Sixth Annual Report,* p. 48.
49. *Calendar of Virginia State Papers,* Vol. XI, p. 363.
50. *Ibid.,* p. 362.
51. J. H. Sullivan to S. P. Chase, December 10, 18, 1861, *Chase Papers.*
52. Baltimore *American and Commercial Advertiser,* December 3, 1861.
53. *Official Records,* I, Vol. V, p. 702; J. H. Sullivan to S. P. Chase, December 10, 1861, *Chase Papers.*
54. "Rosecrans's Campaigns," in *Report of the Joint Committee on the Conduct of the War,* 2d Sess. 38th Cong., pt. 3, p. 14.
55. *Official Records,* I, Vol. V, p. 913.
56. *Ibid.,* pp. 965-966; Allan, *op. cit.,* p. 14.
57. Allan, *op. cit.,* p. 14.
58. *Official Records,* I, Vol. V, p. 944; Allan, *op. cit.,* p. 14.
59. Allan, *op. cit.,* p. 16.
60. *Official Records,* I, Vol. V, pp. 390, 395, 1005; J. H. Sullivan to S. P. Chase, December 10, 1861, *Chase Papers;* Allan, *op. cit.,* pp. 16-17.
61. *Official Records,* I, Vol. V, p. 976.
62. *Ibid.; Thirty-Sixth Annual Report,* p. 49.
63. *Official Records,* I, Vol. V, pp. 1004-1005.
64. Allan, *op. cit.,* p. 20.
65. T. J. Jackson to "Officer Comdg. the United States Forces in & near Hancock, Md.," January 5, 1862, *Lander Papers.* Jackson had approximately 9,000 effectives (*Official Records,* I, Vol. V, pp. 1026-1027).
66. N. P. Banks to F. W. Lander, January 5, 1862, *Lander Papers.*

THE BALTIMORE AND OHIO IN THE CIVIL WAR

67. G. B. McClellan to N. P. Banks, January 7, 1862, Mc-Clellan Papers.

68. R. Morris Copeland, A. A. G., to F. W. Lander, January 7, 1862, Lander Papers.

69. Allan, op. cit., pp. 27-28. See also Official Records, I, Vol. V, p. 1039.

70. Official Records, I, Vol. V, pp. 1047, 1053, 1054; Mary Anna Jackson, Memoirs of Stonewall Jackson, pp. 225-228.

71. F. W. Lander to G. B. McClellan, February 6, 1862, McClellan Papers; Wheeling Intelligencer, February 20, 1862.

72. Thirty-Sixth Annual Report, p. 50.

73. Official Records, I, Vol. XII, pt. 3, p. 6; Edwin M. Stanton to George B. McClellan, March 24, 1862, McClellan Papers; Baltimore American and Commercial Advertiser, March 29, 1862. Other members of the cabinet were instrumental in securing military protection for the Baltimore and Ohio Railroad. Of these Salmon P. Chase, Secretary of the Treasury, and Montgomery Blair, Postmaster General, received most prominent mention. (See Baltimore American and Commercial Advertiser, March 29, 1862.)

74. George B. McClellan to F. W. Lander, February 28, 1862, McClellan Papers.

75. George B. McClellan to F. W. Lander, February 28, 1862, Lander Papers; Official Records, I, Vol. V, p. 731.

76. Wheeling Intelligencer, March 14, 1862; Allan, op. cit., pp. 40-41; L. F. Barstow, A. A. G., Paw Paw, to George B. McClellan, March 2, 1862; James Shields to G. B. McClellan, March 10, 1862, McClellan Papers.

77. Thirty-Sixth Annual Report, pp. 51-52; Official Records, I, Vol. XII, pt. 3, p. 6. The term "burnt district" was applied to that part of the Baltimore and Ohio which had been completely destroyed by the Confederates.

78. Thirty-Sixth Annual Report, pp. 52-53; Baltimore Sun, March 26, 1862; Baltimore American and Commercial Advertiser, March 29, 1862; Wheeling Intelligencer, March 8, 29, and April 3, 1862.

79. Baltimore American and Commercial Advertiser, April 12, 1862; Wheeling Intelligencer, April 5, 17, 21, 1862.

NOTES

CHAPTER VI

1. *Journal of the House of Delegates of the State of Virginia for the Called Session of 1862*, p. 88.
2. Wheeling *Intelligencer*, May 31 and June 6, 1862.
3. *Thirty-Sixth Annual Report*, pp. 55-56.
4. Henderson, *op. cit.*, Vol. II, pp. 366-367; *Official Records*, I, Vol. LI, pt. 2, p. 637.
5. *Thirty-Seventh Annual Report*, p. 42.
6. *Thirty-Sixth Annual Report*, p. 8.
7. *Thirty-Seventh Annual Report*, p. 41; Wheeling *Intelligencer*, October 6, 1862.
8. *Official Records*, I, Vol. XXI, p. 31; John Codman Ropes, *The Story of the Civil War*, Vol. II, p. 454.
9. *See* below, Chapter X.
10. *Address of John W. Garrett, on his Re-Election as President of the Baltimore & Ohio R. R. Co. On the 23d November, 1864, Sketching the Policy and Prospects of the Company*, p. 5.
11. *Thirty-Seventh Annual Report*, p. 43.
12. *Ibid.*, p. 48.
13. *Ibid.*, pp. 48-53; *American Railroad Journal*, August 15, 1863; Wheeling *Intelligencer*, August 12, 1863.
14. *Thirty-Seventh Annual Report*, p. 49.
15. Charles M. Pepper, *The Life and Times of Henry Gassaway Davis*, pp. 30-31.
16. *Address of John W. Garrett, 23d November, 1864*, p. 5.
17. *Thirty-Eighth Annual Report*, pp. 57-58.
18. *Ibid.*, p. 62.
19. *Ibid.*, pp. 57-58.
20. *Ibid.*, pp. 59-62.
21. *Official Records*, I, Vol. XXV, pt. 2, pp. 652, 685, 710-712.
22. *Ibid.*, pp. 652-653.
23. *Ibid.*, p. 685.
24. *Ibid.*, pp. 652, 684-685.
25. *Ibid.*, pp. 710-711.
26. *Ibid.*, 710-712.
27. *Ibid.*, pt. 1, p. 119.

28. *Ibid.*, p. 116.

29. The Federal force consisted of 86 men from parts of Co. G, 23rd Ill., Captain Martin Wallace, and Co. A, 14th (W.) Va., Captain Jacob Smith (John Bigelow, Jr., *The Campaign of Chancellorsville; A Strategic and Tactical Study*, p. 462).

30. William N. McDonald, *A History of the Laurel Brigade*, pp. 121-122.

31. Bigelow, *op. cit.*, p. 463.

32. *Official Records*, I, Vol. XXV, pt. 1, pp. 115-118.

33. *Ibid.*, p. 117. In his *Loyal West Virginia from 1861 to 1865*, p. 260, Lang states that there were but 220 men.

34. *Official Records*, I, Vol. XXV, pt. 1, pp. 127-128; Genevieve Brown, *A History of the Sixth Regiment, West Virginia Infantry Volunteers* (MS), pp. 30-31.

35. *Ibid.*, pp. 114, 118, 122-123; *Thirty-Seventh Annual Report*, p. 46; Baltimore *Sun*, April 30, 1863.

36. *Diary of William L. Wilson*, April 28, 1863 (MS).

37. George Baylor, *Bull Run to Bull Run*, p. 137.

38. John Bayles to author, May 16, 1938; Wilson, *Diary*, April 27, 1863; *Official Records*, I, Vol. XXV, pt. 1, p. 126.

39. Bigelow, *op. cit.*, p. 465; *Official Records*, I, Vol. XXV, pt. 1, p. 126.

40. Baylor, *op. cit.*, p. 138. Efforts of the invaders to propitiate the ladies were however of no avail. When asked to sing or play they gave the "Star-Spangled Banner," "Hooker is Our Leader," or some other decidedly Union sentiment (Bigelow, *op. cit.*, p. 465).

41. *Official Records*, I, Vol. XXV, pt. 1, pp. 113-114, 118.

42. *Ibid.*, p. 118.

43. *Ibid.*, pp. 118, 122-123; *Thirty-Seventh Annual Report*, p. 46; Wheeling *Intelligencer*, May 6, 1863. While in Fairmont the Confederates burned the library of Governor Francis H. Pierpont "in retaliation for a like act on the part of the ambitious little man" (*Official Records*, I, Vol. XXV, pt. 1, p. 120).

44. *Official Records*, I, Vol. XXV, pt. 1, pp. 119, 133; Letter Book, Vol. II, p. 25 (June 8, 1863), *Stanton Papers*.

45. *Official Records*, I, Vol. XXV, pt. 1, p. 119.

NOTES

46. Imboden had 1,825 men on April 20 but next day being reinforced at Hightown his number swelled to about 3,365, of which about 700 were cavalry. General Lee sent him the 25th and 31st Virginia regiments of infantry (Bigelow, *op. cit.*, pp. 124, 460).

47. This force consisted of about 900 men under command of Colonel George R. Latham (Bigelow, *op. cit.*, p. 461).

48. *Official Records*, I, Vol. XXV, pt. 1, pp. 98-101. A body of Imboden's cavalry reached the Baltimore and Ohio and destroyed many of the small bridges between Mannington and Moundsville.

49. *Official Records*, I, Vol. XXV, pt. 1, pp. 119-120.

50. *Ibid.*, p. 120.

51. *Ibid.*

52. *Ibid.*, p. 121.

53. *Ibid.*

54. *Ibid.*, pt. 2, pp. 442, 453.

55. *Ibid.*, pp. 285-286, 299, 300.

56. *Ibid.*, p. 299.

57. *Ibid.*, pp. 279, 295.

58. *Ibid.*, pp. 428-429; Wheeling *Intelligencer*, April 29, 1863.

59. *Official Records*, I, Vol. XXV, pt. 2, p. 295. Bigelow, *op. cit.*, states that the consolidated report of April 30, 1863, shows that Schenck had 34,297 men available for duty in his department (p. 467).

60. *Thirty-Seventh Annual Report*, p. 47. Passengers, freight, mails and baggage were transferred at Fairmont "by wagons and Pontoon Bridge" pending the reconstruction of the railroad bridge over the Monongahela River.

61. *Thirty-Seventh Annual Report*, p. 55.

62. *Official Records*, I, Vol. XXXIII, pp. 499-500; Douglas Southall Freeman, (ed.), *Lee's Dispatches*, p. 134; *Thirty-Eighth Annual Report*, p. 53; Wheeling *Intelligencer*, February 3, 1864; Baltimore *Sun*, February 4, 1864.

63. Harry Gilmor, *Four Years in the Saddle*, p. 194.

64. *Official Records*, I, Vol. XXXIII, pp. 151, 154, and Vol. XLVI, pt. 2, p. 559; *Thirty-Eighth Annual* Report, p. 53;

THE BALTIMORE AND OHIO IN THE CIVIL WAR

Baltimore *Sun,* February 13, 1864; Wheeling *Intelligencer,* February 15, 1864; Gilmor, *op. cit.,* pp. 144-147.

65. *Official Records,* I, Vol. XXXVII, pt. 1, pp. 68, 69, 382, 383, 392; Baltimore *Sun,* May 6, 1864; Baltimore *American and Commercial Advertiser,* May 9, 1864; Wheeling *Intelligencer,* May 9, 1864.

66. *Official Records,* I, Vol. XXXVII, pt. 1, pp. 383, 393, 397, 398, 399, 406, 408, 409.

67. *Ibid.,* Vol. XLIII, pt. 2, p. 385; Wheeling *Intelligencer,* October 17, 1864; Charles Wells Russell, (ed.), *The Memoirs of Colonel John S. Mosby,* pp. 313-321. *See* also James J. Williamson, *Mosby's Rangers,* pp. 260-263.

68. Russell, *op. cit.,* p. 315.

69. Wheeling *Intelligencer,* October 17, 1864.

70. *Official Records,* I, Vol. XLIII, pt. 2, pp. 693, 707; *Thirty-Ninth Annual Report,* p. 40; Wheeling *Intelligencer,* November 29, 30, and December 1, 2, 6, 9, 1864; Baltimore *Sun,* December 6, 1864. Other small raids occurred on December 5, 1864, February 3, and March 30, 1865. *See Thirty-Ninth Annual Report,* pp. 40-44; *Official Records,* I, Vol. XLVI, pt. 2, pp. 182, 188-189, 384, 411-412; Baltimore *Sun,* April 1, 1865; and Wheeling *Intelligencer,* April 1, 1865.

CHAPTER VII

1. W. E. Porter, "Keeping the Baltimore and Ohio in Repair in War Time was a Task for Hercules," in *Book of the Royal Blue,* Vol. X (July, 1907).

2. Ropes, *op. cit.,* Vol. I, pp. 123-124.

3. *Ibid.,* p. 124.

4. Wheeling *Intelligencer,* April 1, 1862. This was in effect a reassignment (See *Official Records,* I, Vol. V, pp. 552, 691).

5. *Official Records,* I, Vol. XII, pt. 3, pp. 30-31.

6. *Ibid.,* p. 350.

7. *Ibid.,* pp. 201-202, 397.

8. The Middle Department embraced all of Pennsylvania and Delaware and all of Maryland except the counties adjacent to the Potomac River (*Official Records Atlas,* Vol. II, plate clxv).

NOTES

9. "Special Orders No. 146," in *Special Orders Issued from the Adjutant General's Office* (1862). Wool had been given command of all forces guarding the railroad between Cumberland and Baltimore on June 17, 1862. Consequently Miles's forces came under Wool's jurisdiction on that date. Kelley's troops were attached to Wool's command by a special order issued from the Adjutant General's Office on June 27, 1862.

10. *Official Records,* I, Vol. XII, pt. 3, p. 477.

11. *Ibid.,* p. 520, and Vol. LI, pt. 1, pp. 713-714.

12. *Ibid.,* Vol. XXI, pp. 864, 874; Wheeling *Intelligencer,* December 30, 1862; Cox, *op. cit.,* Vol. I, p. 444.

13. *Official Records,* I, Vol. XXV, pt. 2, pp. 158-159.

14. *Ibid.,* p. 295.

15. *See* Cox, *op. cit.,* Vol. I, p. 444.

16. *Official Records,* I, Vol. XXIII, pt. 2, pp. 454-455.

17. Wheeling *Intelligencer,* February 12, 1864.

18. Edwin M. Stanton to Horace Greeley, Letter Book III, pt. 1, pp. 83-85, *Stanton Papers;* quotation from New York *Herald* in Wheeling *Intelligencer,* March 1, 1864.

19. Quotations from New York *Herald* and Wellsburg (W. Va.) *Herald* in Wheeling *Intelligencer,* February 26, 1864, March 1, 1864.

20. *Official Records,* I, Vol. XXXVII, pt. 1, pp. 396, 422.

21. *Ibid.,* Vol. XII, pt. 3, pp. 24, 25, 28.

22. Baltimore *Sun,* March 31, 1862.

23. "Letters from Commanding Generals in Relation to Military Protection of Baltimore and Ohio Railroad and Chesapeake and Ohio Canal," in *Miscellaneous Documents of the House of Representatives,* 3d Sess. 37th Cong., No. 15, p. 3.

24. *Ibid.,* p. 4.

25. *Congressional Globe,* January 12, 1863, p. 283.

26. George W. Conrad to James Conrad, November 23, 1862; George W. Conrad to "Father and Mother," December 29, 1862, *The Letters of George W. Conrad.*

27. "The B. & O. R. R. The Base of Operations for the Federal Army in 1863-65: Reminiscences of Maj. S. F. Shaw," in *Book of the Royal Blue,* Vol. II, p. 11 (October, 1898); Wheeling *Intelligencer,* June 16, 1863.

28. Special Orders No. 129 (108A, 1863), *Correspondence of the Adjutant General's Office.*

29. *Official Records,* I, Vol. XXXVII, pt. 1, pp. 355-356. *See also ibid.,* Vol. LI, pt. 1, p. 1069.

30. These "iron clads" were also used to cover the rebuilding and reconstruction of the road following Confederate raids (*Official Records,* I, Vol. XXXVII, pt. 2, p. 397).

31. *Ibid.,* Vol. XXV, pt. 2, p. 482.

CHAPTER VIII

1. Graham A. Barringer, "The Influence of Railroad Transportation on the Civil War," in *Studies in American History Inscribed to James Albert Woodburn,* p. 255.

2. *Official Records,* I, Vol. XII, pt. 3, p. 551; Cox, *op. cit.,* Vol. I, pp. 224-225.

3. *Official Records,* I, Vol. XII, pt. 3, pp. 555, 560.

4. *Ibid.,* pp. 560-561.

5. Cox, *op. cit.,* Vol. I, p. 227.

6. *Ibid.,* pp. 226-229.

7. Wheeling *Intelligencer,* June 15, 1865; Cox, *op. cit.,* Vol. I, p. 228.

8. Wheeling *Intelligencer,* June 15, 1865.

9. Ropes, *op. cit.,* Vol. II, p. 269; Cox, *op. cit.,* pp. 228-231.

10. James Ford Rhodes, *History of the United States from the Compromise of 1850,* Vol. IV, p. 399; Barringer, *op. cit.,* p. 271.

11. Journal, September 24, 1863, *Chase Papers.*

12. Charles A. Dana to Edwin M. Stanton, September 23, 1863, *Stanton Papers.*

13. Journal, September 24, 1863, *Chase Papers.*

14. *Ibid.*

15. *Ibid.*

16. Quoted in *ibid.* by Secretary Chase as Lincoln's own words.

17. *Ibid.*

18. *Ibid.*

19. *Stanton Papers.* It is not improbable that these telegrams were sent before the President and the Cabinet had

NOTES

reached a decision. The message to Felton is dated "Sept. 23d 1863 11-P.M."; to Garrett, "September 23d 1863 11-20 P.M."; and to Scott, "Sept 23 1863 12:15 P.M." The latter date was obviously September 24, 1863, 12:15 A.M.

20. Henry W. Halleck to George G. Meade, September 24, 1863, *Stanton Papers.*

21. John W. Garrett to H. J. Jewett, September 24, 1863; John W. Garrett to Dillard Ricketts, September 24, 1863; and Edwin M. Stanton to Thomas A. Scott, September 28, 1863, *ibid.*

22. John W. Garrett to Joseph Hooker, September 25, 1863; John W. Garrett to H. J. Jewett, September 24, 1863; and John W. Garrett to Edwin M. Stanton, October 4, 1863, *ibid.* Lewis M. Cole was commissioned captain and assigned as aide to Hooker (John W. Garrett to H. J. Jewett, September 24, 1863, *ibid.*). William P. Smith was offered a captaincy but refused it. He stated that he deserved a higher grade (Smith to Stanton, September 27, 1863, *ibid.*).

23. John W. Garrett to Edwin M. Stanton, September 25, 1863, *ibid.*

24. John W. Garrett to H. J. Jewett, September 24, 1863, *ibid.*

25. John W. Garrett to Dillard Ricketts, September 24, 1863, *ibid.*

26. John W. Garrett to L. M. Hubby, J. M. McCullough, L. L. Hommedieu, W. H. Clement, and John Newman, September 24, 1863, *ibid.*

27. John W. Garrett to Joseph Hooker, September 25, 1863; William P. Smith to Edwin M. Stanton, September 28, 1863, *ibid.*

28. J. W. Garrett to E. M. Stanton, September 25, 1863, *ibid.*

29. William P. Smith to Edwin M. Stanton, September 27, 1863, *ibid.*

30. David Homer Bates, *Lincoln in the Telegraph Office,* p. 179.

31. William P. Smith to Edwin M. Stanton, September 27, 1863, *Stanton Papers.*

255

THE BALTIMORE AND OHIO IN THE CIVIL WAR

32. D. C. McCallum to Edwin M. Stanton, September 26, 1863, *ibid.*

33. William P. Smith to D. C. McCallum, September 26, 1863, *ibid.*

34. D. C. McCallum to Edwin M. Stanton, September 28, 1863; Edwin M. Stanton to Thomas A. Scott, September 27, 1863, *ibid.*

35. William P. Smith to Edwin M. Stanton, September 27, 1863, *ibid.*

36. William P. Smith to Edwin M. Stanton, September 27, 1863, *ibid.*

37. Edwin M. Stanton to William P. Smith, September 27, 1863, *ibid.*

38. William P. Smith to Edwin M. Stanton, September 27, 1863, *ibid.*

39. Edwin M. Stanton to Carl Schurz, September 27, 1863, *ibid.*

40. Edwin M. Stanton to William P. Smith, September 27, 1863, *ibid.*

41. Carl Schurz to Edwin M. Stanton, September 28, 1863, *ibid.*

42. Edwin M. Stanton to Carl Schurz, September 28, 1863, *ibid.*

43. William P. Smith to Edwin M. Stanton, September 28, 1863, *ibid.*

44. Edwin M. Stanton to William P. Smith, September 28, 1863, *ibid.*

45. William P. Smith to Edwin M. Stanton, September 28, 1863, *ibid.*

46. William P. Smith to Edwin M. Stanton, October 1, 1863, *ibid.*

47. William P. Smith to Edwin M. Stanton, September 29, 1863, *ibid.*

48. Edwin M. Stanton to Jeremiah T. Boyle, September 24, 1863, *ibid.*

49. Thomas A. Scott to Edwin M. Stanton, September 29, 1863, *ibid.*

50. Thomas A. Scott to Edwin M. Stanton, September 30, 1863, *ibid.*

NOTES

51. Thomas A. Scott to Edwin M. Stanton, October 6, 1863, *ibid.*
52. Lewis M. Cole to Edwin M. Stanton, October 6, 1863, *ibid.*
53. Bates, *op. cit.*, p. 179.
54. John W. Garrett to Edwin M. Stanton, October 4, 1863, *Stanton Papers.*
55. Thomas A. Scott to Edwin M. Stanton, October 5, 1863, *ibid.*
56. John W. Garrett to Edwin M. Stanton, October 12, 1863, *ibid.*
57. Henry W. Halleck to George Meade, September 26, 1863, *ibid.*
58. *Official Records,* I, Vol. XXIX, pt. 1, pp. 149-150.
59. *See* dispatches quoted in Bates, *op. cit.*, pp. 181-182.
60. Thomas A. Scott to Edwin M. Stanton, October 5 and 6, 1863, *Stanton Papers.*
61. Joseph Hooker to Edwin M. Stanton, October 11, 1863, *ibid.*
62. For interesting comment, *see* Edwin A. Pratt, *The Rise of Rail-Power in War and Conquest* (1833-1914), pp. 23-24; also Charles F. Benjamin, "Recollections of Secretary Stanton," in *Century Magazine,* Vol. XXXIII, p. 767 (March, 1887). On September 28, 1863, Secretary Salmon P. Chase wrote: "If this whole movement is carried through to the end as well as it has been thus far, it will be an achievement in the transportation of troops unprecedented, I think, in history (Journal, *Chase Papers*).
63. Less noteworthy movements were made over the Baltimore and Ohio in 1864 and 1865. In June-July, 1864, Major General David Hunter's army having been repulsed in front of Lynchburg fell back to Parkersburg. It was transported immediately over the Baltimore and Ohio to Martinsburg to meet Early's advance down the Valley (*Official Records,* I, Vol. XXXVII, pt. 2, pp. 63, 354). A more extensive movement occurred early in the following year. In January, 1865, Major General John M. Schofield's corps consisting of 15,000 men was transported from Clifton, Tennessee, to Washington, a distance of fourteen hundred miles, in eleven days. The last

257

four hundred miles of this journey were made over the Baltimore and Ohio (*Official Records*, I, Vol. XLVII, pt. 2, pp. 153-154, 204, 214-216, 217, 218, 219, 280).

CHAPTER IX

1. Quotation from Morgantown *Star* in Wheeling *Intelligencer*, September 9, 1861.

2. The Point Pleasant *Register* made comment on this point early in 1863: "Notwithstanding the disproportion of State revenue extorted from the 'uncouth trans-Alleghany country,' out of an aggregate of $40,000,000 expended in internal improvements, we received but the pittance of $1,500,-000—being one dollar in every eighteen. While railroads cover *East Virginia*, we make the sorry show of but one—the Baltimore and Ohio, and the construction of that, after repeated denials, was reluctantly permitted, not to those 'to the manor born,' but to Baltimore capitalists..." (quotation from Point Pleasant *Register* in Wheeling *Intelligencer*, February 9, 1863.)

3. James C. McGregor, *The Disruption of Virginia*, p. 24. Ephraim B. Hall of Marion County made the following observation on the railroad policy of Virginia: "They seem to have constructed their roads as a mere *local convenience* with one or two exceptions, and to have carefully avoided opening up intercourse or communication with any place or people North of the Potomac or West of the Allegheny mountains; ..." (Wheeling *Intelligencer*, March 6, 1863).

4. Wheeling *Intelligencer*, August 10, 1861.

5. *Ibid.*, August 22, 1861; Virgil A. Lewis, *How West Virginia Was Made*, pp. 284-285.

6. L. A. Hagans, Secretary of the Commonwealth of Virginia (Reorganized Government), to John Hall, President of the West Virginia Constitutional Convention, December 4, 1861, *Debates and Proceedings of the West Virginia Constitutional Convention* (1861-1863) (MS).

7. *Debates and Proceedings*, December 6, 1861.

8. *Eighth Census of the United States*, Vol. I, p. 516.

9. Sam M. Hendricks, commander, Henry Kyd Douglas

258

NOTES

Camp, Sons of Confederate Veterans, Shepherdstown, W. Va., to author, November 13, 1937.

10. *Debates and Proceedings,* December 11, 1861.

11. Wheeling *Intelligencer,* March 15, 1862.

12. *See* above, p. 102.

13. One need only examine Virginia's attitude toward the Baltimore and Ohio in the antebellum period to see that this apprehension was based on fact. *See* above, Chapters I and II. That there was genuine hostility to the Baltimore and Ohio during the war period is evidenced in Governor John Letcher's message to the Virginia General Assembly in September, 1862 (*See* above, p. 118). Later this editorial appeared in the Richmond *Enquirer:* "The Baltimore and Ohio railroad—the *teterrima causa* of the only infidelity within the limits of Virginia—is disabled, not so permanently, we fear, as it should be. If our corps of sappers and miners, instead of exploding their mines 'forty yards' without the enemy's works, could put a ton or two of gunpowder into the Kingwood and Boardtree tunnels—if they could blow in the shafts, apply *fowgasses* to the arched masonry, and bring down the whole interior of these important works, it must be months before the road could be repaired and reopened. If it could be permanently closed it would be some small atonement for the folly of ever having permitted its construction" (Baltimore *Sun,* August 17, 1864).

14-17. *Debates and Proceedings,* December 10, 1861.

18-26. *Ibid.,* December 11, 1861.

27. *Ibid. See* also Granville Parker, *The Formation of the State of West Virginia, and Other Incidents of the Late Civil War,* pp. 59-62.

28-36. *Debates and Proceedings,* December 11, 1861.

37-46. *Ibid.,* December 12, 1861.

47. *Ibid.,* December 13, 1861.

48. *Acts of the General Assembly of Virginia* (Reorganized Government, Extra Session) 1862-1863, p. 38; John Marshall Hagans, *Sketch of the Erection and Formation of the State of West Virginia,* p. 72n.

49. *Acts of General Assembly* (Reorganized Government, Extra Session) 1862-1863, p. 66.

THE BALTIMORE AND OHIO IN THE CIVIL WAR

50. *Acts of the Legislature of West Virginia* (First Session), pp. 33-34.
51. *Ibid.*, pp. 103-105.
52. *Congressional Globe*, 39th Cong., 1st Sess., Appendix, p. 426.
53. 11 Wallace, 39-65.

CHAPTER X

1. *See* above, p. 19. The Baltimore and Ohio company collected a charge of 3¾ cents per mile for passengers and from 5 to 8 cents per ton per mile for freight on the Washington Branch (*Senate Documents*, 2d Sess. 37th Cong., No. 1, p. 11).
2. Wheeling *Intelligencer*, October 22, 1861; Ropes, *op. cit.*, Vol. I, p. 181.
3. *Statement of John W. Garrett, President of the Baltimore and Ohio Railroad Company, Made before the Committee on Military Affairs of the House of Representatives, On the 25th of April, 1862, In Opposition to the "Proposition" of the Metropolitan Railroad Company, To Build a Road making Direct Communication between Washington and New York,* p. 7.
4. *See* above, p. 109.
5. *Statement of John W. Garrett before Committee on Military Affairs*, April 25, 1862, p. 19.
6. *House Miscellaneous Documents*, 2d Sess. 37th Cong., No. 65, p. 2.
7. *Ibid.*, pp. 3-5.
8. *Senate Documents*, 2d Sess. 37th Cong., No. 1, p. 11; *Official Records*, III, Vol. I, pp. 705-706. For comment, *see American Railroad Journal*, December 7, 1861.
9. *Statement of John W. Garrett before Committee on Military Affairs*, April 25, 1862, p. 3.
10. *House Executive Documents*, 2d Sess. 37th Cong., No. 79, p. 2.
11. *Ibid.*, p. 2.
12. *Ibid.*, p. 3.
13. *Ibid*, pp. 3-6.
14. *Ibid.*, p. 5.

NOTES

15. *Ibid.,* p. 3.

16. *Ibid.,* p. 7. Garrett's reply to the Secretary of War may be found also in a pamphlet entitled, *Correspondence Between the Secretary of War and the President of the Baltimore and Ohio Railroad Company in Relation to Additional Routes Between Washington and New York, and Improvements of the Established Railway Line* (Baltimore, 1862). *See* also Baltimore *Sun,* March 8, 1862.

17. James D. Richardson, (ed.), *A Compilation of the Messages and Papers of the Presidents 1789-1897,* Vol. VI, p. 46; Lewis Henry Haney, *A Congressional History of Railways in the United States, 1850-1887,* p. 157.

18. *Congressional Globe,* January 21, 1862, p. 427. The bill contained a provision which also gave the President power "to extend, repair and complete the same" *(ibid.,* February 28, 1862, p. 1015).

19. *Ibid.,* January 28, 1862, p. 508.

20. *Ibid.,* pp. 508-509.

21. Haney, *op. cit.,* pp. 158-159.

22. *Official Records,* III, Vol. II, pp. 75, 795. *See* also Richardson, *op. cit.,* Vol. VI, p. 113.

23. It will be recalled that during the movement of Hooker's two corps from the Rappahannock to the Tennessee in September-October, 1863, the United States exercised actual control of the railroads involved.

24. Baltimore *Sun,* April 12, 1862; *Congressional Globe,* April 10, 1862, p. 1612.

25. *Congressional Globe,* April 10, 1862, p. 1612.

26. *Statement of John W. Garrett before Committee on Military Affairs,* April 25, 1862, pp. 3, 4-10, 14-19. The construction of an arm of the Metropolitan Railroad from Washington to Millersville on Round Bay had also been recommended. A memorandum, dated June 25, 1862, contains this comment on the Metropolitan-Millersville route: "The construction of the road to Washington [from Round Bay] will economize in all army transportation & if the Northern Central R. R. should be continued down to Round bay Government can save one dollar per ton on all coal required for the the navy" *(Chase Papers).*

261

27. *Senate Miscellaneous Documents,* 3d Sess. 37th Cong., No. 26, pp. 1-4.

28. *Congressional Globe,* February 7, 1863, p. 773.

29. *Ibid.,* January 14, 1863, p. 314.

30. *Ibid.,* February 9, 12, 14, 1863, pp. 826, 913, 971; also March 3, 1863, p. 1547. The first attempt to report the measure was met by an objection from Vallandigham (Ohio).

31. *Senate Reports,* 3d Sess. 37th Cong., No. 81, p. 1.

32. *Ibid.,* pp. 1, 2.

33. *Congressional Globe,* January 29, February 4, 18, March 3, 1863, pp. 584, 702, and pt. 2, pp. 1042, 1499-1500.

34. *Thirty-Ninth Annual Report,* p. 7.

35. *Address of John W. Garrett on his re-election as President of the Baltimore & Ohio R. R. Co., On the 23d November, 1864,* p. 12; *House Miscellaneous Documents,* 2d Sess. 38th Cong., No. 54, p. 4; *Address of John W. Garrett to the Board of Directors of the Baltimore & Ohio Railroad Company Upon his Re-Election as President of that Company, December, 1865,* p. 6.

36. *Congressional Globe,* February 18, 1865, pp. 911-913.

37. *Ibid.,* pp. 912-913; Haney, *op. cit.,* pp. 161-162.

38. *Journal of the Proceedings of the House of Delegates of the State of Maryland* (January Session, 1865), p. 202.

39. *Ibid.,* p. 297.

40. *House Miscellaneous Documents,* 2d Sess. 38th Cong., No. 54, pp. 1-4.

BIBLIOGRAPHY

Manuscript Material

The Papers of Jonathan M. Bennett. West Virginia University Library. The correspondence of the Auditor of Public Accounts of Virginia from 1857 to 1865. Contain a few items on the Baltimore and Ohio before 1861.

The Papers of Simon Cameron. Manuscript Division of the Library of Congress. A few letters throw light on wartime competition between Baltimore and Ohio and Pennsylvania Central railroads. There are other pertinent items.

The Papers of Salmon P. Chase. Manuscript Division of the Library of Congress. Include a score of letters and a journal containing confidential matter on the Baltimore and Ohio.

The Letters of George W. Conrad. Dr. Roy Bird Cook Private Collection, Charleston, West Virginia. Letters home by a member of the First Regiment, Virginia Cavalry (Union).

The Papers of Robert Garrett and Sons. Manuscript Division of the Library of Congress. Correspondence and business documents of three generations of the Garrett family, chiefly of John Work Garrett, President of the Baltimore and Ohio (1858-1884). A large and invaluable source for this study.

The Papers of Frederick W. Lander. Manuscript Division of the Library of Congress. A small but valuable collection of items on military operations in Virginia and Maryland prior to March, 1862.

The Papers of George B. McClellan. Manuscript Division of the Library of Congress. Indispensable for military operations in northwest and northeast Virginia during the first year of the war.

Diary of Sarah Morgan McKown. West Virginia University Library. A daily record from 1860 to 1866 written by a

263

resident of Berkeley County, (West) Virginia. Some comment on military operations in the vicinity of Martinsburg, (West) Virginia.

The Papers of Francis H. Pierpont. Department of Archives and History, Charleston, West Virginia, and West Virginia University Library, Morgantown. Public and private papers of the Union war governor of Virginia. A few railroad items.

The Papers of Edwin M. Stanton. Manuscript Division of the Library of Congress. Contain much Baltimore and Ohio material not found in printed official records.

War Department Archives. Washington, D. C., and Fort Myer, Virginia. Correspondence of the Secretary of War, the Adjutant General, and the Quartermaster General. Contain a few Baltimore and Ohio items not found in the *Official Records of the Rebellion.*

Debates and Proceedings of the West Virginia Constitutional Convention (1861-1863). Department of Archives and History, Charleston, West Virginia. Stenographic notes by Granville D. Hall, an assistant secretary of the convention. Invaluable for influence of Baltimore and Ohio on the formation of West Virginia.

Diary of William L. Wilson. In temporary possession of author. Daily record by a private in Company B, Twelfth Virginia Cavalry (Confederate). Contains illuminating matter on Jones-Imboden Raid.

Printed Material
(Much Abbreviated)

A Statement showing the Effect That Might be Produced against the State of Maryland and City of Baltimore by the Proposed Increase of the Stockholder Directors in the Baltimore and Ohio R. R. Company, by a Marylander. [Baltimore, 1860].

Acts of the General Assembly of the State of Virginia. Richmond. Various volumes.

Acts of the General Assembly of the State of Virginia (Reorganized Government, 1861-1863). Wheeling.

BIBLIOGRAPHY

Acts of the Legislature of West Virginia (1863-1865). Wheeling.

Address of John W. Garrett on his re-election as President of the Baltimore & Ohio R. R. Co., On the 23d November, 1864, Sketching the Policy and Prospects of the Company. Baltimore, 1865.

Address of John W. Garrett to the Board of Directors of the Baltimore & Ohio Railroad Company Upon His Re-Election as President of that Company, December, 1865. Baltimore, 1865.

Allan, William, *History of the Campaign of General T. J. (Stonewall) Jackson in the Shenandoah Valley of Virginia.* Philadelphia, 1880.

Ambler, Charles Henry, *A History of Transportation in the Ohio Valley.* Glendale, Cal., 1932.

———, *Francis H. Pierpont: Union War Governor of Virginia and Father of West Virginia.* Chapel Hill, 1937.

———, *Sectionalism in Virginia from 1776 to 1861.* Chicago, 1910.

American Railroad Journal (New York).

Andrews, Matthew Page, *History of Maryland: Province and State.* Garden City, N. Y., 1929.

Annual Reports of the President and Directors to the Stockholders of the Baltimore and Ohio Railroad Company (1853-1865). Baltimore, 1853-1866.

"Annual Reports of the Rail Road Companies of the State of Virginia, Made to the Board of Public Works for the Year Ending September 30, 1860," in *Virginia Documents* (1861-1862), Part 3. Richmond, 1862.

Anonymous, "The B & O R. R. The Base of Operations for the Federal Army in 1863-1865: Reminiscences of Maj. S. F. Shaw," in *Book of the Royal Blue,* II, (October, 1898). Baltimore, 1898.

Ashcroft, John, *Railway Directory for 1862.* New York, 1862.

Baltimore *American and Commercial Advertiser.*
Baltimore *Evening Patriot.*
Baltimore *Exchange.*
Baltimore *South.*

THE BALTIMORE AND OHIO IN THE CIVIL WAR

Baltimore *Sun*.

Baltimore and Ohio R. R. Company Extra Dividend Case. Statement Made by the President to the Board of Directors at their Meeting on the 12th September, 1860.... Baltimore, 1860.

Barringer, Graham Andrew, "The Influence of Railroad Transportation on the Civil War," in *Studies in American History Inscribed to James Albert Woodburn*. Bloomington, Indiana, 1926.

Bates, David Homer, *Lincoln in the Telegraph Office; Recollections of the United States Military Telegraph Corps during the Civil War*. New York, 1907.

Baylor, George, *Bull Run to Bull Run or Four Years in the Army of Northern Virginia*. Richmond, 1900.

Benjamin, Charles F., "Recollections of Secretary Stanton," in *Century Magazine*, XXXIII, (March, 1887). New York, 1887.

Bigelow, John, Jr., *The Campaign of Chancellorsville; A Strategic and Tactical Study*. New Haven, 1910.

Brown, Genevieve, *A History of the Sixth Regiment, West Virginia Infantry Volunteers*. Unpublished West Virginia University Master's Dissertation, 1936.

Calendar of Virginia State Papers. 11 vols. Richmond, 1875-1893. Various editors.

Callahan, James Morton, *Semi-Centennial History of West Virginia*. Charleston, 1913.

Congressional Globe.

Cook, Roy Bird, *Lewis County in the Civil War 1861-1865*. Charleston, W. Va., 1924.

Correspondence Between the Secretary of War and the President of the Baltimore and Ohio Rail Road Company in Relation to Additional Routes Between Washington & New York, and Improvement of the Established Railway Line. Baltimore, 1862.

Cox, Jacob Dolson, *Military Reminiscences of the Civil War*. 2 vols. New York, 1900.

BIBLIOGRAPHY

Eighth Census of the United States. 4 vols. Washington, 1864.

Evans, Clement A., (ed.), *Confederate Military History.* 12 vols. Atlanta, 1899.

Freeman, Douglas Southal, (ed.), *Lee's Dispatches.* New York, 1915.

Gill, Richard W., (ed.), *Maryland Court Reports.* 9 vols. Annapolis and Baltimore, 1846-1852.

Gilmor, Colonel Harry, *Four Years in the Saddle.* New York, 1866.

Grattan, Peachy R., (ed.), *Virginia Court Reports.* 33 vols. Richmond, 1860-1881.

Greeley, Horace, *The Great American Conflict: A History of the Great Rebellion in the United States of America, 1860-1865.* 2 vols. Hartford, Conn., 1864-1866.

Hagans, John Marshall, "Sketch of the Erection and Formation of the State of West Virginia, from the Territory of Virginia," in *West Virginia Reports,* Vol. I. Third Edition. Morgantown, 1906.

Hall, Granville Davisson, *The Rending of Virginia.* Chicago, 1902.

Haney, Lewis Henry, "A Congressional History of Railways in the United States, 1850-1887," in *Economics and Political Science Series of the University of Wisconsin,* Vol. VI. Madison, 1910.

Henderson, G. F. R., *Stonewall Jackson and the American Civil War.* 2 vols. New Impression. New York, 1932.

Hollander, Jacob H., *The Financial History of Baltimore.* Baltimore, 1899.

Hungerford, Edward, *The Story of the Baltimore & Ohio Railroad, 1827-1927.* 2 vols. New York, 1928.

Hunt's Merchants' Magazine and Commercial Review (New York).

Jackson, Mary Anna, *Memoirs of Stonewall Jackson.* Louisville, Ky., 1895.

THE BALTIMORE AND OHIO IN THE CIVIL WAR

Johnson, Robert Underwood, and Buell, Clarence Clough, (eds.), *Battles and Leaders of the Civil War.* 4 vols. New York, 1884-1887.

Johnston, Joseph E., *Narrative of Military Operations.* New York, 1874.

Journal of the House of Delegates of the State of Virginia for the Called Session of 1862. Richmond, 1862.

Journal of the Proceedings of the House of Delegates of the State of Maryland (January Session, 1860). Annapolis, 1860.

Journal of the Proceedings of the House of Delegates of the State of Maryland (January Session, 1865). Annapolis, 1865.

Journal of the Proceedings of the Senate of Maryland (January Session, 1860). Annapolis, 1860.

Journal of the Proceedings of the Senate of Maryland (January Session, 1864). Annapolis, 1864.

Lang, Theodore F., *Loyal West Virginia from 1861 to 1865.* Baltimore, 1895.

Letter of H. J. Jewett, President of the Central Ohio Railroad Company, to the President and Directors of the Baltimore and Ohio Railroad Company in Regard to the Connection Between the Two Roads. Baltimore, 1858.

Letter of the President of the Baltimore & Ohio R. R. Co. to the Chairman of the House Committee on the District of Columbia. Baltimore, 1860.

Lewis, Virgil A., *How West Virginia Was Made.* Charleston, 1909.

Lowdermilk, Will H., *History of Cumberland.* Washington, 1878.

McClellan, George B., *McClellan's Own Story.* New York, 1887.

McDonald, Cornelia, *A Diary with Reminiscences of the War and Refugee Life in the Shenandoah Valley, 1860-1865.* Edited by Hunter McDonald. Nashville, Tenn., 1934.

McDonald, William N., *A History of the Laurel Brigade; Originally The Ashby Cavalry of the Army of Northern*

BIBLIOGRAPHY

Virginia and Chew's Battery. Edited by Bushrod C. Washington. Baltimore, 1907.

McGregor, James C., *The Disruption of Virginia.* New York, 1922.

Moody, John, *The Railroad Builders.* New Haven, 1921.

Moore, Frank, (ed.), *The Rebellion Record: A Diary of American Events, with Documents, Narratives, Illustrative Incidents, Poetry, Etc.* 10 vols. New York, 1861-1867.

National Cyclopaedia of American Biography. 24 vols. New York, 1906.

National Intelligencer (Washington).

New York *Herald.*

Nicolay, John G., and Hay, John, *Abraham Lincoln; A History.* 10 vols. New York, 1890.

Objections to Yielding to Northerners the Control of the Baltimore and Ohio Railroad on which Depends the Development of the Farms, Mines, Manufactures and Trade of the State of Maryland, By a Marylander. Baltimore, 1860.

Parker, Granville, *The Formation of the State of West Virginia, and Other Incidents of the Late Civil War.* Wellsburg, W. Va., 1875.

Pepper, Charles M., *The Life and Times of Henry Gassaway Davis.* Garden City, N. Y., 1920.

Philadelphia *Inquirer.*

Porter, W. E., "Keeping the Baltimore and Ohio in Repair in War Time was a Task for Hercules," in *Book of The Royal Blue,* X, (July, 1907). Baltimore, 1907.

Pratt, Edwin A., *The Rise of Rail-Power in War and Conquest, 1833-1914.* Philadelphia, 1916.

Reid, Whitelaw, *Ohio In the War; Her Statesmen, Her Generals, and Soldiers.* 2 vols. New York, 1868.

Reizenstein, Milton, "The Economic History of the Baltimore and Ohio Railroad, 1827-1853," in *Johns Hopkins Uni-*

THE BALTIMORE AND OHIO IN THE CIVIL WAR

versity Studies in Historical and Political Science, Fif-teenth Series, Vols. VII-VIII. Baltimore, 1897.

"Report of a Select Committee of the House of Delegates of Maryland, Relative to Charges of James E. Tyson, Against the Baltimore and Ohio Railroad Company," in *Maryland House Documents,* 1860 (Document BB). Annapolis, 1860.

Report of the Finance Committee of the Baltimore and Ohio Railroad Company, In Opposition to the Payment to the State of Maryland of the Capitation Tax upon Passengers Travelling over the Washington Branch Road. Baltimore, 1869.

Report of the Majority and Minority of the Committee on Western Connections of the Baltimore and Ohio Railroad. Baltimore, 1857.

Reports of the Majority and Minority of the Special Committee of the Baltimore & Ohio Railroad Co. Appointed to Investigate Its Financial Condition, General Line of Policy Heretofore Pursued, Etc. Presented at the Meeting of the Board, April 14, 1858. Baltimore, 1858.

Rhodes, James Ford, *History of the United States from the Compromise of 1850.* 7 vols. New York, 1895-1906.

Rice, Harvey M., *Jonathan McCally Bennett; A Biography.* (Forthcoming).

Richardson, James D., (ed.), *A Compilation of the Messages and Papers of the Presidents, 1789-1897.* 10 vols. Washington, 1896-1899.

Richmond *Enquirer.*

Richmond *Examiner.*

Ringwalt, J. L., *Development of Transportation Systems in the United States.* Philadelphia, 1888.

Ropes, John Codman, *The Story of the Civil War.* 2 vols. New York, 1894-1898.

Russell, Charles Wells, (ed.), *The Memoirs of Colonel John S. Mosby.* Boston, 1917.

Scharf, J. Thomas, *The Chronicles of Baltimore.* Baltimore, 1874.

BIBLIOGRAPHY

——, *History of Western Maryland.* 2 vols. Philadelphia, 1882.

Schotter, Howard Ward, *The Growth and Development of the Pennsylvania Railroad Company.* Philadelphia, 1927.

Smith, Edward Conrad, *The Borderland in the Civil War.* New York, 1927.

Smith, William Prescott, *The Book of the Great Railway Celebrations of 1857.* First Edition. Baltimore, 1858.

Special Orders Issued from the Adjutant General's Office (1862). [United States Government Printing Office.]

Statement of John W. Garrett, President of the Baltimore and Ohio Railroad Company, Made before the Committee on Military Affairs of the House of Representatives, On the 25th of April, 1862, In Opposition to the "Proposition" of the Metropolitan Railroad Company, to Build a Road making Direct Communication between Washington and New York. Baltimore, 1862.

Table of Distances and Epitome of the Route by the Baltimore and Ohio Railroad and Its Chief Connecting Lines, between Baltimore, Cincinnati, St. Louis, etc. Baltimore, 1860.

The War of the Rebellion: A Compilation of the Official Records of the Union and Confederate Armies. 70 vols. in 128 books. Washington, 1881-1901.

United States Congress:
Senate Executive Documents. 1st Session, 37th Congress, No. 1. Washington, 1861.
Senate Documents. 2nd Session, 37th Congress, No. 1. Washington, 1862.
House Executive Documents. 2nd Session, 37th Congress, No. 79. Washington, 1862.
House Miscellaneous Documents. 2nd Session, 37th Congress, No. 65. Washington, 1862.
Reports of Committees of the House of Representatives. 2nd Session, 37th Congress, Vol. II [Government Contracts.] Washington, 1862.

House Miscellaneous Documents. 3rd Session, 37th Congress, No. 15. Washington, 1863.

Senate Miscellaneous Documents. 3rd Session, 37th Congress, No. 26. Washington, 1863.

Senate Reports. 3rd Session, 37th Congress, No. 81. Washington, 1863.

House Miscellaneous Documents. 2nd Session, 38th Congress, No. 54. Washington, 1865.

Report of the Joint Committee on the Conduct of the War. 2nd Session, 38th Congress, Part 3. Washington, 1865.

Wallace, John William, (ed.), *Cases Argued and Adjudged in the Supreme Court of the United States.* 23 vols. Washington, 1870-1876.

Wheeling *Intelligencer.*

Williamson, James J., *Mosby's Rangers; A Record of the Operations of the Forty-Third Battalion of Virginia Cavalry from its Organization to the Surrender.* Second Edition. New York, 1909.

Wilson, William Bender, *History of the Pennsylvania Railroad Company.* 2 vols. Philadelphia, 1899.

Winchester, Paul, *Graphic Sketches from the History of the Baltimore & Ohio Railroad.* Baltimore, 1927.

INDEX

Adams, John Quincy, 15
Adjutant General's Office, U. S., order of, 253 (note 9)
Alexandria, reorganized Virginia government at, 201
Alexandria, Loudoun and Hampshire Railroad, 35
Allegany County, Md., 147; penetrated by B. & O., 17
Alleghany County, Va., 186, 189; inclusion in new state opposed, 191; amendment adopted to exclude, 191
Alleghenies, 67, 107, 108, 145, 152, 154, 172, 182, 183, 188, 194, 223, 224
Allegheny, 159
Allegheny Mountains, 182
Altamont, B. & O. station, 128, 130, 139
Annapolis, Md., 58, 63, 220; military route through, 57
Annapolis and Elk Ridge Railroad, junction of with Washington Branch, 18-19; military route over, 57; heavy government traffic upon, 63
Annapolis Junction, Md., 62, 238 (note 43)
Antietam, battle of, 119, 124, 165
April, 1861, 48, 49, 51, 52, 53, 54, 55, 56, 57, 59, 60, 61
Armored cars, 158
Army, U. S., 156
Army of the Cumberland, defeat of at Chickamauga, 166
Army of the Potomac, 108, 148; Stanton's proposal to aid Rosecrans with, 167; Eleventh and Twelfth Corps of sent to aid of Rosecrans, 169 ff; supplied by Washington Branch Railroad, 205
Army of Virginia, 163

Articles of war, President authorized to take charge of railroads under, 212
Ashby, Turner, lieutenant colonel, assigned to patrol front, 112
Athens, O., Union troops at, 73
Atlantic Ocean, Confederates cut off water communication with, 204
Atlantic States, 33
Augusta Springs, Va., 163
Austro-Sardinian War, 162

Back Creek, tributary of Potomac, 110, 115, 119, 123
Back River, 207, 208
Backbone Mountain, 87
Baltimore, Md., 21, 27, 29, 30, 31, 32, 37, 38, 39, 41, 42, 43, 46, 47, 56, 57, 59, 60, 62, 81, 103, 104, 106, 121, 140, 151, 175, 192, 203, 204, 206, 207, 208, 209, 214, 215, 218, 236 (note 18), 237 (note 28), 238 (note 43), 238 (note 44), 253 (note 9); commercial ambitions of, 15; interested in founding B. & O., 16; eastern terminus of the B. & O., 17; railroad terminal at, 18; interest in B. & O. Railroad, 19; aids Northwestern Virginia Railroad, 22; objections to traffic agreements in, 22-23; loans of to B. & O., 23; sponsor of Northwestern Virginia Railroad, 23; guarantees bonds of Northwestern Virginia Railroad, 23; Federal soldiers expected at, 49-51; April events in, 52; streets of closed to U. S. forces, 53; mob spirit in, 54-55; its isolation recommended, 58; water route opened to, 63; railway connections at restored, 63; interest in destruction of B. & O., 96; effect of destruction of B. & O. on

273

INDEX

INDEX

INDEX

B. & O. Railroad—*Cont'd*
passenger service on, 116; reopening of celebrated at Wheeling, 116; required to hoist U. S. flag at important stations, 116; loyalty of unquestioned, 116-117; a fair prize for the Confederates, 118; base for Federal military operations, 118; value to North, 118; reaction of Confederate government to, 118; Governor Letcher's warning concerning, 118; bridges of damaged by Jackson, 119; damaged by Lee's invasion of Maryland, 119; cut by Jackson near Martinsburg, 119; Southern occupation of, 119; destruction of, 119; Confederate method of destroying rails, 119; report of losses by J. W. Garrett, 119-120; task of rebuilding, 120-121; reopening of main stem of, 121; effect of Gettysburg campaign upon, 121ff; main line of held by Confederates, 121; destruction of, 121-122; purchase of timbers for emergencies, 122; reopened after Gettysburg, 122-123; J. A. Early's campaigns against, 123-124; occupation of by J. A. Early, 123-124; destruction of, 123-124; main stem controlled by J. A. Early, 124; end of Confederate operations in vicinity of, 124; reopening of, 124; harassed by Confederates, 125; objective of Jones-Imboden raid, 125-126; bridges object of Imboden-Jones raid, 127; Jones concerned with attempt to cut, 127-128; bridge of destroyed at Fairmont, 134-135; Jones renews operations against, 136-137; reopened, 139; cut by Rosser, 139-140; blockaded by Gilmor, 141; robbing of passengers of by Confederates, 141; attacked by McNeill's partisans, 141-142; destruction of by McNeill's partisans, 142; reinforcements in defense area of, 142; harassed by Confederates, 142; attacked by Mosby, 142-143; robbery of Federal paymasters on, 142; destruction of train by Mosby, 142-143; raided by Rosser, 143; effects of Confederate raids upon, 144; difficulty of defense, 145; Shenandoah Valley used as base of operations against, 146-147; Kelley assigned to defense of in Mountain Department, 147; defense of eastern portion of, 147; failure of plans for defense of, 147-148; guard of withdrawn by Frémont, 148; Kelley informs war department of insufficiency of guard on, 148; undefended at vulnerable points, 148; Washington authorities note defects in defense of, 148; entire defense of assigned to Major General Wool, 148-149; Wool protests removal of defense troops from, 149; Kelley placed in command of strategic posts along, 149; unsoundness of defense plan of, 150; Schenck succeeds Wool in command of defense of, 150; defense of assigned to Kelley, 150; defects in Schenck's defense plan of, 150-151; defense of tested by Jones' raid, 151; defense of placed in hands of Kelley, 151-153; disposition of defense forces along, 153-154; Federal garrisons increased along, 154; main stem fortified, 154; railroad guards withdrawn from, 154; defenseless condition of, 154; redistribution of defense forces along, 154-155; new defense plans for, 155; Kelley's recommendations to war department concerning defense of, 155-156; plan for defense proposed by Lt. Colonel Gabriel E. Porter, 156; a proposed training ground for troops, 156; war department has free hand in protection of, 157; Federal protection extended, 157; strengthening of military posts along, 157; use of armored cars on, 158; human element in defense of, 158ff; use of raw militia in defense of, 158-159; a training ground for troops, 158; lack of distinguished officers in defense zone of, 160; handicaps in protection of, 160-161; decisive role of in Civil War, 162; stra-

INDEX

277

INDEX

Bridgeport, Ala., 166, 168, 169; arrival of troop trains at, 177, 180
Bridgeport, O., 40
Bridgeport, (W.) Va., 67, 135, 159; railroad guard at, 80
Brooke County, (W.) Va., 34, 191
Brown, George William, Baltimore mayor, interview of with President Lincoln, 56
Brown, John, raid of, 45; B. & O. thanked for assistance in capture of, 234 (note 1)
Brown, Ridgeley, major, 128
Brown's battalion, Confederate, 127
Buchanan County, Va., 186
Buckhannon, (W.) Va., 125, 135, 136, 138
Buffalo Creek, tributary of Monongahela River, destruction of bridges over, 72
Bull Run, B. & O. cars aid Confederate victory at, 100; influence of closing of B. & O., 102, 206
Bunker Hill, (W.) Va., Confederate withdrawal to, 93
Burning Springs oil field, Jones's destruction of, 137
Burnside, Ambrose E., major general, 138, 167
Bushwhacker, described, 132
Butler, Benjamin F., brigadier general, occupies Relay House, 62; restrictive policy of, 62; relaxes restrictions on B. & O., 62; occupies Baltimore, 63

Cabell County, (W.) Va., 194
Cabinet, U. S., members of urged to support recovery of B. & O., 102; discusses Rosecrans's plight, 166-167
Cairo, (W.) Va., 137
Camden Station, B. & O. station in Baltimore, 52, 53; offices at threatened, 54
Camden and Amboy Railroad, 39; monopoly of, 207
Cameron, J. Donald, vice-president Northern Central Railroad, 103
Cameron, Simon, U. S. senator, 42; opposes B. & O. extension, 40-41; interest in Northern Central Railroad, 41; motives of, 41; amendment of, 41-42; secretary of war,

51, 61, 71, 103, 107, 242 (note 27); warns John W. Garrett, 56; his instructions to S. M. Felton, 56; quoted, 57; appoints superintendent of military railway, 57-58; quoted, 59; successful policy of, 63; interest in Northern Central Railroad, 103; resignation of benefits B. & O., 114; favors proposition of Metropolitan Railroad Company, 207; communications to railroad presidents, 208; application of Garrett to, 238 (note 44)
"Cameron's road," 103
Camp Dennison, O., 71, 72, 83
Camp Melvin, Md., 156
Camp Piatt, (W.) Va., 164
Camps of instruction, proposed, 156
Campbell, Archibald W., editor, quoted, 60; denounces destruction of B. & O., 97
Capital, U. S., 147
Capitation tax, imposed on passenger travel by Maryland, 19, 204
Carlile, John S., advocate of division of Virginia, 184
Cars, armored, 158
Carskadon, Thomas R., 195; supports inclusion of Valley counties in W. Va., 190-191
Carson, James H., brigadier general, 112, 113
Case, S. P., 215
"Case Memorial," 215; attacks B. & O., 215; failure of, 215-216
Cave City, Ky., 180
Central, (W.) Va., railroad guard at, 80
Central Ohio Railroad, 17, 23, 24, 27, 33, 39, 170, 171, 178, 233 (note 35); location and extent of, 20; importance of, 21; receives financial aid, 21; completion of, 21; makes agreement with B. & O., 21; warning given by to B. & O., 25; security of, 40; interest of Johns Hopkins and John W. Garrett in, 229 (note 20); B. & O. officials accused of promoting interests of, 232-233 (note 34)
Central West, 20, 40
Chambersburg, Pa., 61, 81
Charleston, (W.) Va., 164

279

INDEX

Charles Town, (W.) Va., 114, 141, 142; mayor of warns Garrett, 52

Charlottesville, Va., 163

Chartier's Valley Railroad, 231 (note 22)

Chase, Salmon P., secretary of the treasury, 71, 106; supports Stanton's plan to aid Rosecrans, 167-168; helps secure military protection for B. & O., 248 (note 73); quoted on movement of troops by rail, 257 (note 62)

Chattanooga, Tenn., 166, 167; arrival of Grant at, 180; relief of, 224

Cheat River, McClellan's plans for strengthening fortifications along, 84

Cheat River bridge, 80, 86, 159; destruction of desired by Lee, 81; President Jefferson Davis orders destruction of, 93; destruction of planned by Imboden, 126; challenge of to Jones, 128; defended by Federals, 128; defense of drawn from West, 161; stand of Sixth (West) Virginia Infantry at, 159

Cherry Run, (W.) Va., B. & O. station at, 65, 67, 109, 115

Chesapeake Bay, 51, 57, 66, 204, 223

Chesapeake and Ohio Canal, 108, 110, 156, 222; cut by Confederates, 204-205

Chickamauga, Ga., defeat of Rosecrans at, 166

Chisholms Mill, Md., 87

Cincinnati, O., 19, 20, 21, 22, 29, 32, 33, 229 (note 20); B. & O. denied a direct approach to, 16; trade of, 31

Cincinnati *Gazette*, attitude of toward B. & O., 101

Cincinnati Merchants' Exchange, advocates opening of B. & O., 101-102

Cis-Allegheny, 69, 149, 189; railroad district of, 147

Cis-Allegheny counties, 199-200; opposition to inclusion of in W. Va,. 184; subject to Confederate attack, 184; inclusion of in new state urged, 189-190

Cismontane counties, Gordon Battelle opposes inclusion of in new state, 191

Civil War, 36, 43, 139; decisive role of B. & O. in, 162, 224-225; establishment of State of West Virginia during, 182, 222

Civilians, interference of with B. & O., 153-154

Clarksburg, (W.) Va., 72, 76, 77, 78; war scare in vicinity of, 52; military forces at, 67, 86, 135, 138, 159; railroad guard at, 80; possible base of McClellan's troops, 83; concentration of Federal troops at, 84; Confederate leaders plan to capture, 136

Cleveland and Ohio Railroad, 17, 32, 33, 40

Clifton, Tenn., 257 (note 63)

Cockeysville, Md., U. S. troops at, 56

Cockpit Point, Va., 204

Cole, Lewis M., B. & O. general ticket agent, 169, 179; role of in troop movement, 169; captain, 176; assigned as aide to Hooker, 255 (note 22)

Columbia, District of, 205, 220

Columbia and Reading Railroad Company, petitions Congress for authority to build New York to Washington railroad, 215, 216

Columbus, O., 169, 174; railroad center at, 20

Columbus and Xenia Railroad, 20

Committee on Military Affairs, U. S. House of Representatives, 156; hears testimony of J. W. Garrett, 205; bill for Metropolitan plan returned to, 214; J. W. Garrett opposes Metropolitan plan before, 214-215; Chairman Wright agrees with Garrett's views on Metropolitan plan, 215; fails to report Metropolitan plan bill to House, 215; bill for construction of New York-Washington railroad referred to, 216; memorial of corporation of the City of Washington to, 216; memorial perishes in, 217

INDEX

281

INDEX

INDEX

Dayton, O., 20

Delaware, state of, 215, 216; included in Middle Department, 148, 252 (note 8)

Dennison, William, governor, 52, 71, 242-243 (note 31); concludes arrangements for moving Ohio troops, 49; reaction of to Garrett's refusal to transport Ohio troops, 50; message of to War Department, 50; request of for military protection for B. & O., 70; dispatch of to secretary of war, 235 (note 13)

Department of Harpers Ferry and Cumberland, created, 104; Lander placed in command of, 104

Department of the Ohio, 69, 138; extended, 70

Department of the Potomac, creation of railroad districts in, 147; partly absorbed by Middle Department, 148

Department of West Virginia, reinforcements on B. & O. in, 142; created, 151; commanded by Kelley, 151; Confederate thrusts into, 152

Department of Western Virginia, 106

Diffey, Alexander, B. & O. general supervisor of trains, 169; role in troop movement, 169; describes difficulties, 237 (note 28)

Discipline, lack of in railroad guard, 159

District of Columbia, 40, 108, 205, 220

Doddridge County, (W.) Va., 189, 196

Done, John H., master of transportation, quoted, 21

Duffields, B. & O. station at, 120

Dumont, Ebenezer, colonel, orders to, 78-79; night march of against Philippi, 79

Early, Jubal A., lieutenant general, Shenandoah Valley campaign of, 123; occupation of B. & O. by, 123-124; withdrawal of from Maryland, 124; controls main stem of B. & O., 124; defeat of, 124; advance down the Valley by, 257 (note 63)

East, the, 21, 59, 186

Eastern Panhandle of West Virginia, 186-187; reasons for erection of, 188

Edwards Ferry, battle of, 104

Eighteenth Ohio Infantry, 73

Eleventh Corps of Army of Potomac, aid of to Rosecrans, 168, 170, 172, 180

Eleventh Indiana Zouaves, enter Cumberland, 92

Eleventh Virginia Cavalry, 127, 128, 129

Ellenboro, (W.) Va., railroad guard at, 80

Engineers, U. S. military, design blockhouse, 157-158

Europeans, 43

Evansville, (W.) Va., 129

Fairfax Stone, 90, 194

Fairmont, (W.) Va., 67, 74, 80, 86, 134, 138, 139, 172; military company at, 69; Union movement against, 72; Kelley sends troops to protect bridge at, 243 (note 32); Confederates burn library of Governor Francis H. Pierpont at, 250 (note 43)

Farmington, (W.) Va., railroad guard at, 80

Farnsworth, John F., congressman, introduces Pennsylvania Railroad Bill, 220

Fayetteville, (W.) Va., 164

Federal armies, B. & O. proposed as training ground for, 156

Federal authorities, place Kelley in command of strategic posts, 149; arrange schedule for B. & O. between Baltimore and Washington, 238 (note 44)

Federal blockhouses, description of, 157-158

Federal force, 73, 74, 138, 163, 201, 250 (note 29)

Federal government, 45, 62; seat of threatened, 19; loyalty of northwestern Virginia to, 70; importance of Chesapeake and Ohio Canal to, 108; B. & O. convenient

INDEX

284

INDEX

Frémont, John C., major general, 140, 149, 150, 154, 160; withdraws railroad guard, 148; commands Mountain Department, 148; Valley campaign of against Jackson, 148
French, 162
Front Royal, Va., 146

Garfield, James A., major general, 166
Garnett, Robert S., brigadier general, supersedes Porterfield as commander in northwest, 81; occupies Laurel Hill and Rich Mountain, 81; correspondence with Lee concerning B. & O., 82; plans concerning B. & O., 82; McClellan thwarts plans of, 82; evacuates Laurel Hill, 85; killed near Corricks Ford, 85; supports Johnston in Trans-Allegheny, 92
Garrett, John W., president B. & O. R. R., 33, 38, 66, 121, 175, 176, 229 (note 20), 235 (note 13); leads private stockholders of B. & O., 25; elected president of B. & O., 26; business connections of, 27; appointed B. & O. director, 27; personality of, 27; managerial policy of, 27-28; early successes as president, 27-28; opposition to policies of, 28; retaliatory policy of, 29; long-and-short-haul policy of, 29; questioned by legislative committee, 30; defends policies before legislative committee, 30-31; economic philosophy of, 31; favors central route to Cincinnati, 31; opposes Wheeling bridge, 35-36; internal reform program of, 37; favors change in board of directors, 37; sponsor of railroad bill in Maryland Senate, 37; desires controlling interest in Central Ohio R. R., 39-40; expansion program of, 40; purchases Central Ohio securities, 40; plan for expansion south, 40; plans extension of Pittsburgh and Connellsville Railroad, 42-43; success of as B. & O. president, 43; surplus account established by, 43; his policies vindicated, 43; partisan of the South, 45; co-operation of with authorities in 1859, 45; attitude and behavior of in 1859, 45; southern background of, 45; speech of on John Brown raid, 45-46; declares B. & O. a Southern line, 45-46; changed policy of, 46; assures travelers and shippers, 47; alleges unfairness by rival lines, 47; criticizes rival lines, 48; pledges indemnity for losses, 48; repeats guarantees to shippers, 48-49; alleged disloyalty of, 49; excoriates Pennsylvania Central Railroad, 49; non-partisan statement of, 49; instructions to Western agents, 49; neutral policy of outlined, 49; agrees to transport Ohio troops, 49; refuses the Ohio troops, 49; explains refusal of Ohio troops, 49-50; his action explained, 50-51; difficulty of his position explained, 51; his acts criticized and defended, 51-52; vindication of found in events, 51-52; co-operation of with city and state authorities, 53; action of during Baltimore riots, 54; intimidation of, tried, 54-55; anonymous letter to quoted, 55; warned by U. S. secretary of war, 56; warned by governor of Virginia, 56; action of on April 21, 1861, 56, 57; new dilemma of, 58; application of for safe conduct of trains, 58-59; his rebuff by Secretary Cameron, 58-59; negotiations of with Virginia, 59; protests Butler's restrictive policies at Relay House, 62; assists military authorities in northwest Virginia, 81; asks military protection for B. & O. reconstruction, 102; requests military protection for restoration of B. & O., 105-106; service of to B. & O., 116; reports B. & O. losses, 119-120; summoned to Washington by Stanton, 168; role in troop movement, 169ff; given military powers, 169; instructions to President Jewett of Central Ohio Railroad, 169-170; instructions to President Ricketts of Jeffersonville Railroad,

INDEX

INDEX

Green, John Shac, lieutenant colonel, 129
Green Spring, (W.) Va., 105
"Greenback Raid," 142
Greenbrier County, (W.) Va., 193, 194
Greenland Gap, 88, 128, 130
Gwinn, Charles J. M., B. & O. general counsel, confers with Virginia authorities, 59; visits Harpers Ferry, 238-239 (note 45); negotiations with Virginians, 238-239 (note 45)

Hagans, George M., quoted, 70
Hagerstown, Md., 90, 101, 205; occupied by Patterson, 92
Hall, Ephraim B., attacks attempt to exclude Pendleton County from new state, 195; points out Virginia's hostility to B. & O., 195; favors inclusion of B. & O. counties, 195-196; insists upon inclusion of B. & O. in new state, 197; offers resolution, 200; quoted on Virginia railroad policy, 258 (note 3)
Halleck, Henry W., general in chief, 167; sends caustic telegram to Schenck, 151; approves use of B. & O. to move troops, 164; summoned to meeting by Stanton, 166; supports President Lincoln, 168; opposes Stanton's plan to aid Rosecrans, 168; instructions of to Meade, 179; instructions of to Kelley, 179
Hampshire County, (W.) Va., 184, 185, 186, 189, 191, 192, 194, 195, 196, 197, 199, 200
Hancock, Md., 105, 114, 115, 120, 123, 150, 151, 152, 154, 157; Jackson attacks Lander's force at, 110-111; Jackson withdraws from, 111
Hancock County, (W.) Va., 34, 191
Hardy County, (W.) Va., 184, 185, 186, 189, 191, 194, 196, 197, 199, 200
Harman, Asher W., colonel, 128, 130, 132, 133, 135, 136, 137
Harman, M. G., colonel, moves to Grafton, 69

Harney, William S., brigadier general, arrest and release of, 65-66
Harper, Kenton, major general, attitude of toward B. & O., 59; promise of to B. & O., 59; activities of at Harpers Ferry, 60; colonel, C. S. A., 67; succeeded by Thomas J. Jackson, 239 (note 47)
Harpers Ferry, (W.) Va., 17, 51, 55, 59, 60, 61, 62, 63, 66, 68, 73, 74, 78, 90, 94, 99, 100, 104, 105, 109, 114, 119, 121, 123, 124, 138, 142, 145, 149, 154, 156, 157, 217, 221, 235 (note 13), 236 (note 19); railroad junction at, 18; raid at, 45; U. S. arsenal at, 52; occupation of by Virginia troops, 52; secessionist forces at, 65; importance of to Confederate military authorities, 91; key to Shenandoah Valley, 91; arrival of Johnston at, 91; Johnston proposes evacuation of, 91; Johnston prepares to evacuate, 92; machinery of arsenal dismantled by Confederates at, 92; use of Winchester and Potomac Railroad in evacuation of, 92; bridge at rebuilt, 115; bridge at destroyed by Federal force, 122; Garrett urged to prevent removal of arms from, 236 (note 18); visited by C. J. M. Gwinn, 238-239 (note 45)
"Harriett Lane", revenue cutter, 58, 63
Harrisburg, Pa., 103, 104, 219
Harrisonburg, Va., 145-146, 163
Haymond, Thomas, major general, defense recommendations of, 67, 240 (note 5)
Hempfield Railroad, 33, 231 (note 22)
Hervey, James, offers resolution to exclude Valley counties from new state, 192ff
Hicks, Thomas H., governor, cooperation of with Baltimore authorities, 53; Governor Letcher to on relations with Maryland, 240 (note 64)
Highland County, Va., 186, 189, 192, 194; excluded from new state, 195
Hightown, Va., 251 (note 46)

287

INDEX

Hill, Ambrose P., colonel, 93; major general, 119; destroys New Creek railroad bridge, 245 (note 10)
Hill, Charles W., brigadier general, assigned defense of railroad, McClellan's orders to, 83-84; authorized by McClellan to increase troops in railroad defense area, 84; ordered by McClellan to cut off Confederate retreat, 86; arrives at Oakland with troops, 87; resumes pursuit of Confederates, 88; ordered to stop pursuit, 88
Hollidays Cove Railroad, chartered, 34; charter provisions of, 35, 231 (note 22)
Hooker, Joseph, major general, 173, 174, 176, 178, 179; prompt action saves Federal line of communication, 180; Lewis M. Cole assigned as aide to, 255 (note 22); railroad movement of troops of, 261 (note 23); "Hooker is Our Leader", 250 (note 40)
Hopkins, Johns, leads private stockholders of B. & O., 25, 229 (note 20)
House Committee on Roads and Canals, given plan of Metropolitan Railroad Company, 207
House of Delegates, Maryland, opposes Pennsylvania Railroad bill, 221; emphasizes interest in railroad matter, 221; report of select committee of, 230 (note 7); committee accepts Garrett's explanation of discrimination, 230-231 (note 13); B. & O. commended by committee of, 230-231 (note 13)
House of Representatives, 205; resolution on railroads, 207-208; failure of "Case Memorial", 216; R. E. Fenton introduces bill for proposed New York-Washington railroad in, 216; Fenton bill referred to special committee of, 216; J. F. Farnsworth introduces railroad bill in, 220; communication of John W. Garrett to, 221
Hubby, L. M., advises Garrett on movement of troops to Washington, 237 (note 32)
Hughes River, tributary of the Little Kanawha River, 76

Hungerford, Edward, 236 (note 18)
Hunter, David, major general, B. & O. transports troops of, 257 (note 63)
Huntersville, (W.) Va., 108

Illinois, state of, 220
Imboden, John D., 127, 129, 135, 136, 137, 138; captain, 66; instructions to, 67; brigadier general, 125; submits campaign plan to Lee, 126; reinforced, 251 (note 46); destroys bridges, 251 (note 48)
Immigrants, 143
Independence, (W.) Va., 129, 139
Indiana, state of, troops of, 74, 77, 78; progress of troop trains through, 174, 175
Indiana Central Railroad, 175
Indianapolis, Ind., 169, 170, 175, 178; delay of military movement at, 179
"Iron Clads", 254, (note 30)
Irvine, James, colonel, commander of Sixteenth Ohio Infantry, 73, 86, 87
Irvine, Robert, 196, 197

Jackson, Thomas (Stonewall), colonel, 67, 119, 148, 150, 154; commands at Harpers Ferry, 65; captures B. & O. trains, 65; cunning of, 66; interference of with B. & O. schedule, 66, 68; replaced by Joseph E. Johnston, 91; regards Harpers Ferry as strategic point, 91; given B. & O. destruction task, 94; destroys B. & O., 94ff; withdraws to Winchester, 99; major general, 107; commands Valley District, 107; plans campaign in northwest, 107; appeal for aid to Confederate war department, 108; sends out detachments to impede B. & O. reconstruction, 108; destruction of Dam No. 5, 109; hinders work on B. & O., 109; decides against campaigning in Trans-Allegheny, 110; attacks Federals at Bath, 110; demands surrender of Union forces at Hancock, 111; unsuccessful in attack upon Hancock,

INDEX

INDEX

Lamb, Daniel, 196, 199; offers motion in W. Va. constitutional convention on boundary question, 196

Lander, Frederick W., colonel, 77, 78; aide to G. B. McClellan, 75; action of at Parkersburg, 77; orders of to T. T. Crittenden, 77; arrives at Grafton, 77; brigadier general, 106; placed in command of Department of Harpers Ferry and Cumberland, 104; wounded at Edwards Ferry, 104; succeeded by Kelley, 104-105; Rosecrans ordered to aid, 107; attacked by Jackson at Hancock, 110-111; impatience of, 111; counterattack of, 113-114; death of, 115

Lane, James H., colonel, 119

Lang, Theodore F., 239 (note 52), 250 (note 33)

Latham, George R., colonel, 251 (note 47)

Laurel Brigade, 140

Laurel Hill, part of Allegheny chain, 79; occupied by Garnett, 81; objective of Morris's movement from Philippi, 84; evacuated by Garnett, 85

Lee, Robert E., general, 68, 70, 121, 122, 150, 155, 167, 168, 201, 251 (note 46); orders protection of B. & O., 68; defense plans of, 69; instructions of, 69; sends troops to Grafton, 69; desires destruction of Cheat River bridge at Rowlesburg, 81; invasion of Maryland by, 119; receives Imboden's plan for campaign, 126; grants Jones major role in campaign against B. & O., 126-127; orders start of Imboden-Jones raid, 127; Jones's account to of destruction of oil at Burning Springs, 137; report of Jones to, 137; quoted on Jones-Imboden raid, 138

Lee County, Va., 186

Leesburg, Va., 156

Letcher, John, governor, warns John W. Garrett, quoted, 56; attitude of toward Maryland, 59; special order of, 59; urgent report to, 67; warns B. & O., 118; correspondence of with Governor

Hicks on Maryland relations, 240 (note 64); instructions to Colonel Jackson, 240 (note 64); Judge George W. Thompson writes on defense of northwest Virginia to, 240-241 (note 5); dispatch of to George A. Porterfield, 242 (note 27); hostility of to B. & O., 259 (note 13); message of to Virginia General Assembly, 259 (note 13)

Lewis County, (W.) Va., 196

Lewisburg, (W.) Va., 163

Lincoln, Abraham, President, 49, 57, 58, 207; changed itinerary of, 46-47; returns U. S. troops to Pennsylvania, 56; angles for support of German element, 152; appoints Sigel to command Department of West Virginia, 153; goes to War Department office to discuss Rosecrans's plight, 166-167; recommendations of on aid to Rosecrans, 167; opposes Stanton's plan to send part of Army of Potomac to Chattanooga, 167; supported by Halleck in opposition to Stanton's plan, 168; uncertain attitude of toward public control and ownership of railroads, 211; favors war department supervision of railroads, 211; advocates construction of a railroad at government expense, 211-212; depression following election of, 233 (note 41)

Little Cacapon River, tributary of the Potomac, 105, 111, 120

Little Kanawha River, tributary of the Ohio, 16

Little Kanawha Valley, recovery of for South planned by Jackson, 107

Little Miami Railroad, 20

Locust Point, Md., water route to, 63

London, Eng., 217

Long Bridge, 170, 178, use of for railroad connection, 42

Loring, Alonzo, major, 68

Loring, William W., brigadier general, joins Jackson at Winchester, 108; assigned to hold Romney, 112-113; strained relations of with Jackson, 113; complains to Confederate war department, 113

290

INDEX

Louisville, Ky., 29, 169, 171, 176, 179, 180
Louisville and Nashville Railroad, 176, 180
Lynchburg, Va., 257 (note 63)

McCallum, Daniel C., colonel, U. S. director of military railroads, 169; complaint of to war department, 171-172; W. P. Smith's reply to, 171-172
McClellan, George B., major general, 71, 72, 77, 81, 92, 105, 106, 107, 111, 114, 154, 160, 162, 165, 223, 242-243 (note 31), 244 (note 66); appeals to, 69-70; commands the department of the Ohio, 69; military policy of, 70; views of on military occupation of B. & O., 71; rebuked by General Scott, 71; action of on Ohio River, 71-72; first offensive operations of, 72; orders of to James Irvine, 73; assigns Thomas A. Morris to command, 74; instructions of to J. B. Steedman, 75; policy of after Philippi, 79; policy of justified, 79-80; places B. & O. under guard, 80; watches Confederate activity on Laurel Hill and Rich Mountain, 82; thwarts Garnett's plans concerning B. & O., 82; telegram to General Morris, 82; orders Morris to strengthen position at Rowlesburg, 83; authorizes Morris to evacuate Clarksburg and Philippi, 83; arrives at Parkersburg, 83; orders Rosecrans to Parkersburg, 83; goes to Grafton, 83; relieves Morris of railroad defense, 83; assigns railroad defense to Charles W. Hill, 83-84; plans concerning strengthening of Cheat River fortifications, 84; authorizes Hill to increase troops in railroad defense area, 84; plans for offensive, 84; orders Morris to move against Laurel Hill, 84-85; engagement at Rich Mountain, 85; plan to blockade Northwestern Turnpike, 86; order to Hill, 86; orders Hill to stop fruitless pursuit of Confederates, 88; end of campaign in

northwestern Virginia, 88; assumes higher command, 88; successful in defense of railroad, 88-89; influence of campaigns of upon northwest Virginia, 89; opens east-west corridor by military campaign, 89; occupies B. & O. in northwestern Virginia, 92; dispatch of General Scott to, 242-243 (note 31)
McDonald, Angus, colonel, 245 (note 11); sent to destroy B. & O. Cheat River bridge, 93; petition of to Garrett, 236 (note 18)
McDonald, Edward H., captain, 128
McDowell, Irwin, major general, defeated by Confederates, 100
McDowell, Va., battle of, 146
McDowell County, (W.) Va., 193
McNeill, John H., captain, 128; attacks B. & O., 141-142; captures Federal soldiers, 142; consequences of raid by, 142
Main Stem, gross earnings of, 29
Manassas, Va., 106, 108; second battle of, 160, 165
Manassas Gap Railroad, 94; use of captured B. & O. rolling stock on, 100
Mannington, (W.) Va., 74, 80, 251 (note 48); destruction of bridge at, 72; arrival of Union troops at, 73; railroad guard at, 80
Marietta, O., 138; Union forces at, 72, 73
Marietta and Cincinnati Railroad, 18, 20, 22; concludes agreement with B. & O., 22; operates Ohio River ferry, 22
Marion County, (W.) Va., 195, 197, 200, 258 (note 3)
Marshall County, (W.) Va., circuit court of, 21
Martinsburg, (W.) Va., 91, 93, 94, 105, 109, 110, 112, 114, 115, 116, 120, 121, 123, 124, 141, 154, 171; railroad shops at, 67; B. & O. cut by Jackson at, 119; B. & O. transports Hunter's troops to, 257 (note 63)
Maryland, state of, 15, 17, 19, 20, 37, 38, 39, 40, 43, 45, 47, 53, 57, 59, 61, 62, 93, 110, 147, 183, 192, 197, 207, 208, 209, 212, 214, 215,

291

INDEX

Maryland, state of—*Cont'd*
216, 218, 219, 220, 221, 224; concern of people of, 15-16; interested in founding B. & O., 16; soldiers of, 56; its subjugation recommended, 58; secessionist sympathizers in, 58; possible Confederate "liberation" of, 90; Confederate plans for secession of, 93-94; attitude of on destruction of B. & O., 96; *quasi* enemy to the South, 99; J. A. Early's withdrawal from, 124; placed in Middle Department, 148; part of in the Department of West Virginia, 151; invasion of by Confederates, 155; imposes capitation tax on passenger travel, 204; vested interest of in B. & O., 204; interest in Washington Branch, 204; creates Metropolitan Railroad Company, 205; undecided as to course in war, 215; willing ally of B. & O., 222; dependence of B. & O. on, 223; interest of in B. & O., 227 (note 8); Governor Letcher writes Governor Hicks on relations with, 240 (note 64); included in Middle Department, 252 (note 8)

Maryland general assembly, 30, 239-240 (note 62); charters B. & O. Railroad Co., 15; opposes Pennsylvania Railroad Bill, 220-221; protests to Congress, 220-221; petition of Baltimore business men to, 239-240 (note 62)

Maryland House of Delegates, 105; opposes Pennsylvania Railroad Bill, 221; emphasizes interest in railroad matter, 221; report of select committee of, 230 (note 7); committee of accepts Garrett's explanation of discrimination, 230-231 (note 13); B. & O. commended by committee of, 230-231 (note 13)

Maryland Senate, 37
Marylanders, 16; interest of in B. & O., 227 (note 8)
Mason and Dixon line, 44, 57, 58
Massanutten Mountains, 146
Meade, George G., major general, 167, 168; Halleck's instructions to, 179

Meem, Gilbert, S., brigadier general, 112
Memphis, Tenn., 166
Mercer County, (W.) Va., 193, 194
Metropolitan Railroad, 220; petitions Congress, 205ff; created by Maryland, 205; plan of, 207; Secretary of War Simon Cameron favors proposition of, 207; fails to get immediate support in Congress, 207; change in plan, 207; bill for acceptance of, 213-214; J. W. Garrett opposes, 214; Garrett's arguments against, 214-215; H. B. Wright's position on, 215; failure of, 215; reviving of, 213-214; memorandum on route of, 261 (note 26)
Middle Department, 138, 152; created by U. S. secretary of war, 148; composition of, 148, 252 (note 9); commanded by Wool, 148; Wool given control of all railroad troops in, 148-149; limits of extended, 150; Confederate success in, 151
Middle Fork Bridge, 84
Miles, Dixon S., colonel, 148, 253 (note 9); commands Cis-Allegheny railroad district, 147
Military posts, strengthening of, 157
Militia, used in defense of B. & O., 158-159
Millersville, Md., 261 (note 26)
Milroy, Robert H., major general, 126, 138
Mississippi River, 71, 166, 188
Monocacy, Md., battle of, 124
Monocacy Bridge, Md., 55, 119, 120, 154
Monocacy Junction, Md., 61, 123, 150, 153, 221; viaducts at, 61
Monongahela basin, 20
Monongahela River, 80, 243 (note 32), 251 (note 60)
Monongahela Valley, recovery of for South planned by Jackson, 107
Monongalia County, (W.) Va., 132, 192
Monopoly, freight and passenger held by B. & O., 203-204
Monroe County, (W.) Va., 193, 194
Monterey, Va., 88

INDEX

Moorefield, (W.) Va., 112, 126, 127, 154
Morgan County, (W.) Va., 109, 110, 184, 186, 189, 190, 192, 194, 196, 197, 199, 200
Morgantown, (W.) Va., 128, 132, 133, 159; occupied by Confederates, 133; re-entered by Confederates, 134
Morgantown-Kingwood Turnpike, 129, 133
Morgantown *Star*, quoted, 182-183
Morris, Thomas A., brigadier general, assignment of to command, 74; takes command at Grafton, 77; modifies B. F. Kelley's plan, 78; orders of, 78-79; McClellan's telegram to, 82; ordered to strengthen position at Rowlesburg, 83; authorized to evacuate Clarksburg and Philippi, 83; relieved of railroad defense, 83; ordered to move against Laurel Hill by McClellan, 84-85; delays pursuit of Garnett, 85; fails to follow up victory at Corricks Fords, 85
Morton, Thomas, colonel, 88
Mosby, John S., colonel, 143; "Greenback Raid" of, 142; destroys B. & O. train, 142-143
Moundsville, (W.) Va., 68, 251 (note 48)
Mountain Department, 160; creation of railroad districts in, 147; Kelley assigned to railroad defense in, 147; commanded by John C. Frémont, 148; Wool given control of all railroad troops in, 148-149
Mulligan, James A., colonel, 130, 136
Murfreesboro, Tenn., 180

Nashville, Tenn., 169
Nashville and Chattanooga Railroad, 176; cut by Confederates, 180
National Capital, 107, 147; B. & O. instrumental in security of, 222
National *Intelligencer*, quoted on destruction of B. & O., 96
National Road, 15

Navy, United States, 158; dependence of on B. & O. for coal supply, 102
Newburg, (W.) Va., 129, 139
New Creek, (W.) Va., 88, 90, 105, 112, 115, 126, 143, 149, 154, 156, 157; threatened by Confederates, 82-83; destruction of B. & O. bridge at, 245 (note 10)
New Jersey, state of, 207, 215, 216
New York, state of, a commercial rival of Maryland, 15
New York Central Railroad, competes for Cincinnati traffic, 19, 28, 211
New York City, commercial rival of Baltimore, 15, 21, 29, 207, 208, 209, 210, 215, 216, 220; B. & O. discrimination in favor of, 230-231 (note 13)
New York *Commercial Advertiser*, denounces destruction of B. & O., 97
New York *Herald*, 143
New York and Erie Railroad, 28, 211
Ninth Indiana Infantry, 78
North, the, 35, 49, 56, 59, 203; severance of rail communication with, 54; sympathy of for Maryland in B. & O. destruction, 97
North Branch Bridge, 87, 100, 105, 140
North Carolina, state of, 211
North Fork, tributary of Hughes River, 76
North Mountain, 115, 119, 121, 154
Northeast Virginia, partly included in Middle Department, 148
Northern Central Railroad, 41, 103, 170, 178, 203, 205, 211, 214, 219, 221, 261 (note 26); southern terminal of, 18; movement of Federal troops over, 51; Baltimore station of, 52; closing of, 53-54; trains of, mentioned, 56; Secretary Cameron's interest in, 57; military route over temporarily abandoned, 57; re-opening of, 63; rate discrimination by, 103-104; bill introduced in Congress concerning, 219-220; Pennsylvania Central acquires controlling interest in, 233 (note 41); quotation in

INDEX

INDEX

INDEX

Pocahontas County, (W.) Va., 193, 194
Point of Rocks, Md., 65, 67, 92, 100, 119, 216, 217
Point Pleasant, (W.) Va., 164
Point Pleasant *Register*, quoted, 258 (note 2)
Politics, influences selection of military officers, 160
Pomeroy, Joseph, supports resolution to exclude Valley counties from W. Va., 191; opposition to proslavery character of Valley counties, 192; moves rejection of Bath County, 193
Pope, John, major general, 150, 163, 165; approves use of B. & O. to move troops, 164
Port Republic, Va., battle of, 146
Port Tobacco, Md., 216
Porter, Gabriel E., lieutenant colonel, proposes a railroad defense plan, 156
Porterfield, George A., colonel, assignment to command, 68; takes command at Grafton, 69; mobilization orders of, 69; establishes outpost at Fetterman, 72; orders destruction of railroad, 72; asks aid of Joseph E. Johnston, 73; withdrawal of to Philippi, 74; designs of against B. & O. quoted, 74; defeat of at Philippi, 79; retreat of from Philippi, 79; dispatch of Governor Letcher to, 242 (note 27)
Potomac, Army of the. See Army of the Potomac.
Potomac, Department of. See Department of the Potomac.
Potomac Bridge, 94
Potomac River, 17, 40, 66, 90, 93, 104, 106, 107, 108, 111, 112, 114, 122, 140, 145, 150, 156, 157, 188, 204, 209, 210, 218, 222, 223, 235 (note 13), 252 (note 8); bridge across at Harpers Ferry, 52; eastern boundary of West Virginia, 202
Potomac Valley, new Confederate military policy in, 93-94
President, U. S., authorized to take charge of railroads under articles

of war, 212; power given to, 261 (note 18)
President Street Station, (Baltimore), 53
Preston County, (W.) Va., 132
Princeton, (W.) Va., 164
Pruntytown-Philippi Turnpike, 79
Public ownership of railroads, attitude of President and Congress toward, 211

Quantico Creek, tributary of the Potomac, 204
Quincy Siding, B. & O. station, 123, 142

Railroad, the, first use of for invasion, 162; increasing use of in transportation of troops, 164ff
Railroads, bill for government operation of introduced in Senate, 212; government control of, 212-213; war department directs and supervises repair of, 239-240 (note 62)
Railway executives, fear public control and ownership of railroads, 211
Raisin, W. I., captain, 132
Raleigh Court House, (W.) Va., 164
Rappahannock River, 127, 165, 168, 180, 224, 261 (note 23)
Rattling Bridge, 123
Rawlings Station, B. & O. station, 121
Red House, Md., 87, 88, 128
Reid, Whitelaw, book by mentioned, 242-243 (note 31)
Relay House, Md., railroad junction at, 18, 121, 154, 178, 207, 208, 209, 217, 237 (note 28), 238 (note 43); Federal occupation of, 62
Reorganized Government of Virginia, designs of Confederates against, 125; general assembly of, 200
Republicans, 55
Rich Mountain, part of Allegheny chain, 79; occupied by Confederates, 81; victory of Federal troops at, 85
Richmond, Va., 35, 45, 65, 67, 114, 146, 148, 163, 217; secession con-

296

INDEX

INDEX

Secretary of War, Confederate, 113
Secretary of War, U. S., 58, 104, 107, 171, 214; urged to recover control of B. & O., 102; charged with suppression of B. & O., 102-103; creates Middle Department, 148; places defense of B. & O. in hands of Kelley, 153; appreciates seriousness of Rosecrans's plight, 166; House of Representatives directions to, 207-208; authorized to use railroads for transportation of troops and supplies, 212; places B. & O. under control of war department, 213; dispatch of Governor Dennison to, 235 (note 13); Garrett's reply to, 261 (note 16)
Senate, U. S., bill introduced for government operation of railroads in, 212; J. A. Pearce's speech on railroad bill in, 212-213; ignores "Case Memorial," 215-216; memorial of the Corporation of the City of Washington to, 216; ignores memorial of Corporation of City of Washington, 217
Seventh Indiana Infantry, 78
Seventh Virginia Cavalry, Confederate, 127, 129
Seward, William H., U. S. secretary of state, supports Stanton's plan to aid Rosecrans, 167-168
Shenandoah Mountain, Va., 135
Shenandoah River, tributary of the Potomac, 146
Shenandoah Valley, 18, 65, 106, 114, 127, 145, 154, 161, 224; flour mills of, 63; a gateway to the South, 81; strategic importance of, 90; Harpers Ferry key to, 91; new Confederate military policy in, 93-94; J. A. Early's campaign in, 123; Federal movements in, 124; control of by Sheridan, 142; devastated by Sheridan, 143; used as avenue of approach and base of operations, 146-147; partly included in Middle Department, 150; effect of unsettled military situation in on boundary question, 200
Shepherdstown, (W.) Va., 90
Sheridan, Philip H., major general, 160; repulses J. A. Early at Win-

chester, 124; controls lower Shenandoah Valley, 142; devastates the Shenandoah, 143
Shields, James, brigadier general, succeeds Lander, 115
Shipping Point, Va., 204
Showalter, John H., major, 159
Sigel, Franz, major general, 149, 160
Simpsons Creek Bridge, 242 (note 28)
Sir Johns Run, tributary of the Potomac, 111
Sir Johns Run Depot, B. & O. station, 109
Sixteenth Ohio Infantry, 73, 78
Sixth Indiana Infantry, arrival of at Parkersburg, 77
Sixth Massachusetts Regiment, 54, 237 (note 28); attack upon in Baltimore, 53
Sixth Virginia Cavalry, Confederate, 129
Sixth (W.) Va., Volunteer Infantry, Union, 128; stand of at Cheat River bridge, 159; retreat of, 159
Sleepy Creek, tributary of the Potomac, 115
Smith, Jacob, captain, 250 (note 29)
Smith, William P., B. & O. master of transportation, 168, 175, 176, 235 (note 12); receives notice of arrival of Federal troops, 51; role in troop movement, 169; reports progress of troop trains, 171; reply to McCallum's complaint to war department, 171-172; reports Schurz's interference, 173; instructions of to B. & O. agents, 173; goes to Indianapolis, 179; explanation of, 235 (note 13); refuses captaincy, 255 (note 22)
Smithfield, (W.) Va., 93
Soldier's House, Indianapolis, 176
South, the, 39, 56
South Branch basin, 161
South Branch of Potomac, 105, 112, 123, 127
South Branch Valley, 88, 154
Southern cause, 45
Southern men, 60
Speaker of House of Representatives, U. S., communication of J. W. Garrett to, 221

INDEX

INDEX

301

INDEX

Virginia, state of—*Cont'd*
placed in command of strategic
posts in northwestern part of,
149; northwestern part of, 161;
dismemberment of, 182; cismontane part of, 182; eastern part of,
183; northwest part of, 183; transmontane policy of, 183; dislike of
for B. & O., 188; E. B. Hall points
out hostility to B. & O. by, 195;
reorganized general assembly of,
200; formal thanks of to B. & O.
for assistance in John Brown affair, 234 (note 1); B. & O. injured
by attitude of, 235 (note 9); E. B.
Hall quoted on railroad policy
of, 258 (note 3); attitude of toward B. & O. in antebellum
period, 259 (note 13)
Virginia general assembly, 34; unfriendly attitude of toward the
B. & O., 16; denies charter to
Hollidays Cove Railroad, 34; con-
ciliation policy of, 35; message of
Governor John Letcher to, 259
(note 13); act of, 228 (note 16)
Virginia government, policy in possible recovery of northwestern
Virginia, 93-94
Virginia Military Institute, 65, 113
Virginia Piedmont, 146
Virginia Supreme Court of Appeals,
36
Virginia troops, 236 (note 19), 242-
243 (note 31), 251 (note 46)
Virginians, 35, 61, 62, 65; policy of
in 1860, 35; activities of at Harp-
ers Ferry, 59

Walcutt, Charles C., major, 87
Wallace, Lew, colonel, enters Cumberland, 92
Wallace, Martin, captain, 250 (note
29)
War Department, Confederate,
plans removal of B. & O. property, 94; creates Valley District,
107
War Department, U. S., 50, 57, 70,
114, 152, 153, 157, 208, 242-243,
(note 31); determination of to
pass troops through Baltimore,
56; obstinacy of, 59; watchful
waiting policy of, 61; permission

to B. & O. granted by, 62-63; indifference of to B. & O. plea for
military protection, 102; policy of
toward B. & O. criticised, 104;
creates Department of Harpers
Ferry and Cumberland, 104;
strengthening of B. & O. defense
after McNeill raid, 142; informed
of insufficiency of railroad guard,
148; places Major General John
E. Wool in defense of entire B.
& O., 148-149; new experiment of,
151; creates Department of West
Virginia, 151; recommendations
of Kelley to, 155-156; informed
of plight of Rosecrans's forces,
166; plan to send aid to Rosecrans, 168-169; McCallum's complaint to, 171-172; notified by W.
P. Smith of Schurz's interference,
173; anxiety over troop trains,
175; sends T. A. Scott to Louisville, 177; reliance on Garrett,
178; President Lincoln favors supervision of railroads by, 211;
B. & O. placed under control of,
213; directs and supervises repairing of railroads, 239-240 (note
62)
War of 1812, 15
Warfare, modern, innovations of,
157
Warford, A. B., president Northern
Central Railroad, 103
Warm Springs, Va., 163
Washington, D. C., 15, 18, 19, 40,
45, 47, 49, 52, 54, 55, 56, 57, 61,
63, 90, 98, 101, 103, 106, 108, 121,
160, 163, 165, 166, 169, 170, 171,
178, 203, 208, 209, 210, 214, 215,
216, 217, 218, 220, 221, 222, 223,
235 (note 13), 235-236 (note 15),
236-237 (note 24), 237 (note 28),
237 (note 32), 238 (note 43), 238
(note 44), 242 (note 27), 257 (note
63), 261 (note 26); railroad terminal at, 18; railroad convention at,
46; severance of rail communication with, 53-54; military route to
described, 57; military situation
in vicinity of, 61; railroad facilities of, 63; Confederate plans for
military investment of, 93-94; requests to authorities at, 105; J. A.

302

INDEX

INDEX

Wheeling *Intelligencer*, extra of unfriendly, 55-56; quoted, 60; denounces destruction of B. & O., 97

Whetstone Point, Md., troops landed at, 63

White Sulphur Springs, (W.) Va., 35

White's battalion, Confederate, 127

Willey, Waitman T., U. S. senator, 133, 192; quoted on significance of B. & O. to Trans-Allegheny, 187; opposes inclusion of Alleghany County in new state, 191; stresses importance of B. & O. to northwest Virginia, 192; opposes arbitrary annexation of Valley counties, 198; resolutions on boundary question, 198-199; opposition in constitutional convention to boundary plan of, 199

Willey, William J., colonel, orders received by, 72; destroys B. & O. bridges, 72

Williams, Alpheus, brigadier general, 114, 115

Williamsport, Md., 90, 92, 93, 109, 114, 205

Wilson, John L., B. & O. master of road, 169, 171; role in troop movement, 169

Winchester, Va., 91, 92, 93, 99, 100, 105, 106, 107, 108, 110, 113, 126, 138, 145, 146, 150, 154, 156, 236 (note 18); 245 (note 11); withdrawal of Stuart and Jackson to, 99; occupied by Federals, 115, 120; Sheridan defeats Early at, 124

Winchester and Potomac Railroad, 18; used in evacuation of Harpers Ferry, 92

Wise County, Va., 186

Witcher's battalion, Confederate, 127

Wood County, (W.) Va., 192

Wool, John E., major general, 160; defends B. & O, 148-149; commands Middle Department, 148; protests to Stanton on removal of railroad troops, 149; maintains jurisdiction over B. & O. defense, 149; superseded by Major General Robert C. Schenck, 150; jurisdiction of, 253 (note 9)

Wright, Hendrick B., congressman, introduces bill for acceptance of Metropolitan plan, 213-214; agrees with views of Garrett on Metropolitan plan, 215

Wynkoop, George C., brigadier general, 56

York, Pa., 57, 220

PENNSYLVA

McConnelsburg ⬤

Cumberland ⬤

⬤ Fairmont

Piedmont ⬤

Green
Spring ⬤

Rowlesburg
⬤

⬤ New
Creek

R. R.

Ohio

⬤ D

Pa ⬤

and

⬤

⬤
Creek

Springfield

Martir
Darkesvi
Bunker
Op

Romney ⬤

Winchester ⬤

⬤
Philippi

Corricks Ford
⬤

Greenland ⬤

Cedar Creek ⬤
Kernstown ⬤

Moorefield ⬤

⬤ Laurel Hill
⬤ Rich Mountain

⬤ ·· Fishers Hill ⬤

Strasburg ⬤
⬤

⬤ Beverly

WEST
VIRGINIA

Woodstock ⬤

Br

Mt. Jackson ⬤

⬤ Cheat Mountain

New Market ⬤